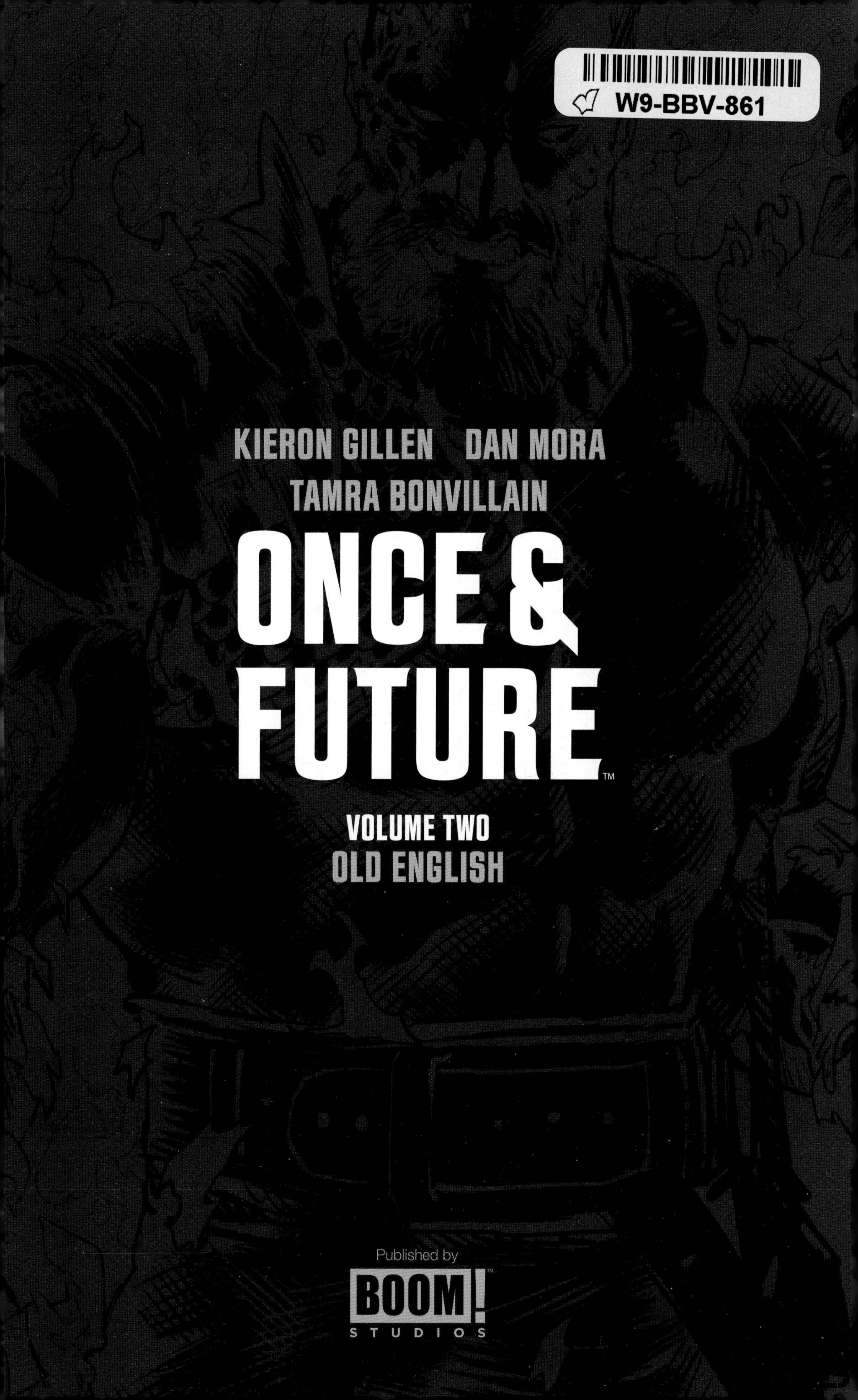

KIERON GILLEN DAN MORA
TAMRA BONVILLAIN

ONCE & FUTURE™

VOLUME TWO
OLD ENGLISH

Published by
BOOM! STUDIOS

DESIGNER
SCOTT NEWMAN

ASSOCIATE EDITOR
AMANDA LaFRANCO

EDITOR
MATT GAGNON

Ross Richie CEO & Founder
Joy Huffman CFO
Matt Gagnon Editor-in-Chief
Filip Sablik President, Publishing & Marketing
Stephen Christy President, Development
Lance Kreiter Vice President, Licensing & Merchandising
Arune Singh Vice President, Marketing
Bryce Carlson Vice President, Editorial & Creative Strategy
Kate Henning Director, Operations
Spencer Simpson Director, Sales
Scott Newman Manager, Production Design
Elyse Strandberg Manager, Finance
Sierra Hahn Executive Editor
Jeanine Schaefer Executive Editor
Dafna Pleban Senior Editor
Shannon Watters Senior Editor
Eric Harburn Senior Editor
Sophie Philips-Roberts Associate Editor
Amanda LaFranco Associate Editor
Jonathan Manning Associate Editor
Gavin Gronenthal Assistant Editor
Gwen Waller Assistant Editor
Allyson Gronowitz Assistant Editor
Ramiro Portnoy Assistant Editor
Kenzie Rzonca Assistant Editor
Shelby Netschke Editorial Assistant
Michelle Ankley Design Coordinator
Marie Krupina Production Designer
Grace Park Production Designer
Chelsea Roberts Production Designer
Samantha Knapp Production Design Assistant
José Meza Live Events Lead
Stephanie Hocutt Digital Marketing Lead
Esther Kim Marketing Coordinator
Breanna Sarpy Live Events Coordinator
Amanda Lawson Marketing Assistant
Holly Aitchison Digital Sales Coordinator
Morgan Perry Retail Sales Coordinator
Megan Christopher Operations Coordinator
Rodrigo Hernandez Operations Coordinator
Zipporah Smith Operations Assistant
Jason Lee Senior Accountant
Sabrina Lesin Accounting Assistant

ONCE & FUTURE Volume Two, November 2020. Published by BOOM! Studios, a division of Boom Entertainment, Inc. Once & Future is ™ & © 2020 Kieron Gillen, Ltd. Originally published in single magazine form as ONCE & FUTURE No. 7-12. ™ & © 2020 Kieron Gillen, Ltd. All rights reserved. BOOM! Studios™ and the BOOM! Studios logo are trademarks of Boom Entertainment, Inc., registered in various countries and categories. All characters, events, and institutions depicted herein are fictional. Any similarity between any of the names, characters, persons, events, and/or institutions in this publication to actual names, characters, and persons, whether living or dead, events, and/or institutions is unintended and purely coincidental. BOOM! Studios does not read or accept unsolicited submissions of ideas, stories, or artwork.

BOOM! Studios, 5670 Wilshire Boulevard, Suite 400, Los Angeles, CA, 90036-5679. Printed in USA. First Printing.

ISBN: 978-1-68415-637-5, eISBN: 978-1-64668-092-4

WRITTEN BY
KIERON GILLEN

ILLUSTRATED BY
DAN MORA

COLORED BY
TAMRA BONVILLAIN

LETTERED BY
ED DUKESHIRE

COVER BY
DAN MORA

ONCE & FUTURE ™

CREATED BY **KIERON GILLEN** AND **DAN MORA**

CHAPTER SEVEN

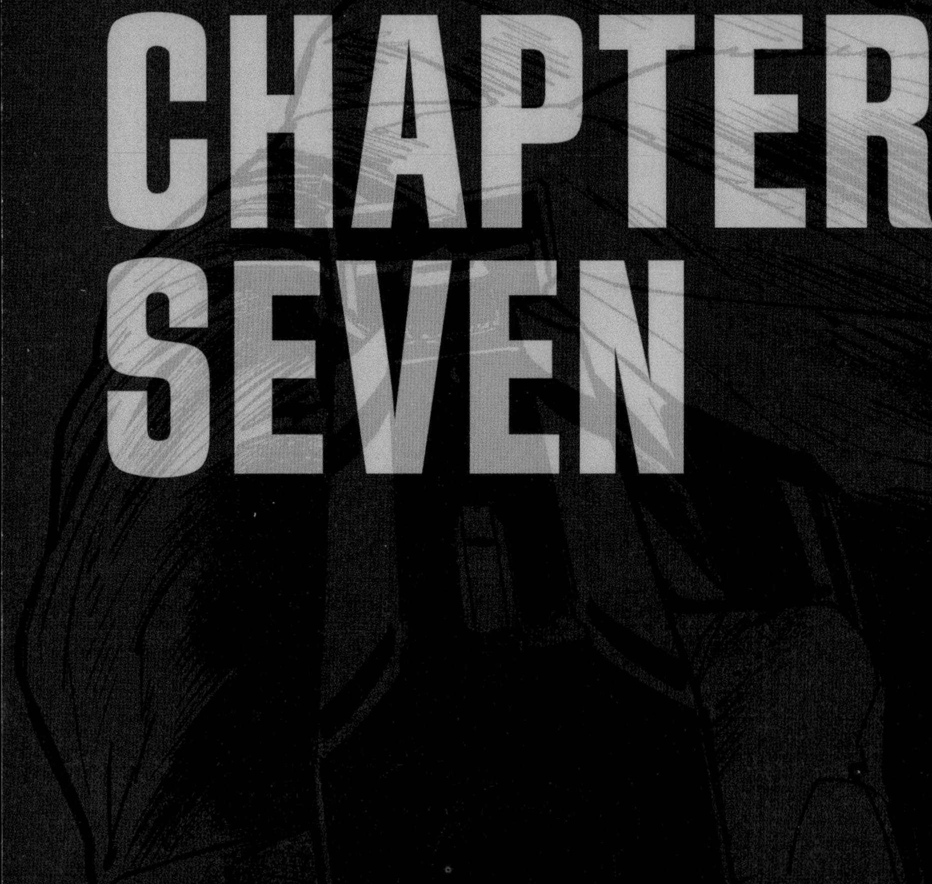

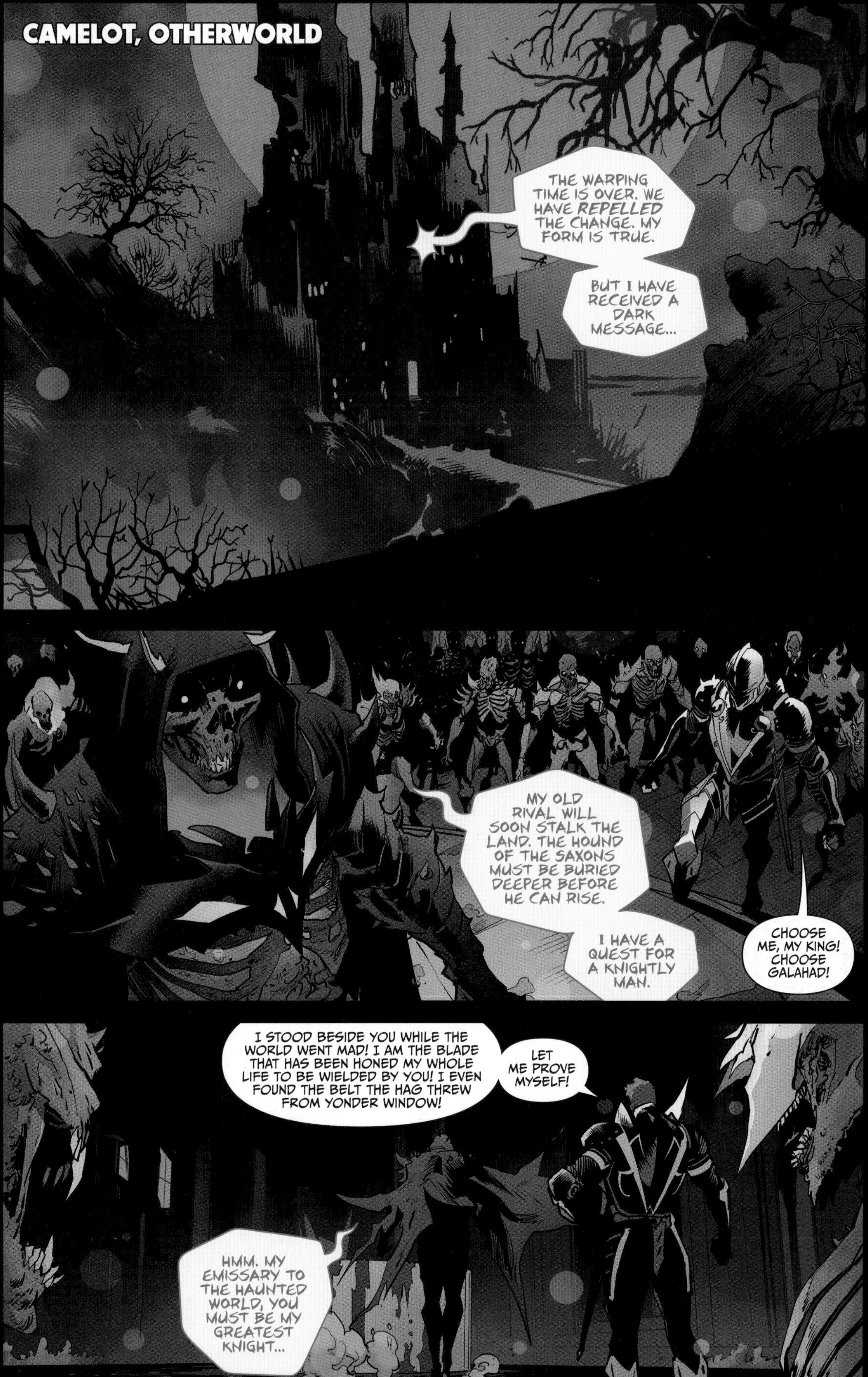
CAMELOT, OTHERWORLD
THE WARPING TIME IS OVER. WE HAVE REPELLED THE CHANGE. MY FORM IS TRUE.
BUT I HAVE RECEIVED A DARK MESSAGE...
MY OLD RIVAL WILL SOON STALK THE LAND. THE HOUND OF THE SAXONS MUST BE BURIED DEEPER BEFORE HE CAN RISE.
I HAVE A QUEST FOR A KNIGHTLY MAN.
CHOOSE ME, MY KING! CHOOSE GALAHAD!
I STOOD BESIDE YOU WHILE THE WORLD WENT MAD! I AM THE BLADE THAT HAS BEEN HONED MY WHOLE LIFE TO BE WIELDED BY YOU! I EVEN FOUND THE BELT THE HAG THREW FROM YONDER WINDOW!
LET ME PROVE MYSELF!
HMM. MY EMISSARY TO THE HAUNTED WORLD, YOU MUST BE MY GREATEST KNIGHT...

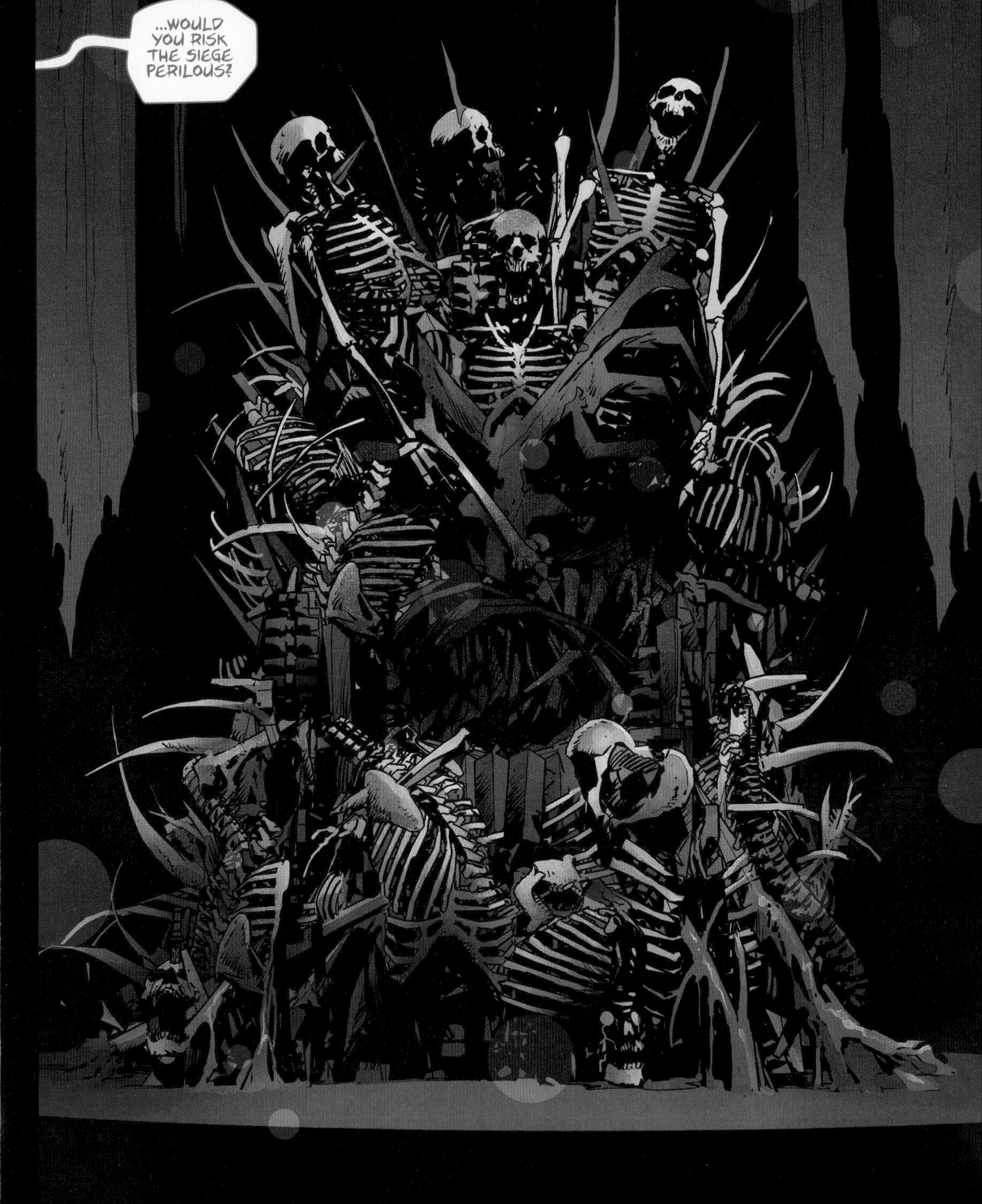
...WOULD YOU RISK THE SIEGE PERILOUS?

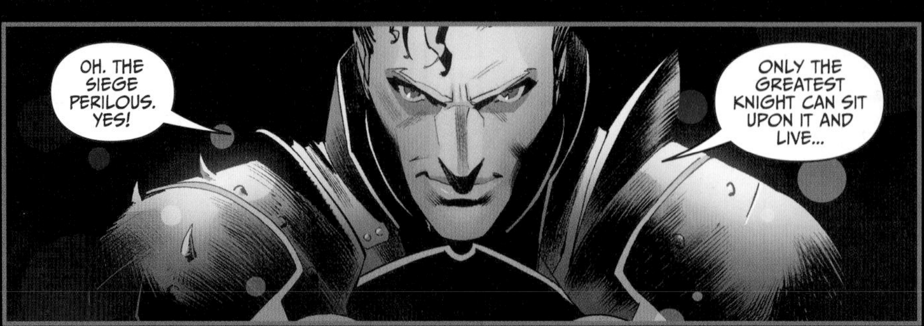
OH. THE SIEGE PERILOUS. YES!
ONLY THE GREATEST KNIGHT CAN SIT UPON IT AND LIVE...

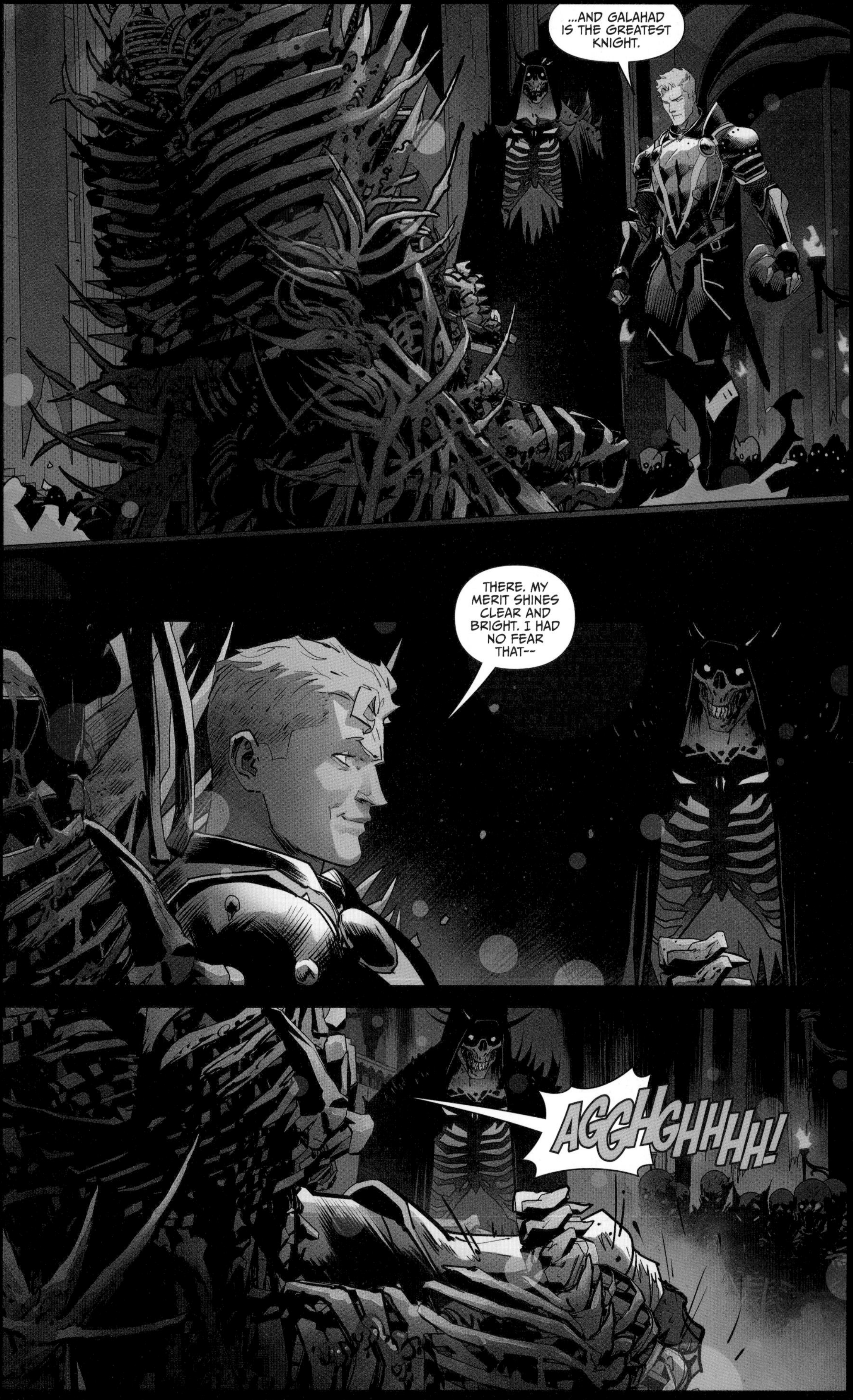
...AND GALAHAD IS THE GREATEST KNIGHT.
THERE. MY MERIT SHINES CLEAR AND BRIGHT. I HAD NO FEAR THAT--
AGGHGHHHH!

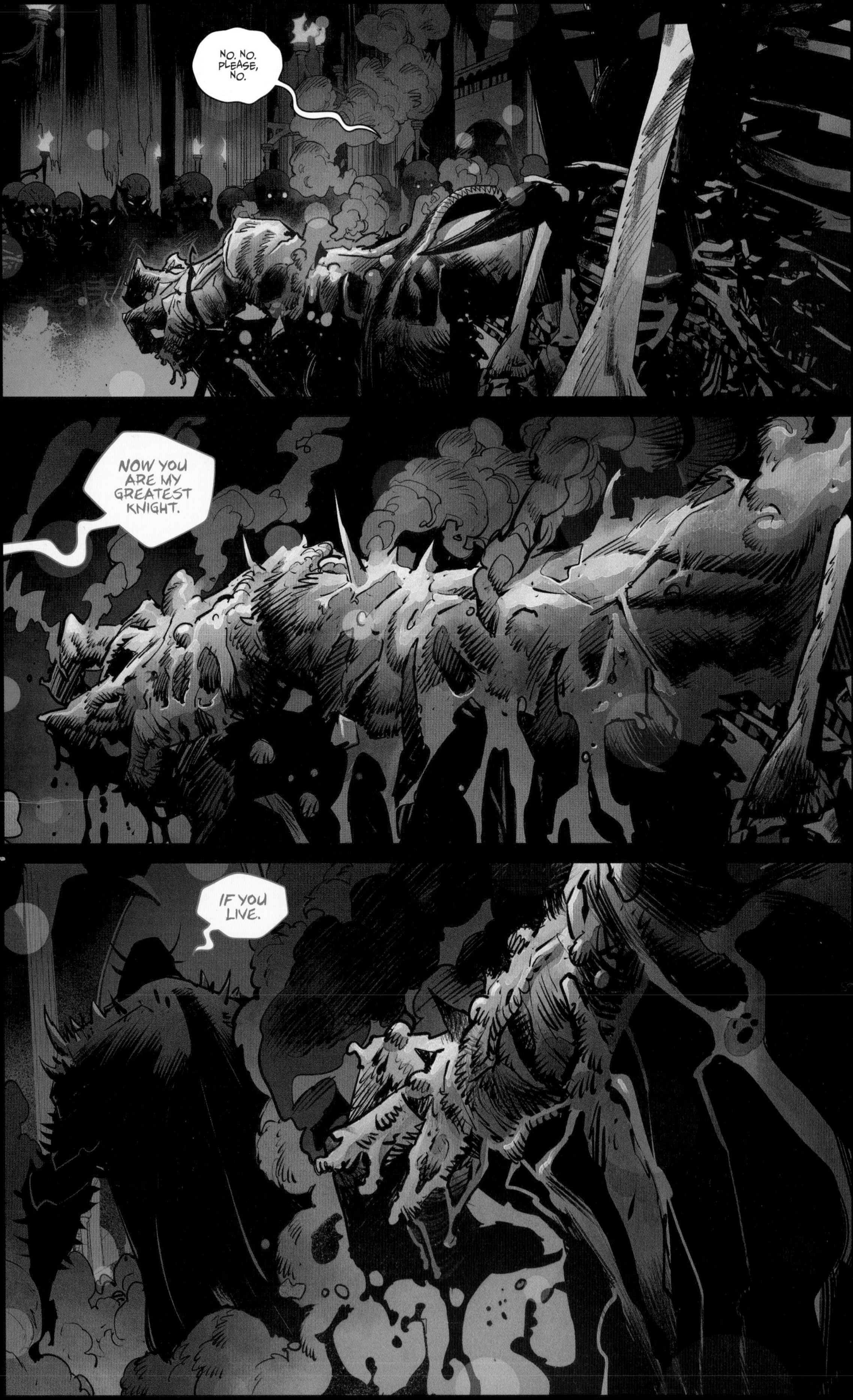
NO. NO. PLEASE, NO.
NOW YOU ARE MY GREATEST KNIGHT.
IF YOU LIVE.

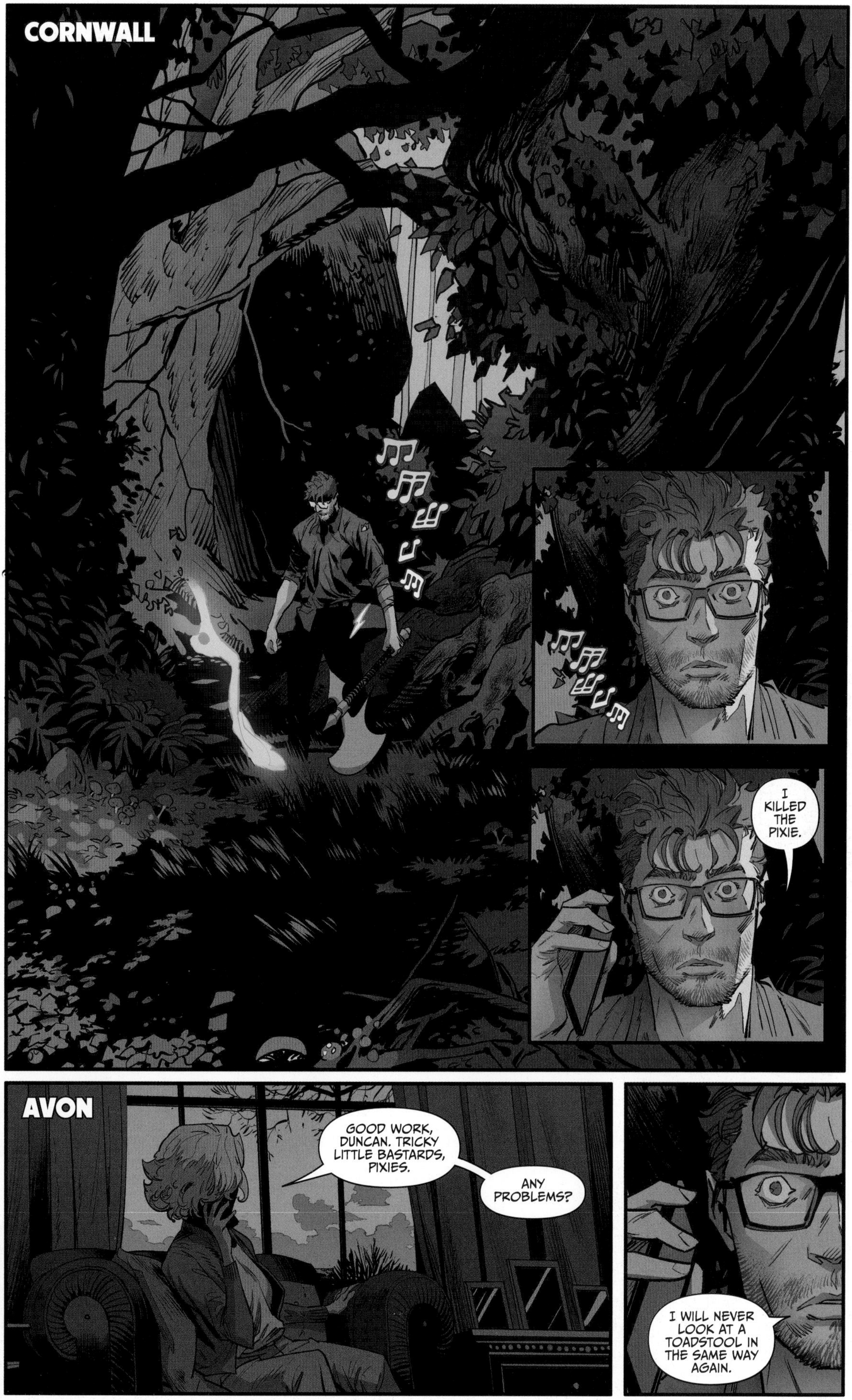
CORNWALL
I KILLED THE PIXIE.
AVON
GOOD WORK, DUNCAN. TRICKY LITTLE BASTARDS, PIXIES.
ANY PROBLEMS?
I WILL NEVER LOOK AT A TOADSTOOL IN THE SAME WAY AGAIN.

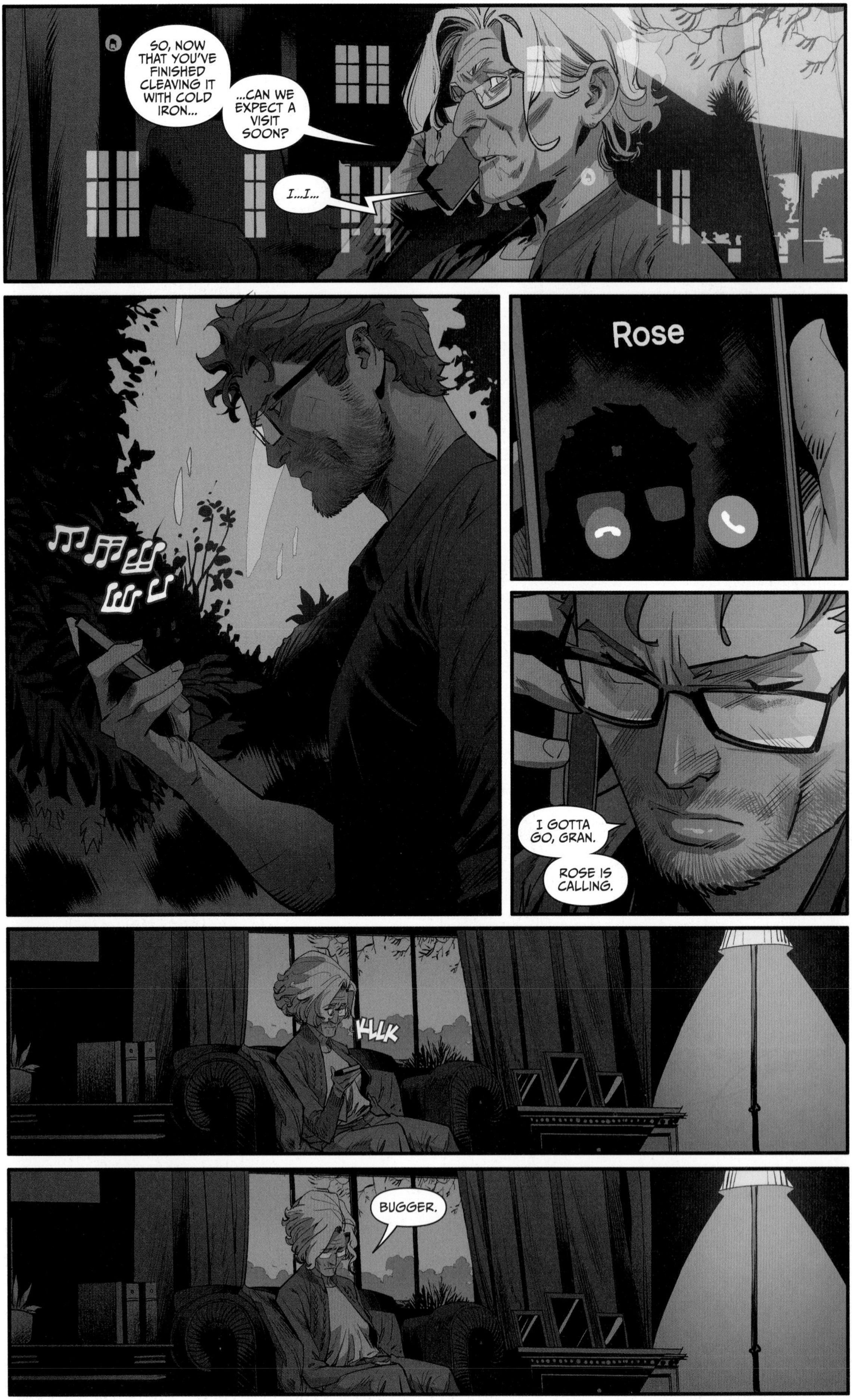
SO, NOW THAT YOU'VE FINISHED CLEAVING IT WITH COLD IRON...
...CAN WE EXPECT A VISIT SOON?
I...I...
Rose
I GOTTA GO, GRAN.
ROSE IS CALLING.
KLLK
BUGGER.

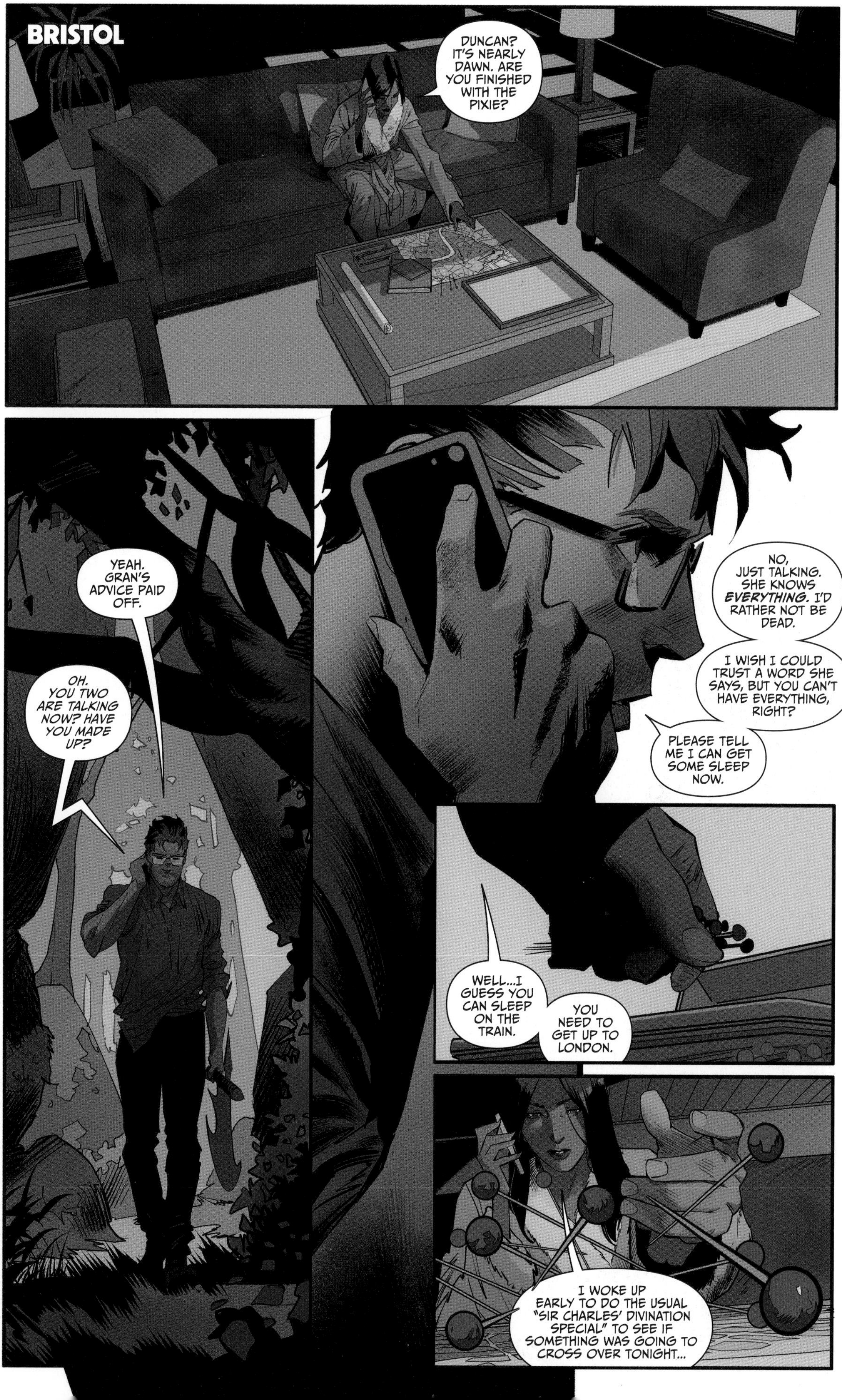
BRISTOL
DUNCAN? IT'S NEARLY DAWN. ARE YOU FINISHED WITH THE PIXIE?
YEAH. GRAN'S ADVICE PAID OFF.
OH. YOU TWO ARE TALKING NOW? HAVE YOU MADE UP?
NO, JUST TALKING. SHE KNOWS *EVERYTHING.* I'D RATHER NOT BE DEAD.
I WISH I COULD TRUST A WORD SHE SAYS, BUT YOU CAN'T HAVE EVERYTHING, RIGHT?
PLEASE TELL ME I CAN GET SOME SLEEP NOW.
WELL...I GUESS YOU CAN SLEEP ON THE TRAIN.
YOU NEED TO GET UP TO LONDON.
I WOKE UP EARLY TO DO THE USUAL "SIR CHARLES' DIVINATION SPECIAL" TO SEE IF SOMETHING WAS GOING TO CROSS OVER TONIGHT...

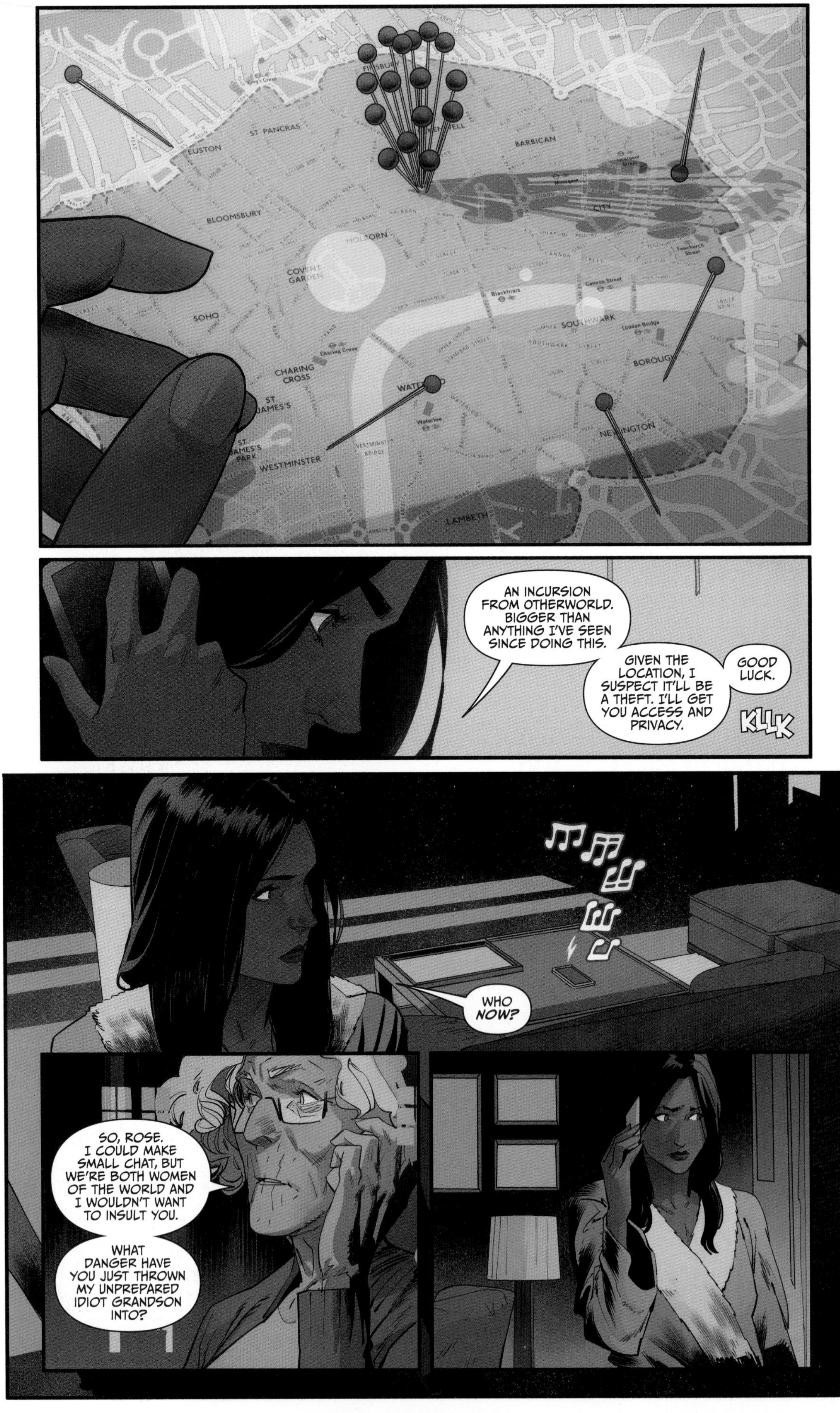
FINSBURY
EUSTON
ST. PANCRAS
BARBICAN
CITY
BLOOMSBURY
HOLBORN
COVENT GARDEN
SOHO
CHARING CROSS
ST. JAMES'S
ST. JAMES'S PARK
WESTMINSTER
WATE
SOUTHWARK
BOROUG
NEWINGTON
LAMBETH
AN INCURSION FROM OTHERWORLD. BIGGER THAN ANYTHING I'VE SEEN SINCE DOING THIS.
GIVEN THE LOCATION, I SUSPECT IT'LL BE A THEFT. I'LL GET YOU ACCESS AND PRIVACY.
GOOD LUCK.
KLLK
WHO NOW?
SO, ROSE. I COULD MAKE SMALL CHAT, BUT WE'RE BOTH WOMEN OF THE WORLD AND I WOULDN'T WANT TO INSULT YOU.
WHAT DANGER HAVE YOU JUST THROWN MY UNPREPARED IDIOT GRANDSON INTO?

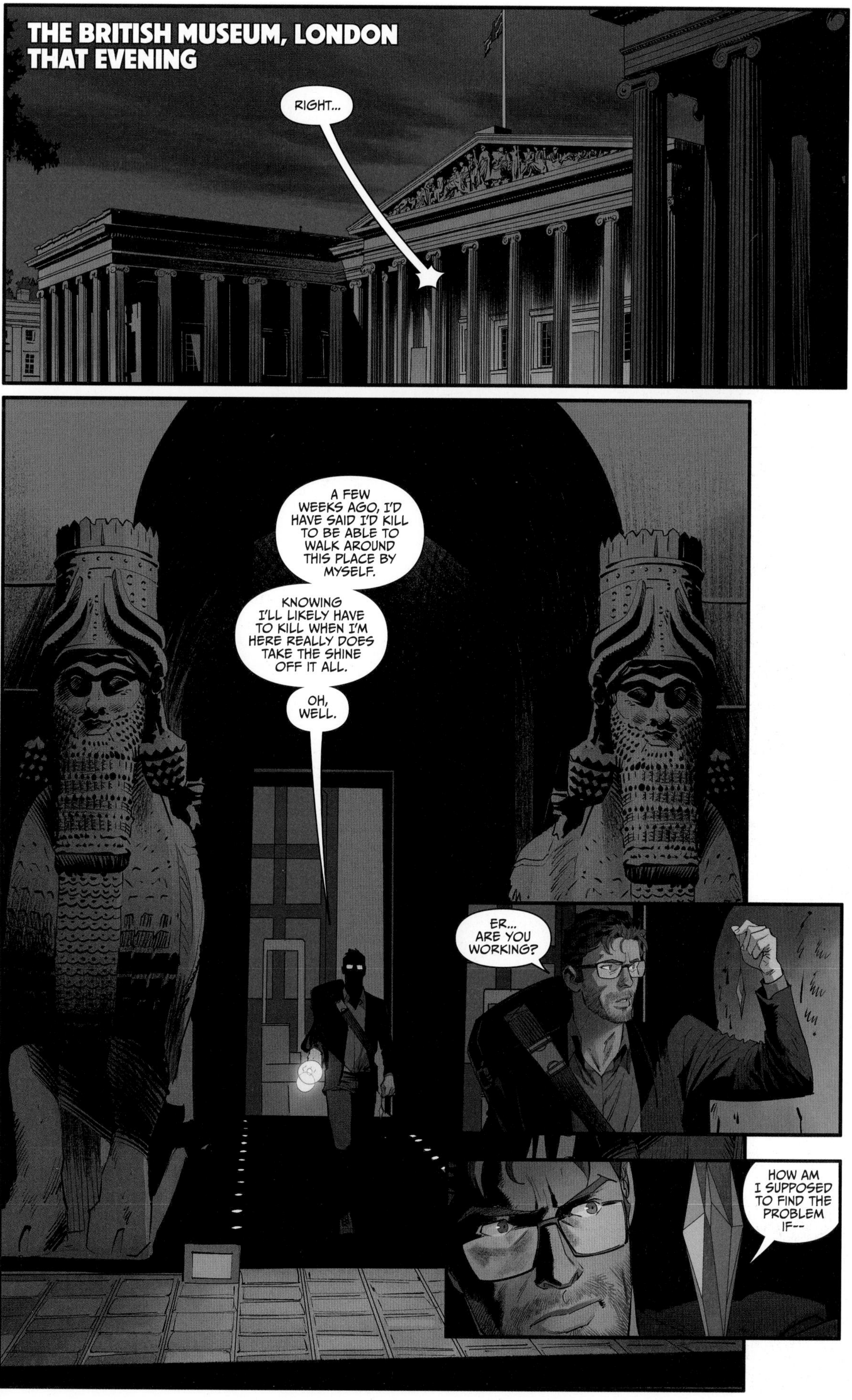
THE BRITISH MUSEUM, LONDON
THAT EVENING
RIGHT...
A FEW WEEKS AGO, I'D HAVE SAID I'D KILL TO BE ABLE TO WALK AROUND THIS PLACE BY MYSELF.
KNOWING I'LL LIKELY HAVE TO KILL WHEN I'M HERE REALLY DOES TAKE THE SHINE OFF IT ALL.
OH, WELL.
ER... ARE YOU WORKING?
HOW AM I SUPPOSED TO FIND THE PROBLEM IF--

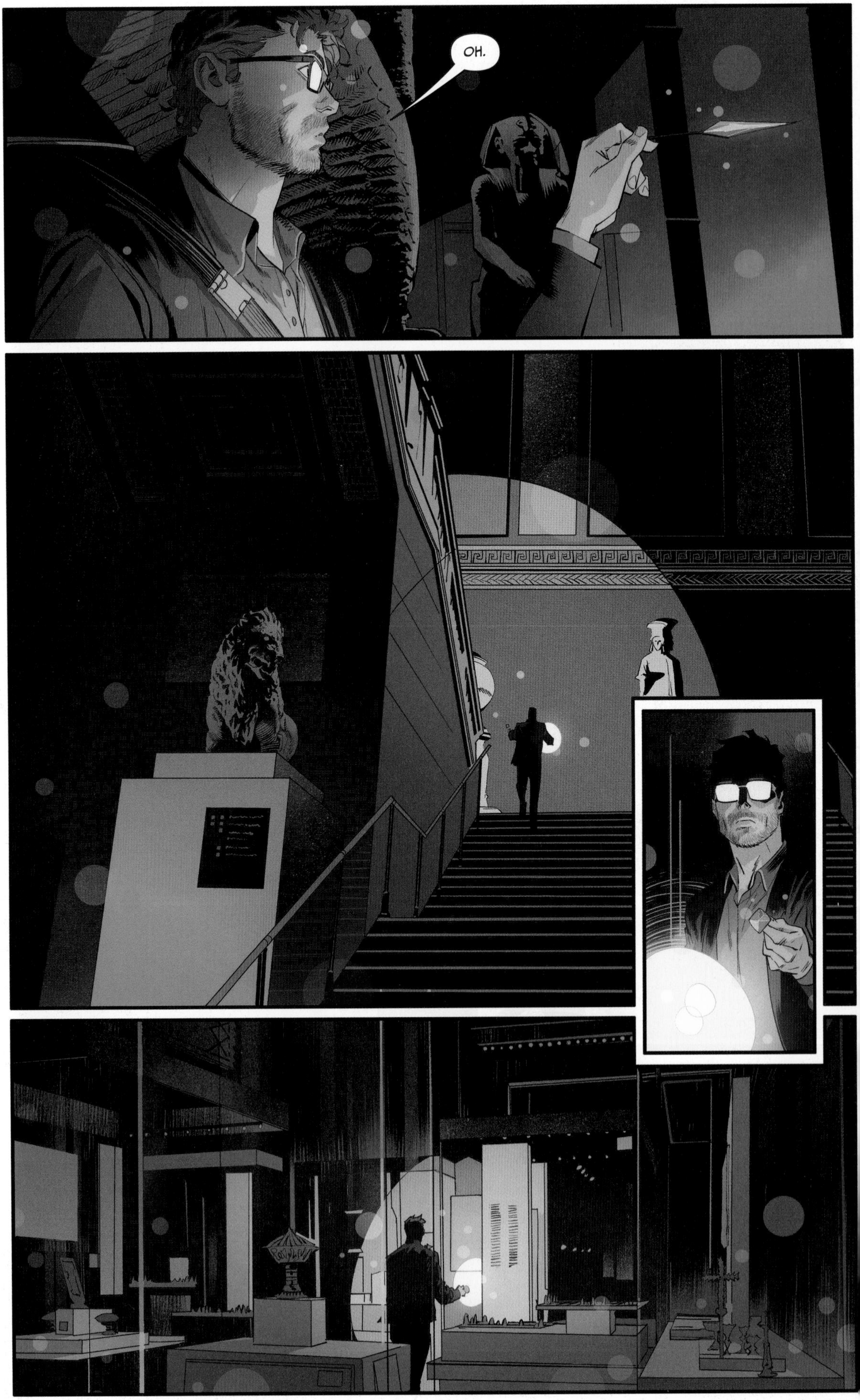
OH.

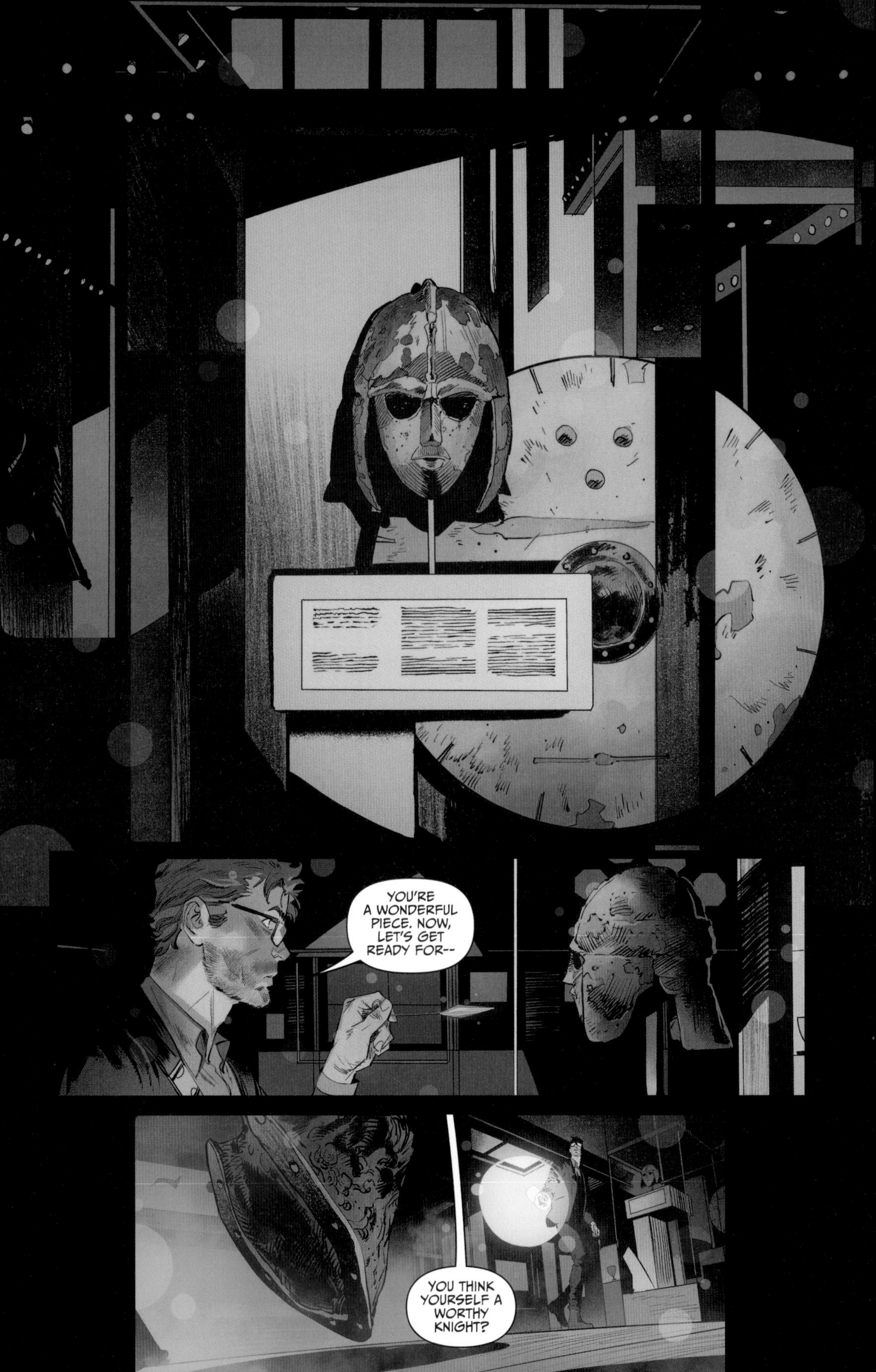
YOU'RE A WONDERFUL PIECE. NOW, LET'S GET READY FOR--
YOU THINK YOURSELF A WORTHY KNIGHT?

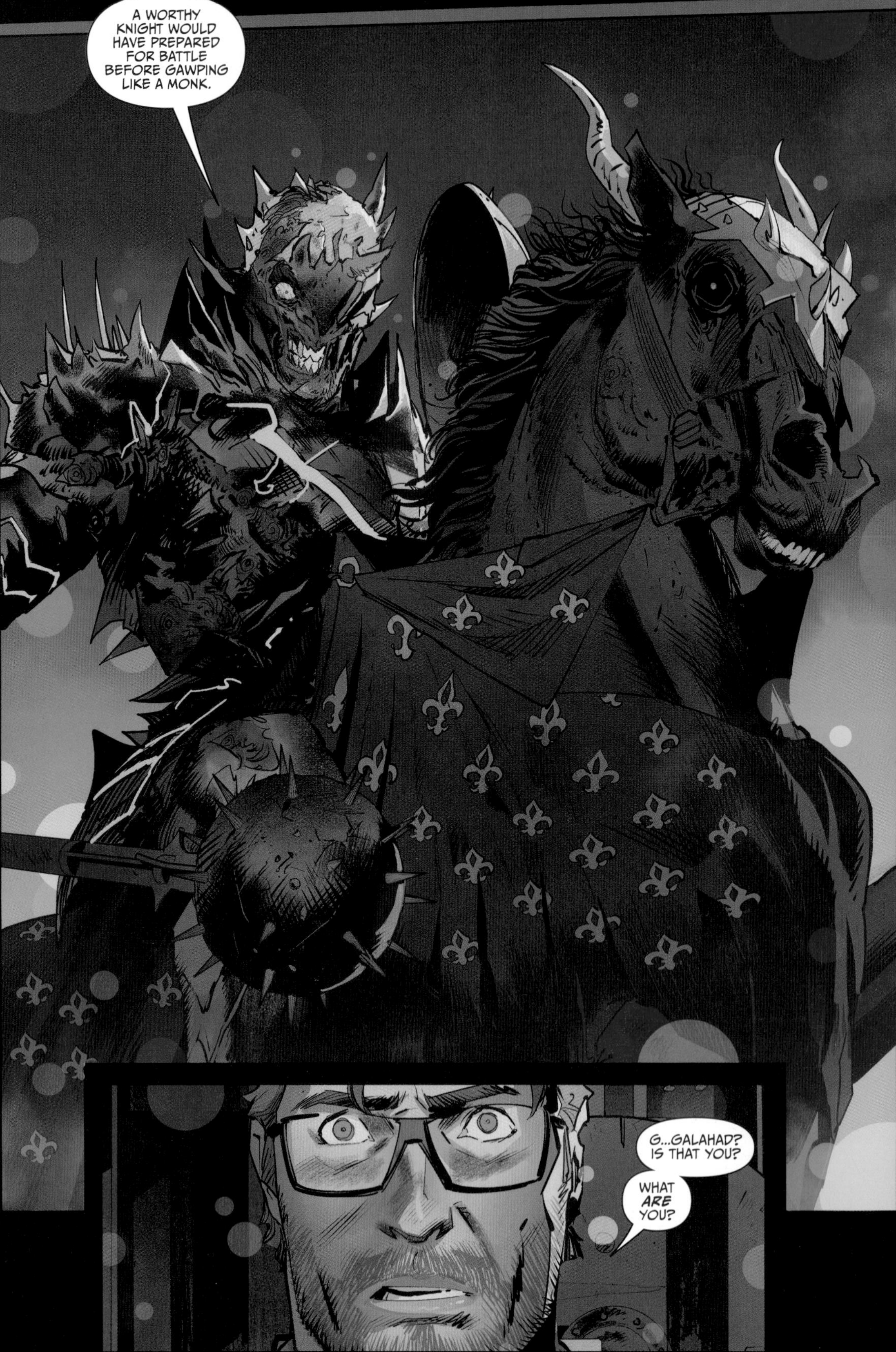
A WORTHY KNIGHT WOULD HAVE PREPARED FOR BATTLE BEFORE GAWPING LIKE A MONK.
G...GALAHAD? IS THAT YOU?
WHAT *ARE* YOU?

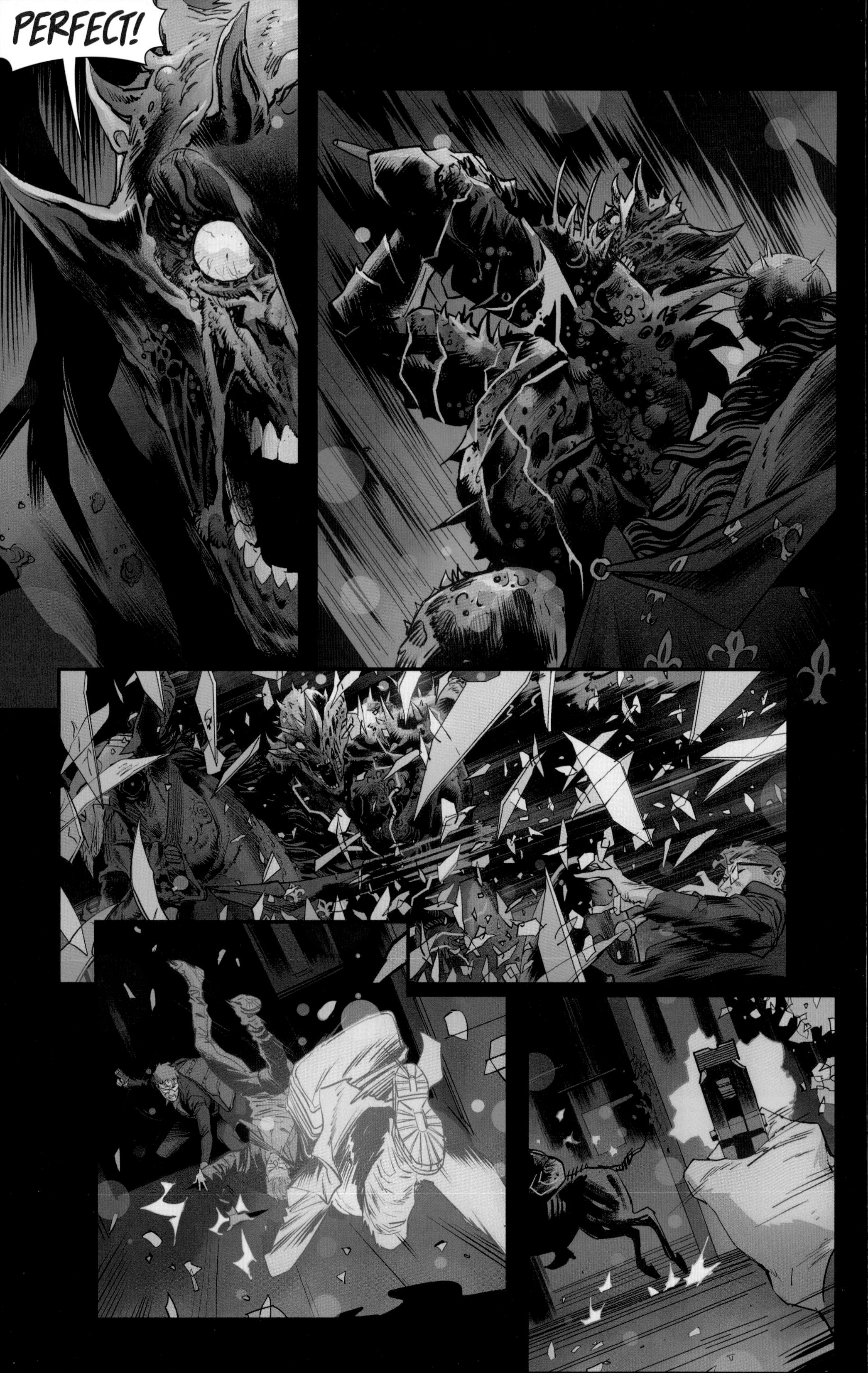
PERFECT!

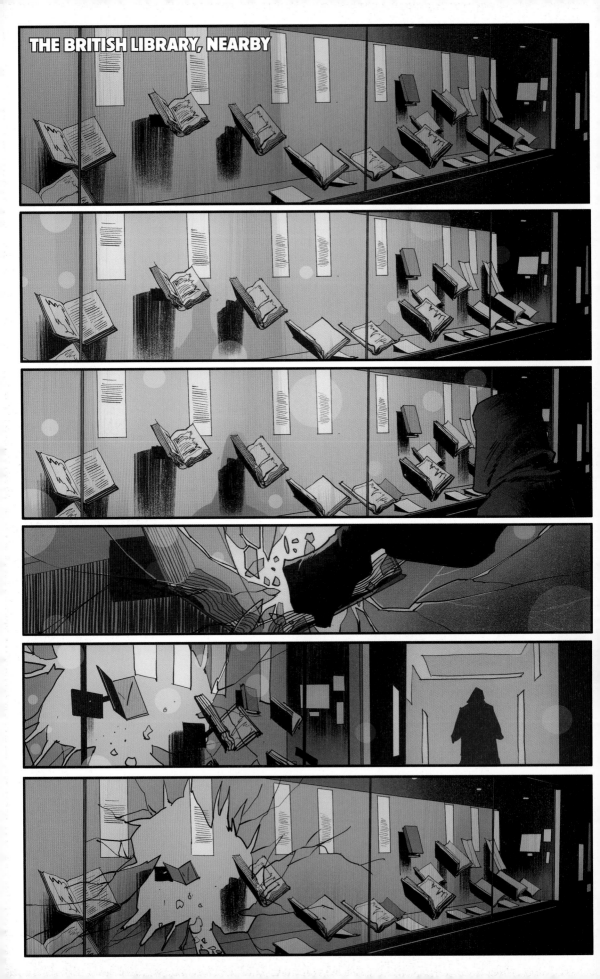

THE BRITISH LIBRARY, NEARBY

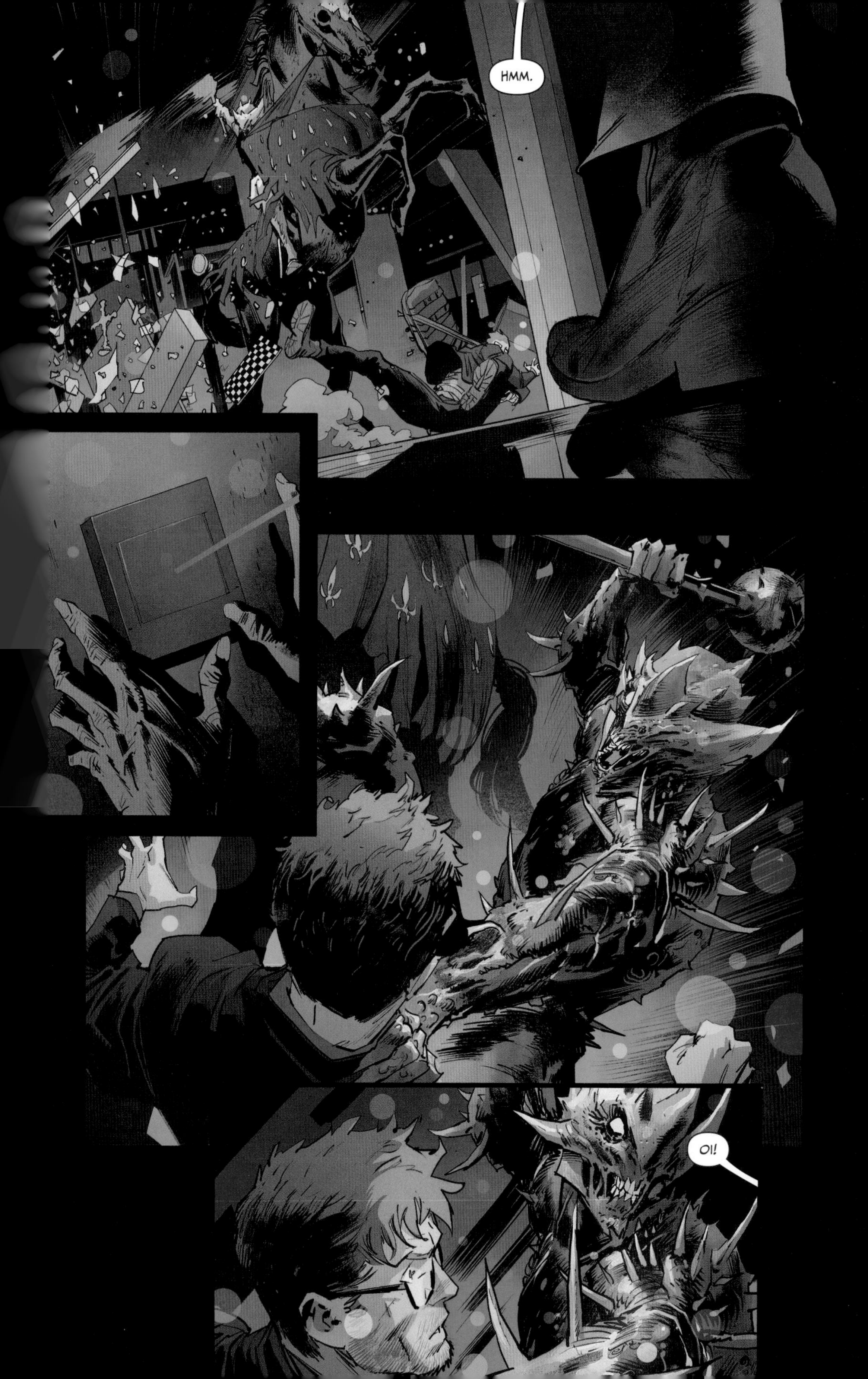
HMM.
OI!

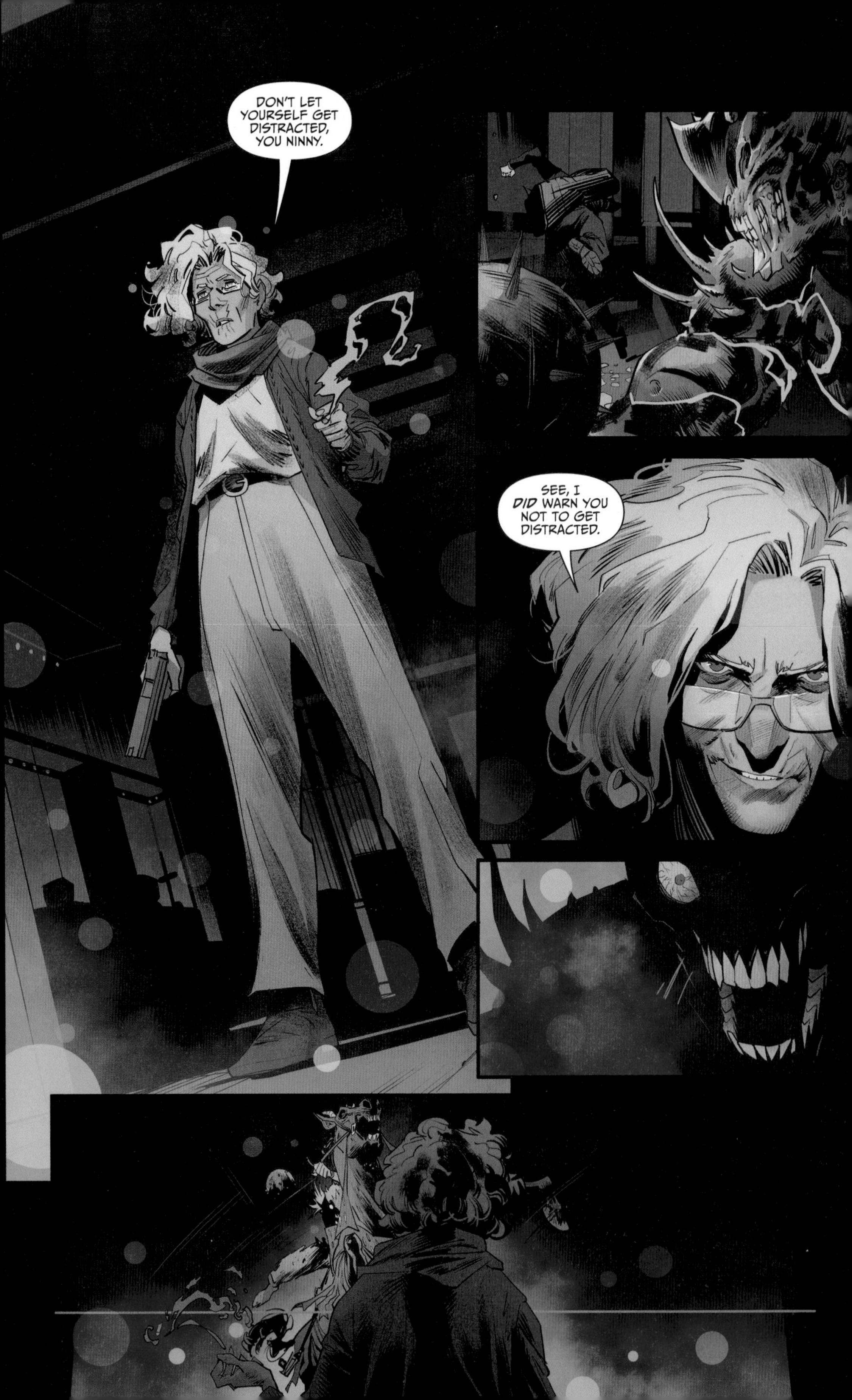
DON'T LET YOURSELF GET DISTRACTED, YOU NINNY.
SEE, I DID WARN YOU NOT TO GET DISTRACTED.

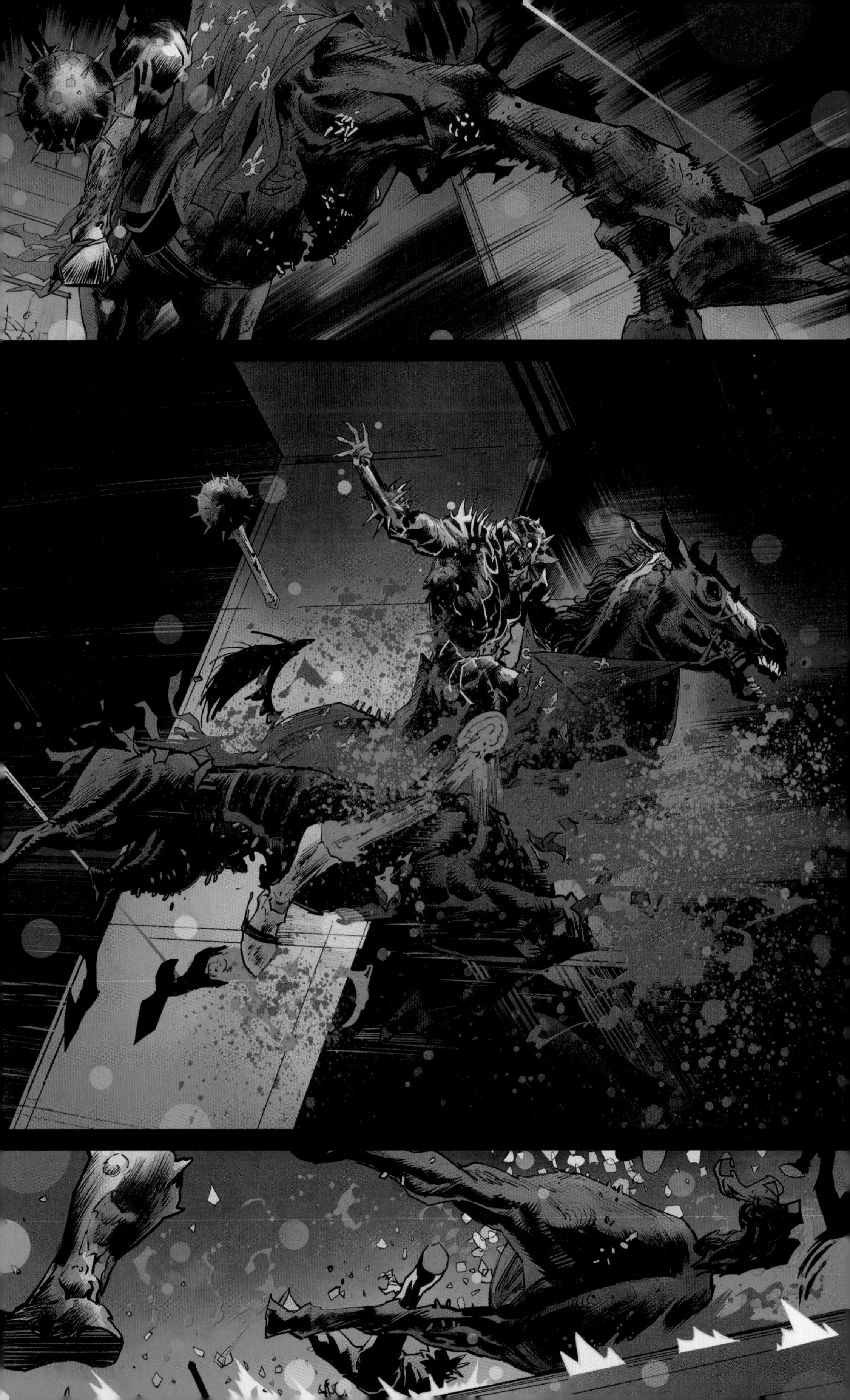

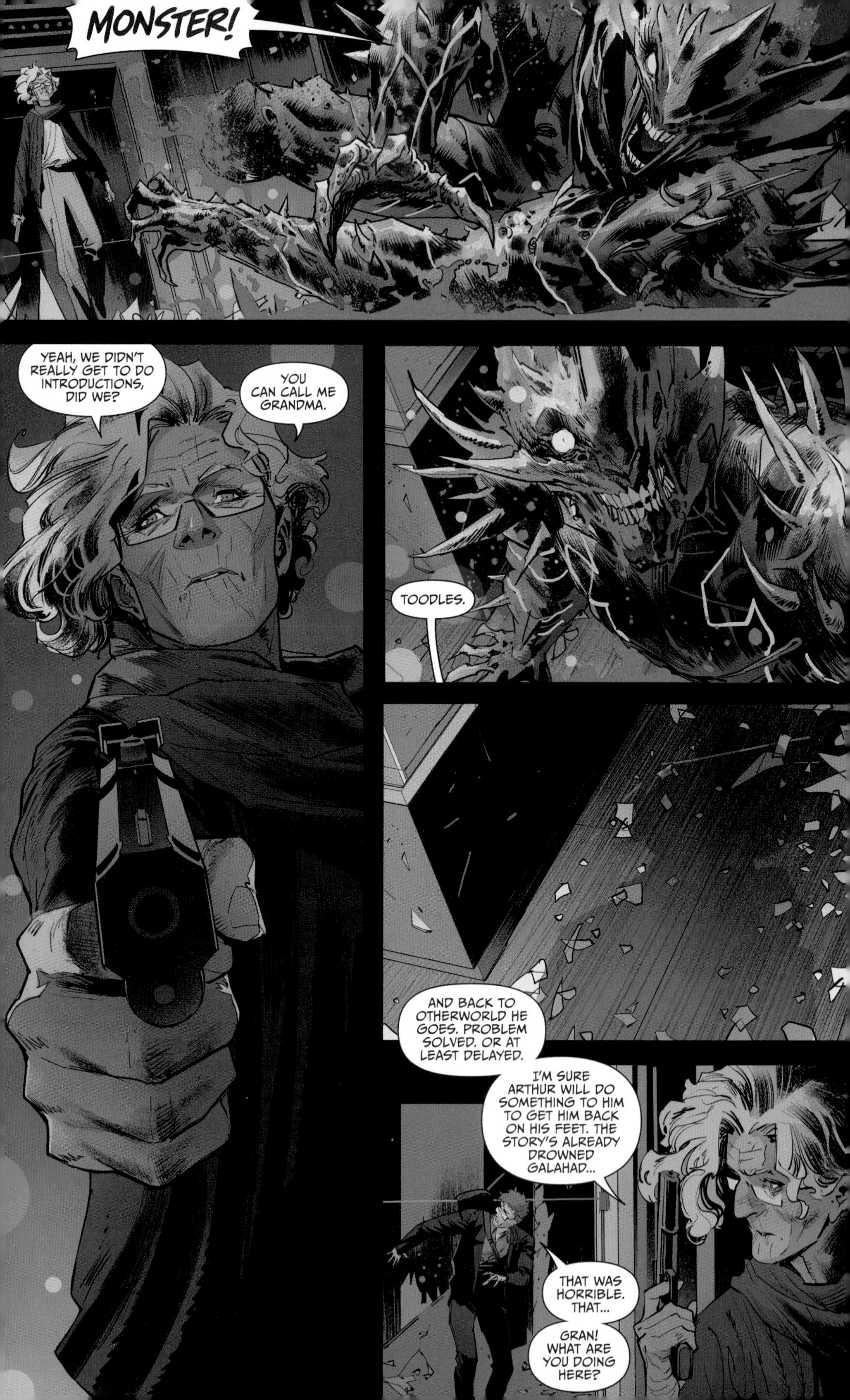
MONSTER!
YEAH, WE DIDN'T REALLY GET TO DO INTRODUCTIONS, DID WE?
YOU CAN CALL ME GRANDMA.
TOODLES.
AND BACK TO OTHERWORLD HE GOES. PROBLEM SOLVED. OR AT LEAST DELAYED.
I'M SURE ARTHUR WILL DO SOMETHING TO HIM TO GET HIM BACK ON HIS FEET. THE STORY'S ALREADY DROWNED GALAHAD...
THAT WAS HORRIBLE. THAT...
GRAN! WHAT ARE YOU DOING HERE?

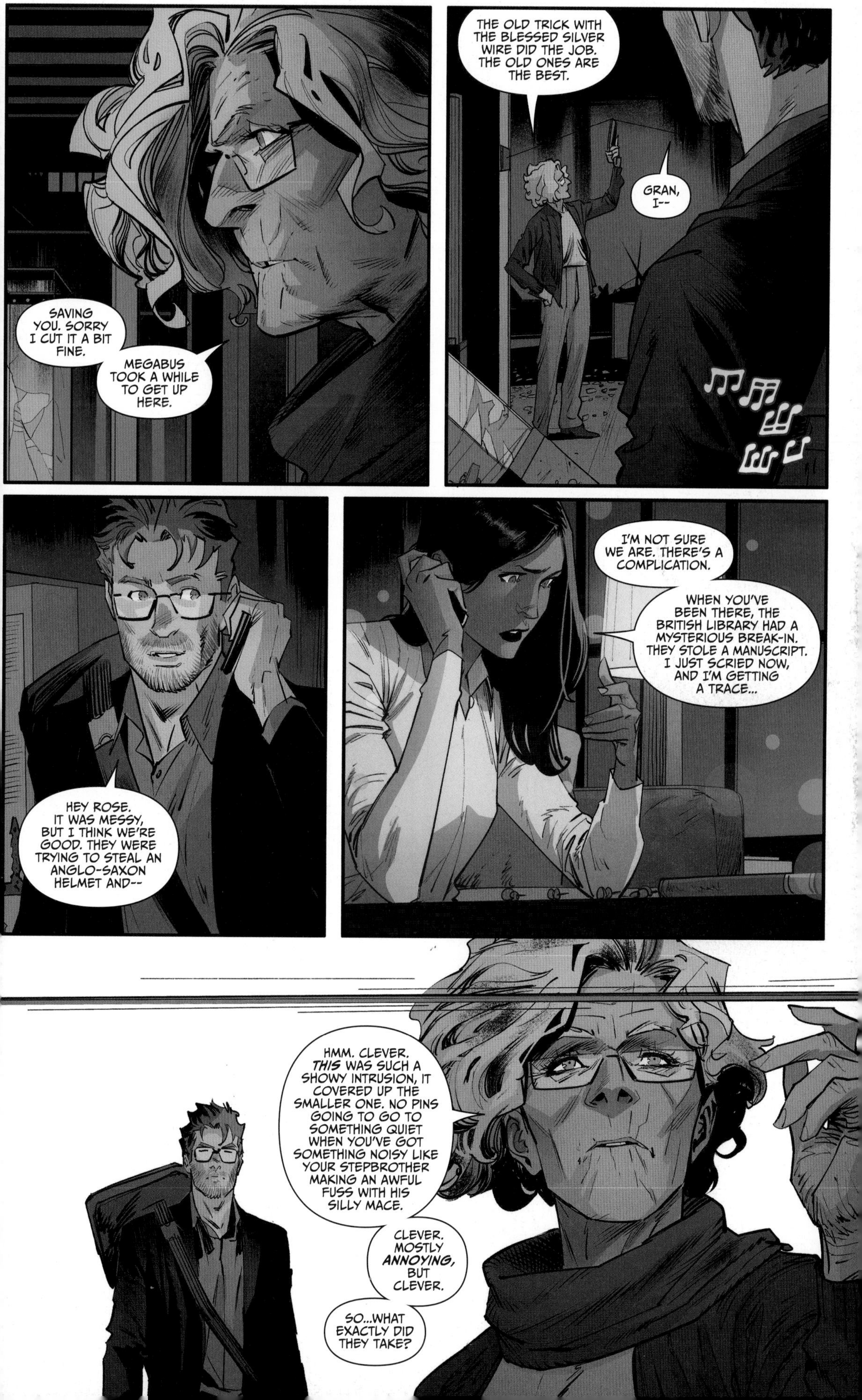
SAVING YOU. SORRY I CUT IT A BIT FINE.
MEGABUS TOOK A WHILE TO GET UP HERE.
THE OLD TRICK WITH THE BLESSED SILVER WIRE DID THE JOB. THE OLD ONES ARE THE BEST.
GRAN, I--
HEY ROSE. IT WAS MESSY, BUT I THINK WE'RE GOOD. THEY WERE TRYING TO STEAL AN ANGLO-SAXON HELMET AND--
I'M NOT SURE WE ARE. THERE'S A COMPLICATION.
WHEN YOU'VE BEEN THERE, THE BRITISH LIBRARY HAD A MYSTERIOUS BREAK-IN. THEY STOLE A MANUSCRIPT. I JUST SCRIED NOW, AND I'M GETTING A TRACE...
HMM. CLEVER. *THIS* WAS SUCH A SHOWY INTRUSION, IT COVERED UP THE SMALLER ONE. NO PINS GOING TO GO TO SOMETHING QUIET WHEN YOU'VE GOT SOMETHING NOISY LIKE YOUR STEPBROTHER MAKING AN AWFUL FUSS WITH HIS SILLY MACE.
CLEVER. MOSTLY *ANNOYING,* BUT CLEVER.
SO...WHAT EXACTLY DID THEY TAKE?

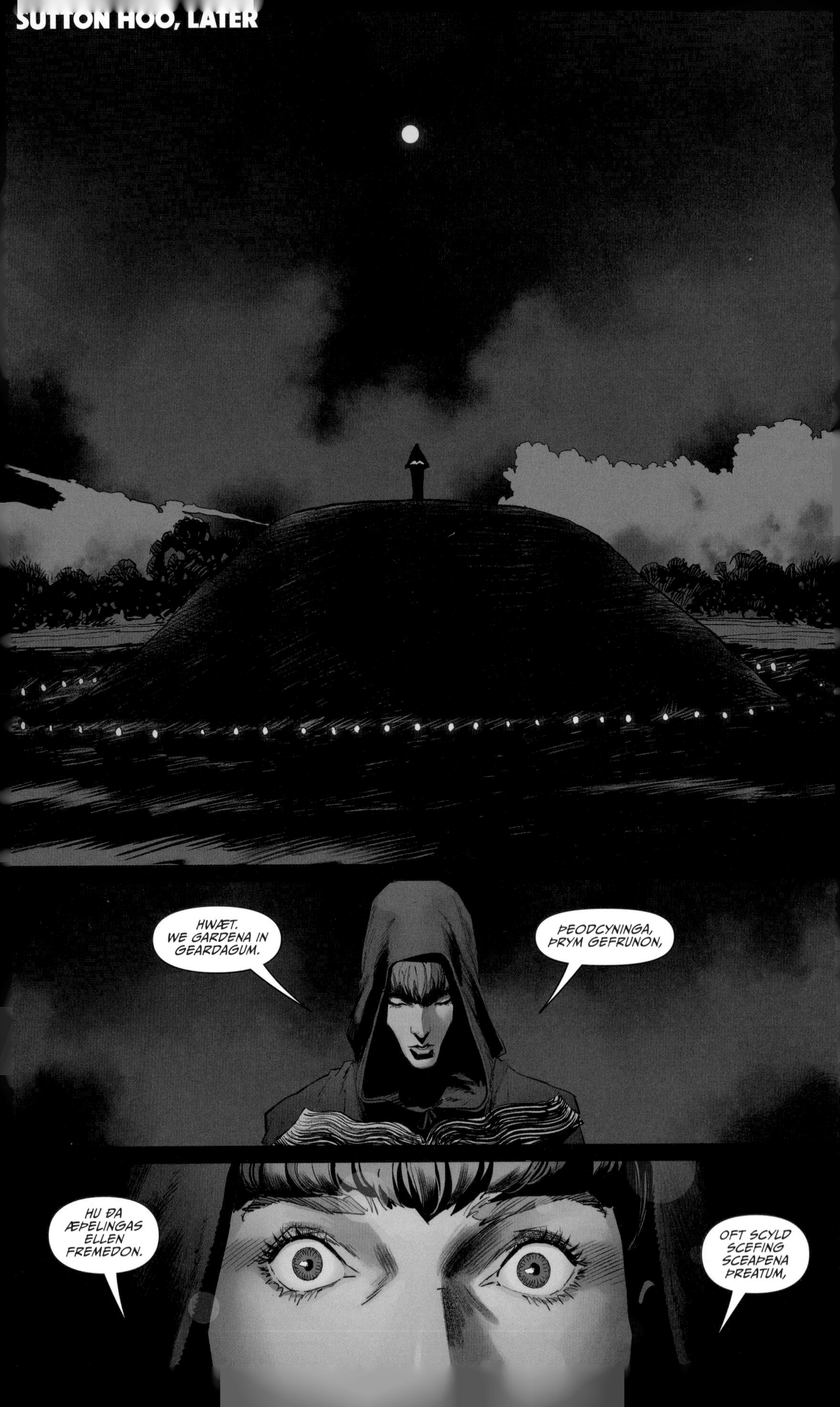
SUTTON HOO, LATER
HWÆT. WE GARDENA IN GEARDAGUM.
ÞEODCYNINGA, ÞRYM GEFRUNON,
HU ÐA ÆÞELINGAS ELLEN FREMEDON.
OFT SCYLD SCEFING SCEAÞENA ÞREATUM,

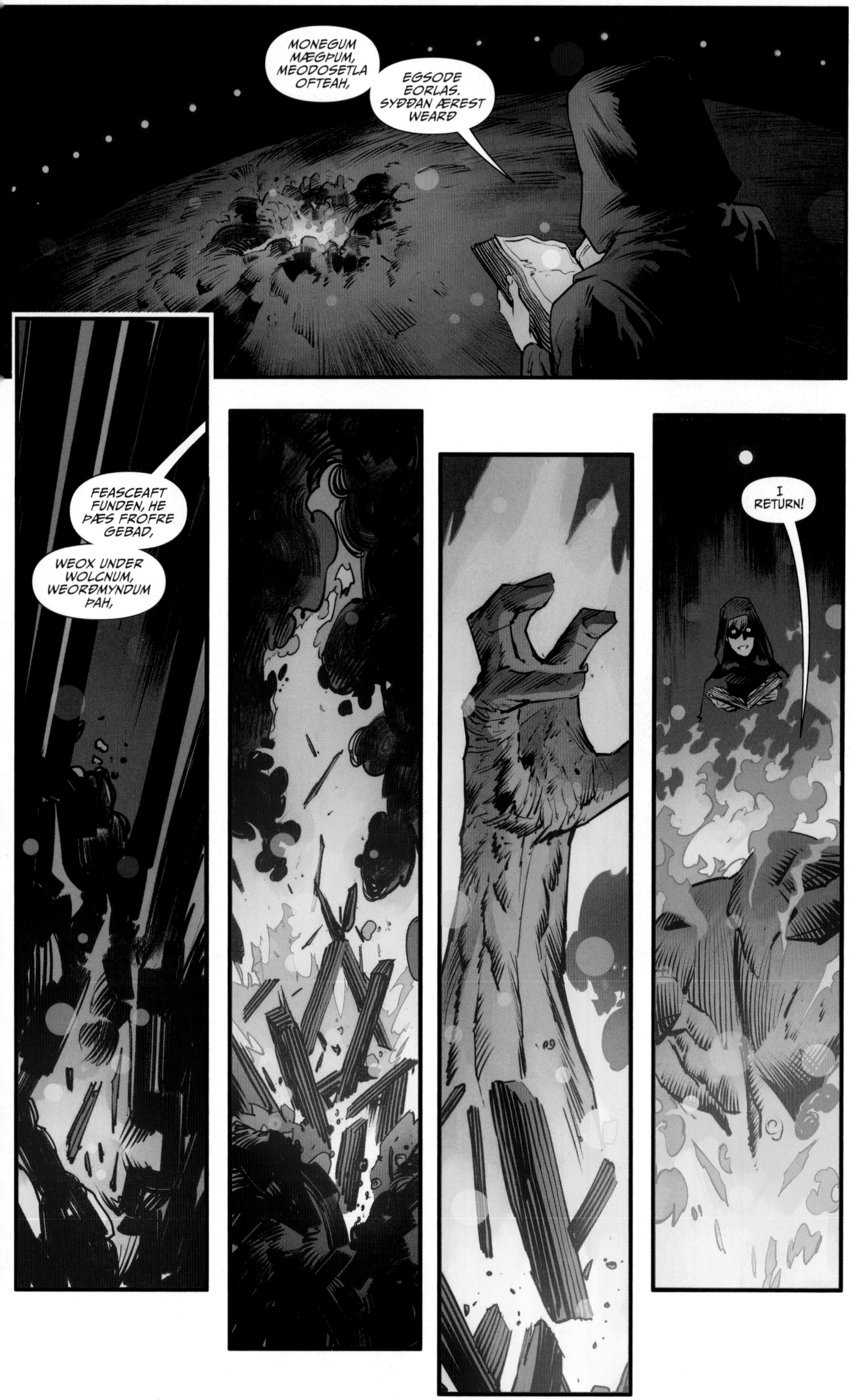
MONEGUM MÆGÞUM, MEODOSETLA OFTEAH,
EGSODE EORLAS. SYÐÐAN ÆREST WEARÐ
FEASCEAFT FUNDEN, HE ÞÆS FROFRE GEBAD,
WEOX UNDER WOLCNUM, WEORÐMYNDUM ÞAH,
I RETURN!

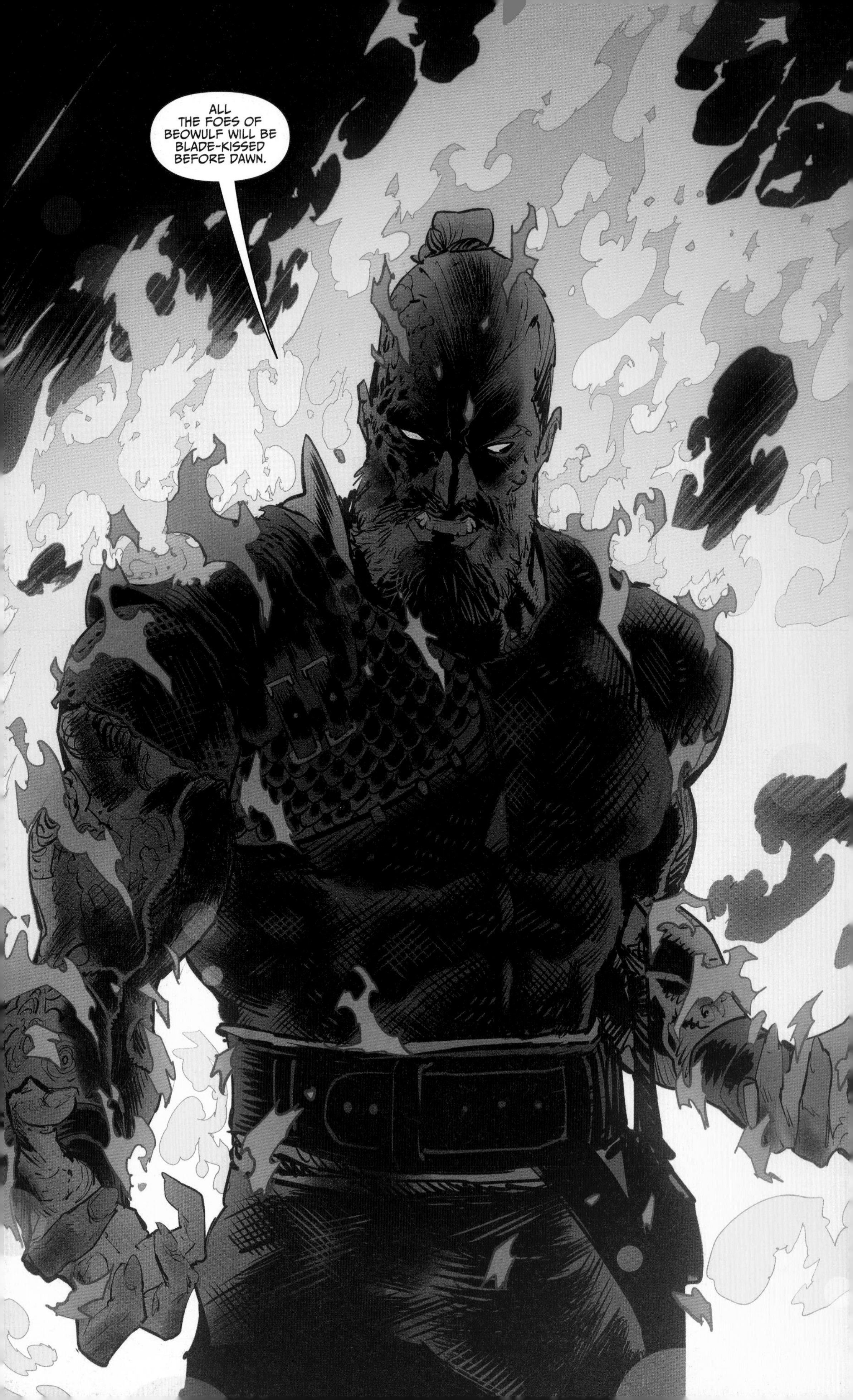
ALL THE FOES OF BEOWULF WILL BE BLADE-KISSED BEFORE DAWN.

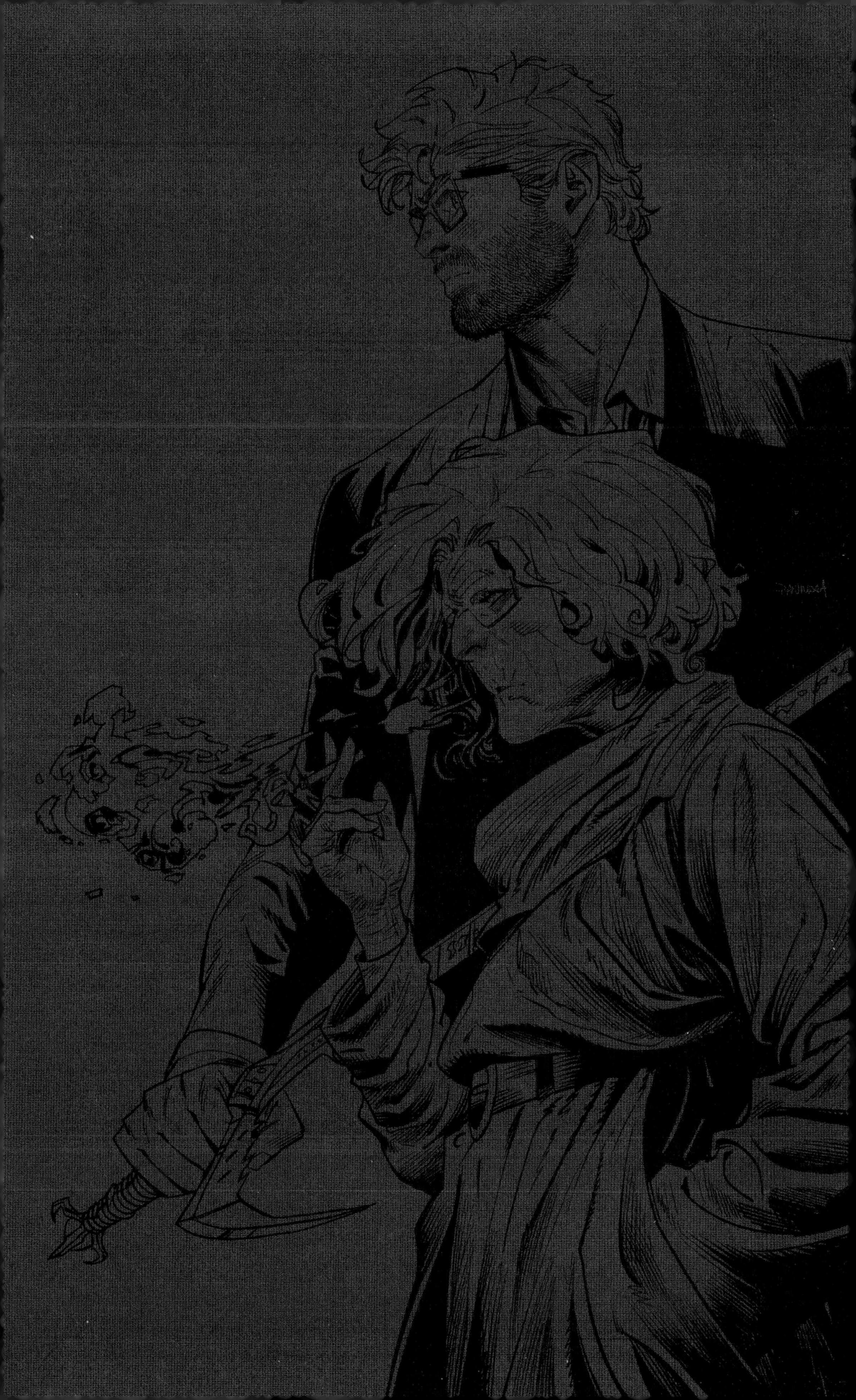

CHAPTER EIGHT

SUTTON HOO

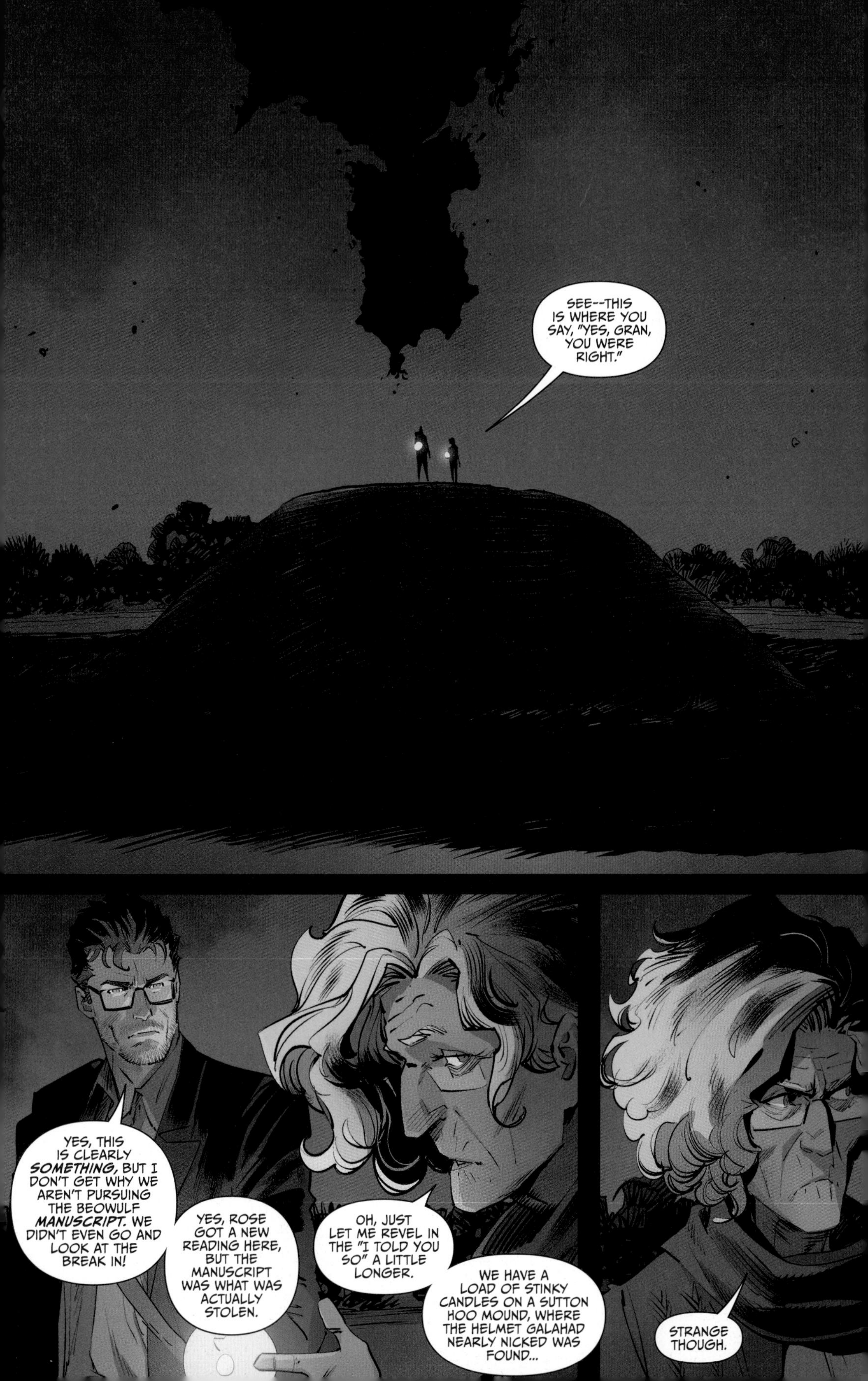
SEE--THIS IS WHERE YOU SAY, "YES, GRAN, YOU WERE RIGHT."
YES, THIS IS CLEARLY SOMETHING, BUT I DON'T GET WHY WE AREN'T PURSUING THE BEOWULF MANUSCRIPT. WE DIDN'T EVEN GO AND LOOK AT THE BREAK IN!
YES, ROSE GOT A NEW READING HERE, BUT THE MANUSCRIPT WAS WHAT WAS ACTUALLY STOLEN.
OH, JUST LET ME REVEL IN THE "I TOLD YOU SO" A LITTLE LONGER.
WE HAVE A LOAD OF STINKY CANDLES ON A SUTTON HOO MOUND, WHERE THE HELMET GALAHAD NEARLY NICKED WAS FOUND...
STRANGE THOUGH.

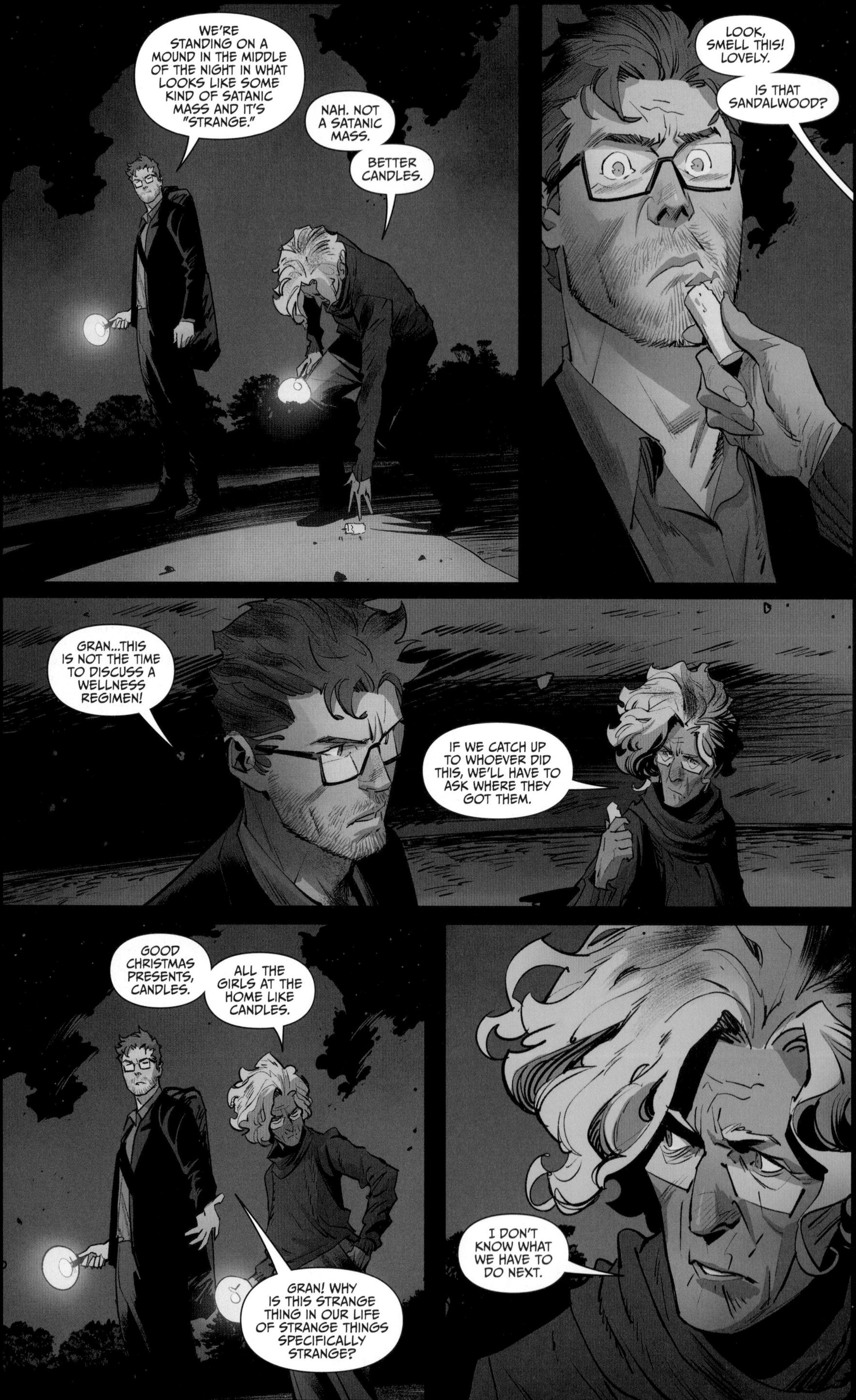
WE'RE STANDING ON A MOUND IN THE MIDDLE OF THE NIGHT IN WHAT LOOKS LIKE SOME KIND OF SATANIC MASS AND IT'S "STRANGE."
NAH. NOT A SATANIC MASS.
BETTER CANDLES.
LOOK, SMELL THIS! LOVELY.
IS THAT SANDALWOOD?
GRAN...THIS IS NOT THE TIME TO DISCUSS A WELLNESS REGIMEN!
IF WE CATCH UP TO WHOEVER DID THIS, WE'LL HAVE TO ASK WHERE THEY GOT THEM.
GOOD CHRISTMAS PRESENTS, CANDLES.
ALL THE GIRLS AT THE HOME LIKE CANDLES.
GRAN! WHY IS THIS STRANGE THING IN OUR LIFE OF STRANGE THINGS SPECIFICALLY STRANGE?
I DON'T KNOW WHAT WE HAVE TO DO NEXT.

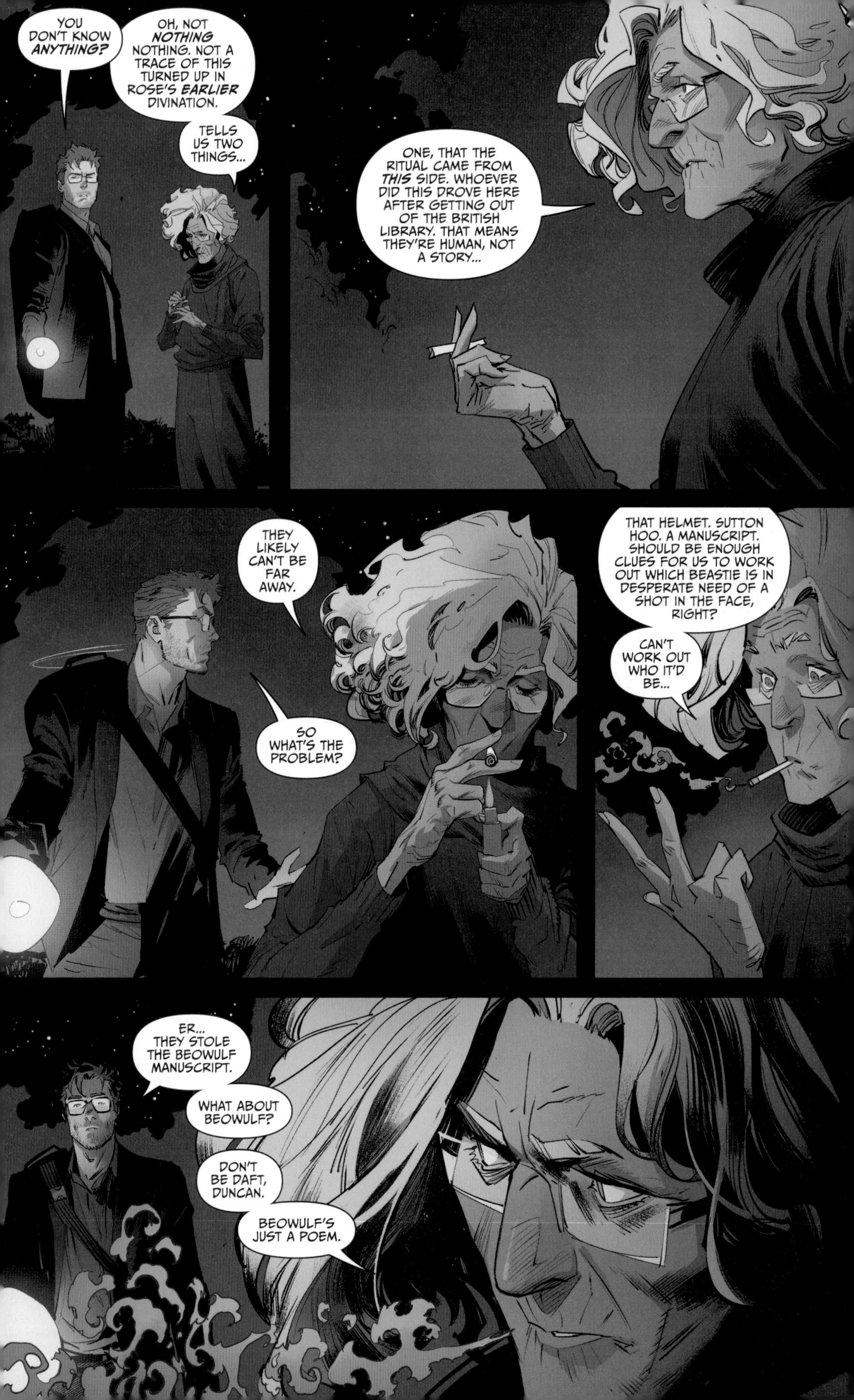

YOU DON'T KNOW *ANYTHING?*
OH, NOT ***NOTHING*** NOTHING. NOT A TRACE OF THIS TURNED UP IN ROSE'S ***EARLIER*** DIVINATION.
TELLS US TWO THINGS...
ONE, THAT THE RITUAL CAME FROM ***THIS*** SIDE. WHOEVER DID THIS DROVE HERE AFTER GETTING OUT OF THE BRITISH LIBRARY. THAT MEANS THEY'RE HUMAN, NOT A STORY...
THEY LIKELY CAN'T BE FAR AWAY.
SO WHAT'S THE PROBLEM?
THAT HELMET. SUTTON HOO. A MANUSCRIPT. SHOULD BE ENOUGH CLUES FOR US TO WORK OUT WHICH BEASTIE IS IN DESPERATE NEED OF A SHOT IN THE FACE, RIGHT?
CAN'T WORK OUT WHO IT'D BE...
ER... THEY STOLE THE BEOWULF MANUSCRIPT.
WHAT ABOUT BEOWULF?
DON'T BE DAFT, DUNCAN.
BEOWULF'S JUST A POEM.

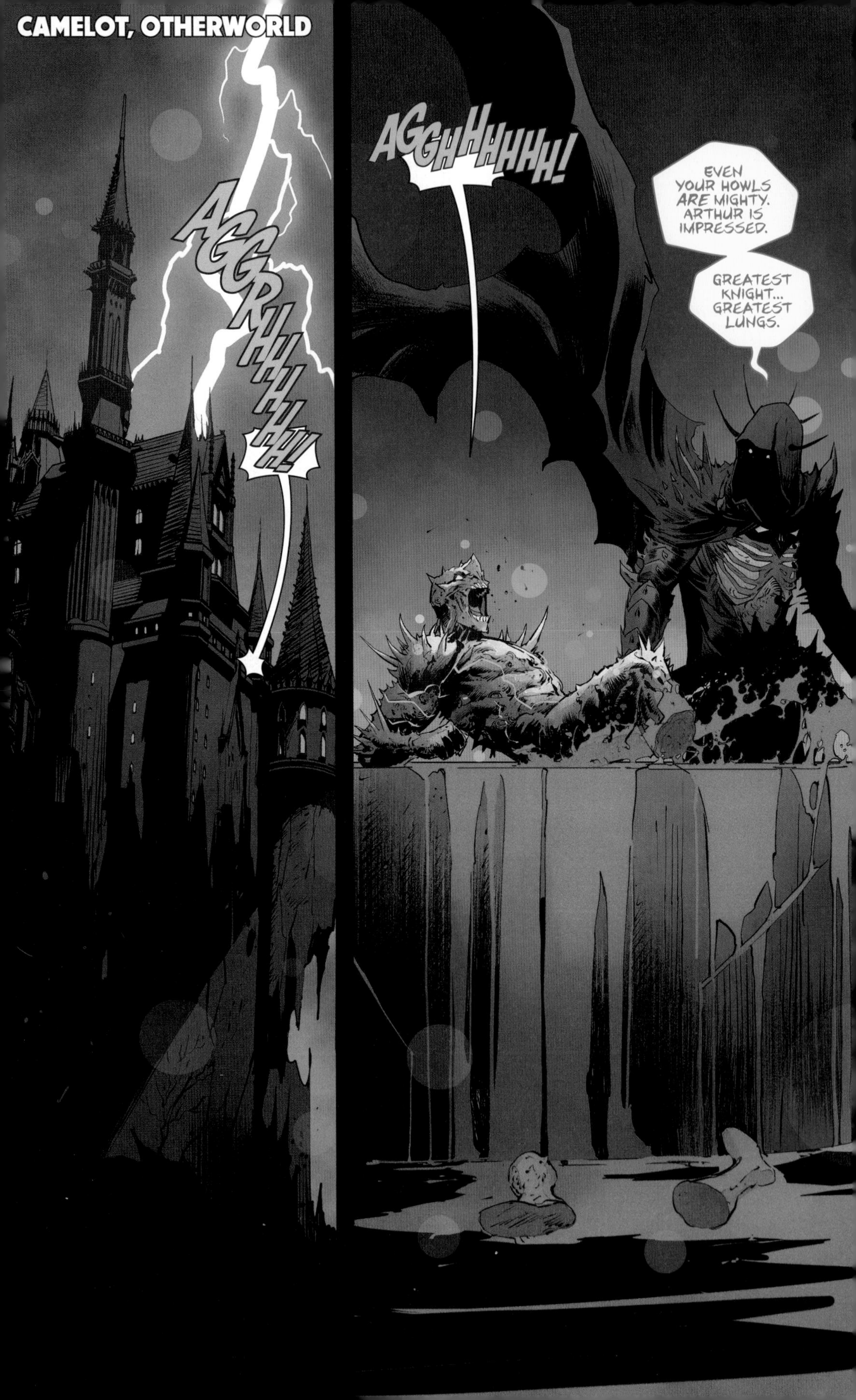
CAMELOT, OTHERWORLD
AGGRHHHHH!
AGGHHHHHH!
EVEN YOUR HOWLS ARE MIGHTY. ARTHUR IS IMPRESSED.
GREATEST KNIGHT... GREATEST LUNGS.

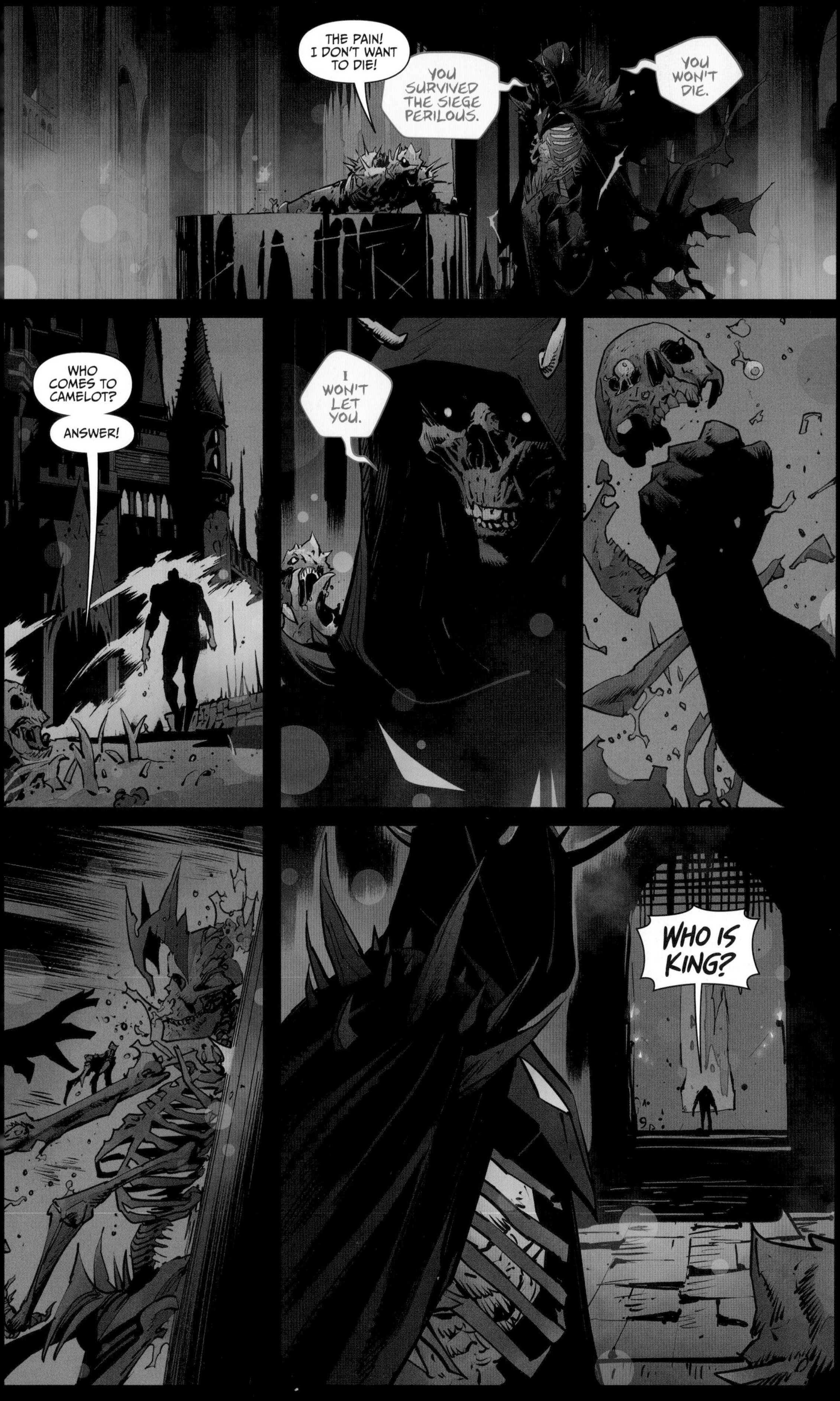

THE PAIN! I DON'T WANT TO DIE!
YOU SURVIVED THE SIEGE PERILOUS.
YOU WON'T DIE.
WHO COMES TO CAMELOT?
ANSWER!
I WON'T LET YOU.
WHO IS KING?

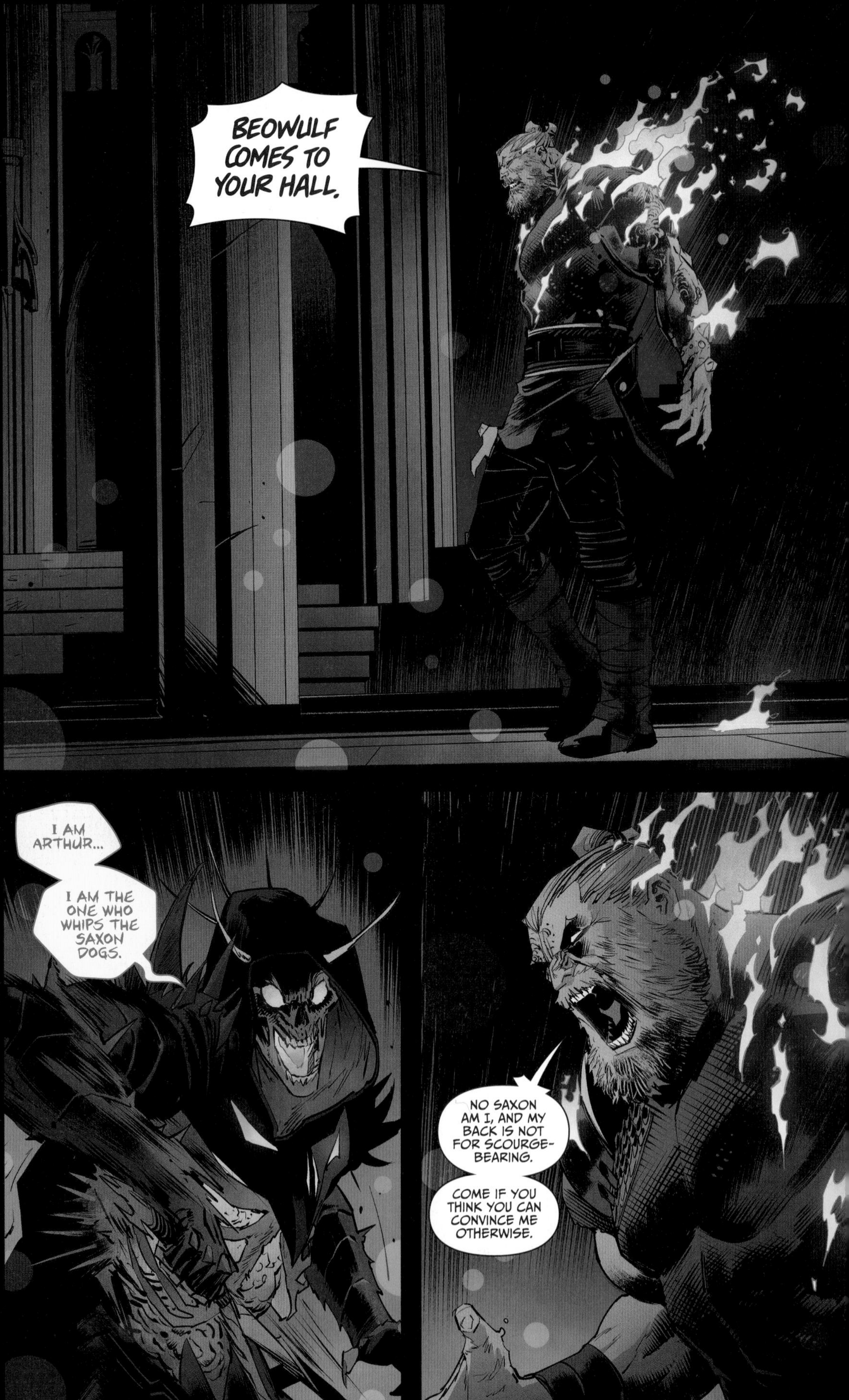
BEOWULF COMES TO YOUR HALL.
I AM ARTHUR...
I AM THE ONE WHO WHIPS THE SAXON DOGS.
NO SAXON AM I, AND MY BACK IS NOT FOR SCOURGE-BEARING.
COME IF YOU THINK YOU CAN CONVINCE ME OTHERWISE.

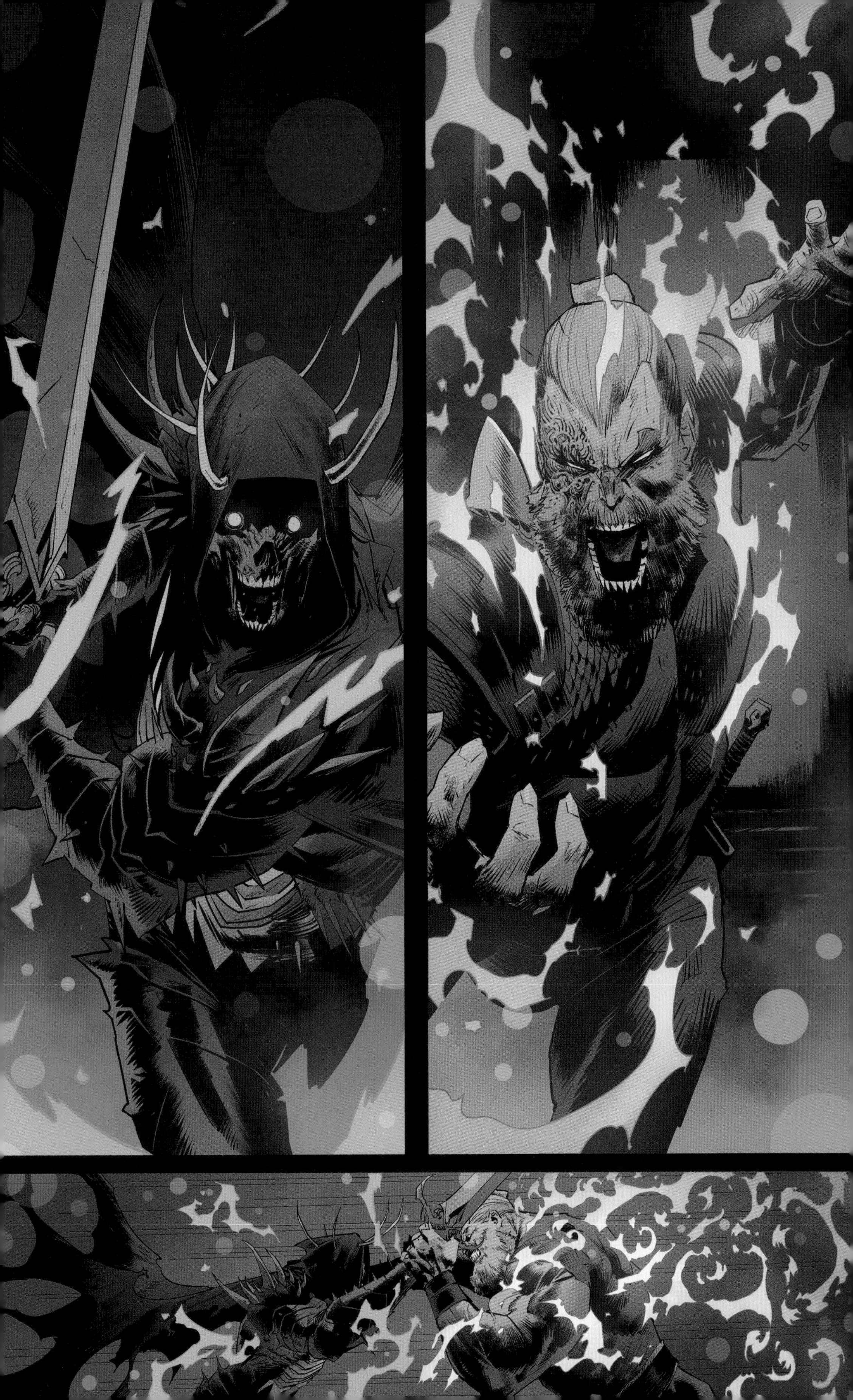

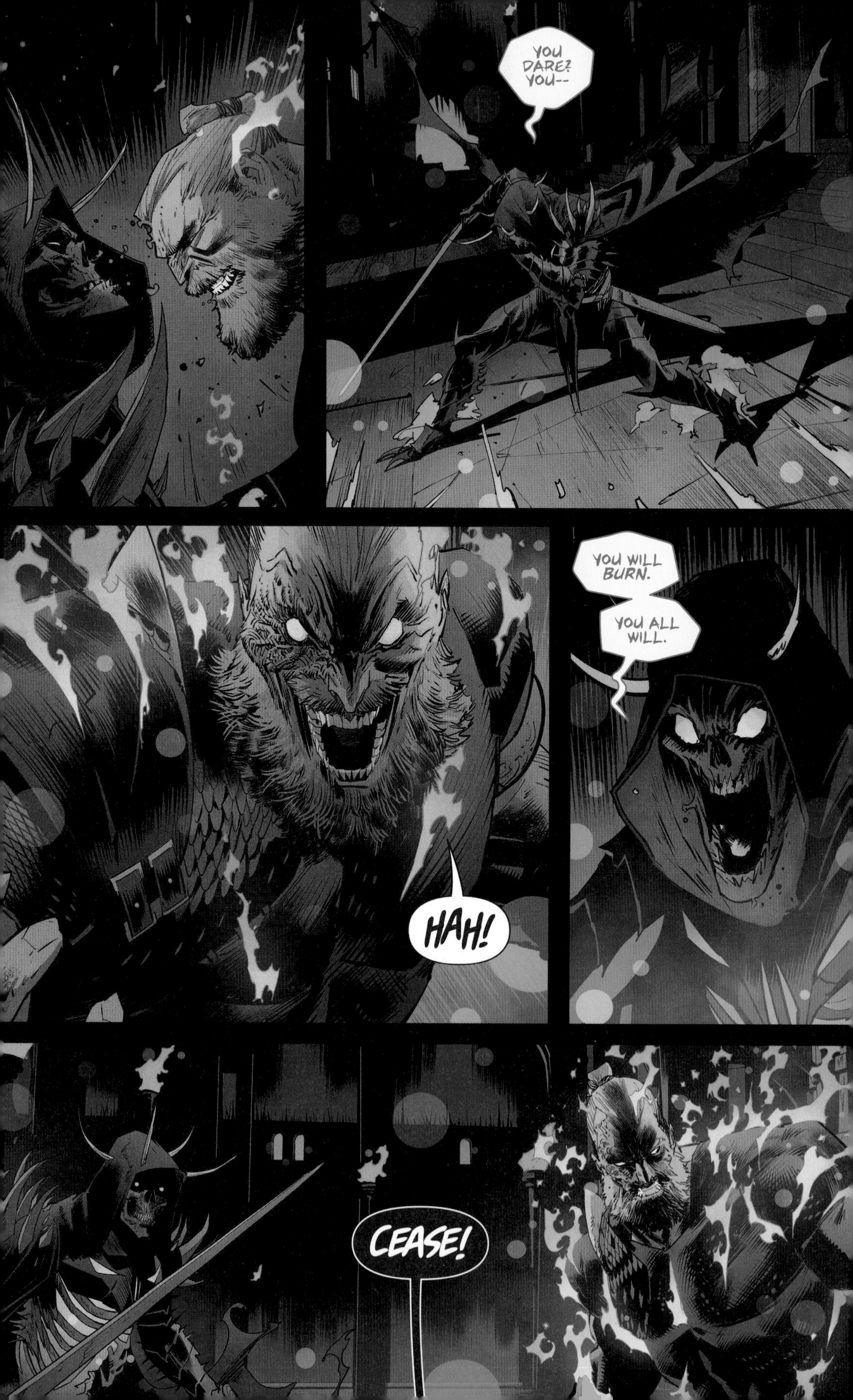
YOU DARE? YOU--
HAH!
YOU WILL BURN.
YOU ALL WILL.
CEASE!

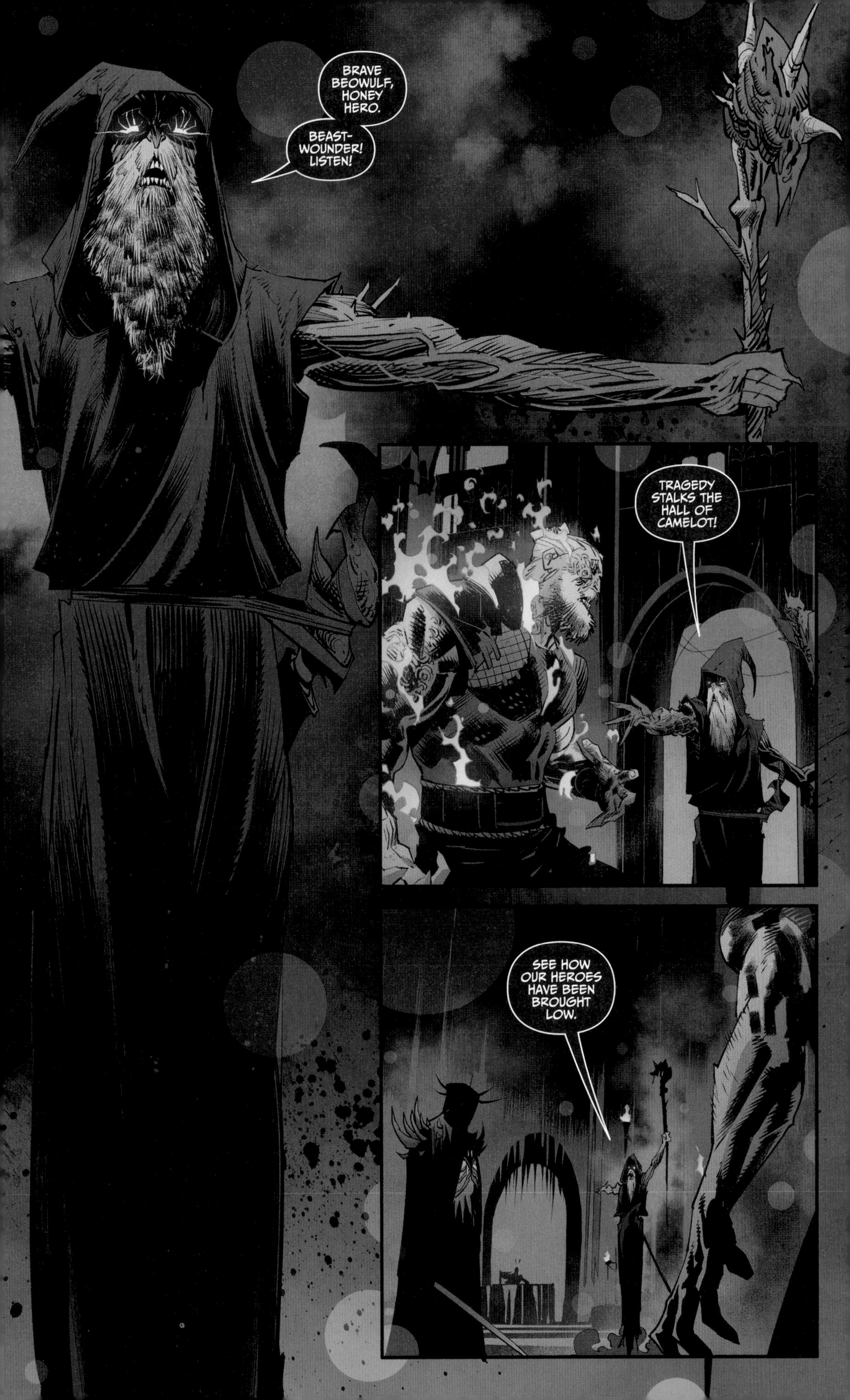

BRAVE BEOWULF, HONEY HERO.
BEAST-WOUNDER! LISTEN!
TRAGEDY STALKS THE HALL OF CAMELOT!
SEE HOW OUR HEROES HAVE BEEN BROUGHT LOW.

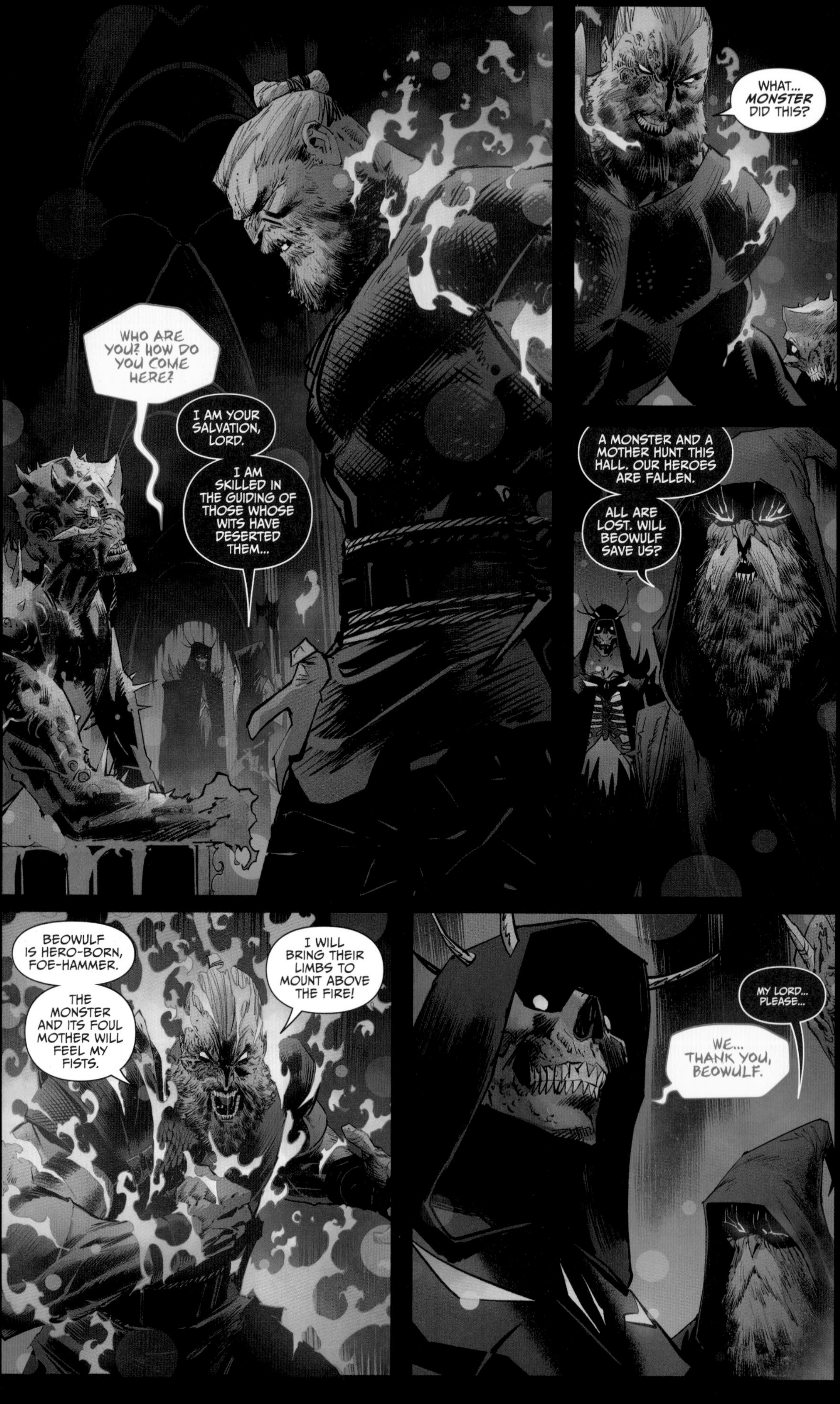
WHO ARE YOU? HOW DO YOU COME HERE?
I AM YOUR SALVATION, LORD.
I AM SKILLED IN THE GUIDING OF THOSE WHOSE WITS HAVE DESERTED THEM...
WHAT... MONSTER DID THIS?
A MONSTER AND A MOTHER HUNT THIS HALL. OUR HEROES ARE FALLEN.
ALL ARE LOST. WILL BEOWULF SAVE US?
BEOWULF IS HERO-BORN, FOE-HAMMER.
THE MONSTER AND ITS FOUL MOTHER WILL FEEL MY FISTS.
I WILL BRING THEIR LIMBS TO MOUNT ABOVE THE FIRE!
MY LORD... PLEASE...
WE... THANK YOU, BEOWULF.

I FOUGHT HIM, I THINK. IN ANOTHER TIME. HE IS NOT A SAXON, THOUGH HE FIGHTS WITH THEM? I...

ALL IS CONFUSION.

IT WILL BECOME CLEAR.

WHO ARE YOU?

I AM THE ONE WHO WARNED YOU OF HIS RETURN.

THE ONE WHOSE ADVICE YOU FOLLOWED WHEN YOU SENT FORTH YOUR PERFECT KNIGHT TO TRY AND PREVENT HIS COMING...

HE FAILED, YES, BUT WE MAKE THE BEST OF THE SITUATION. WE CAN *USE* THIS, MY LORD...

I AM *MERLIN.*

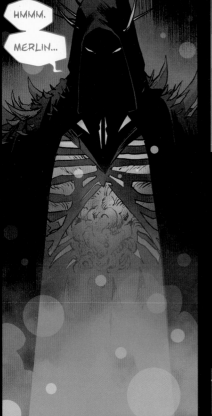

HMMM.

MERLIN...

I KNOW YOU NOT.

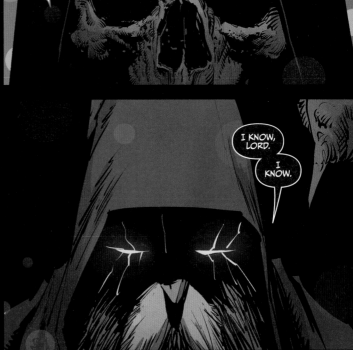

I KNOW, LORD.

I KNOW.

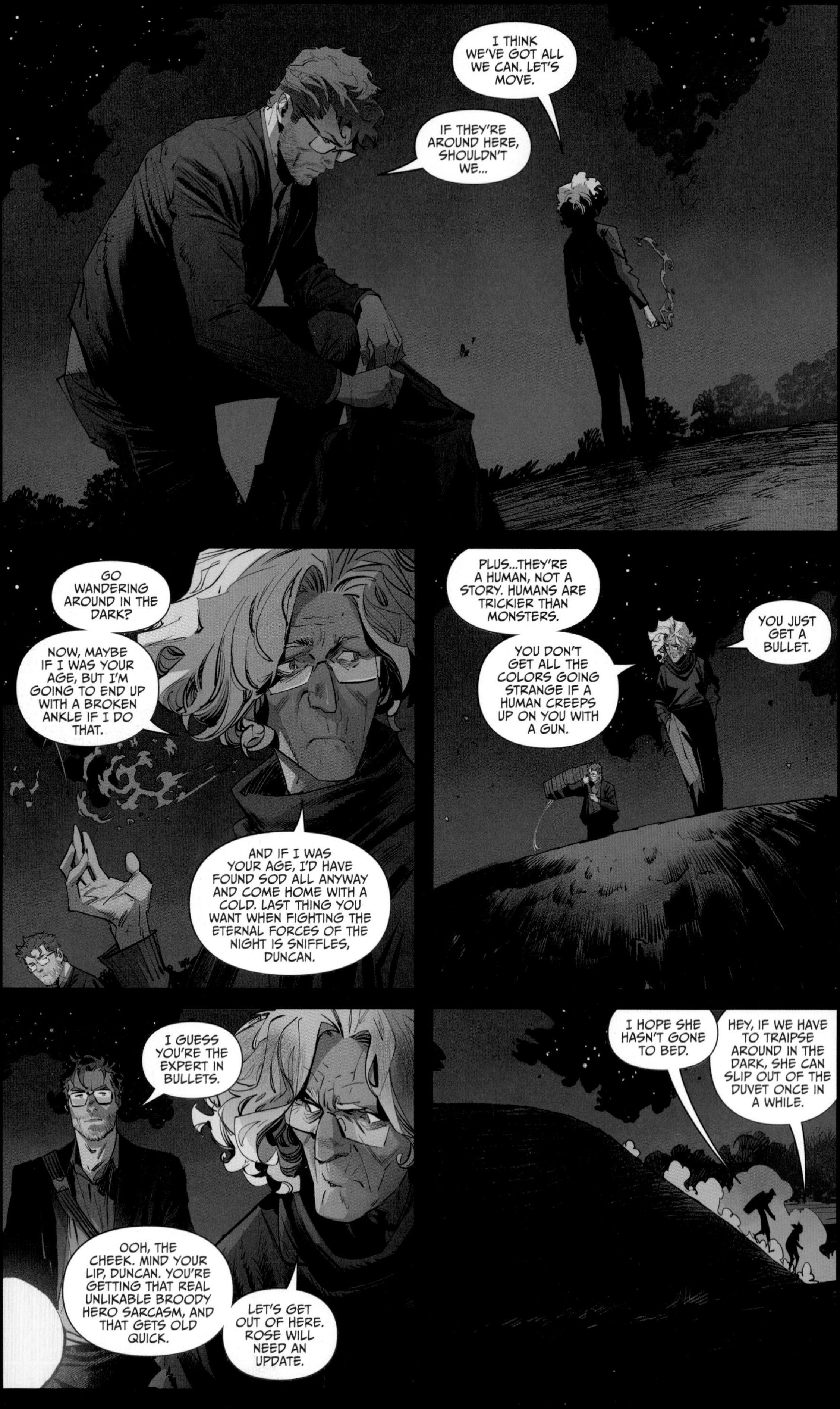
I THINK WE'VE GOT ALL WE CAN. LET'S MOVE.
IF THEY'RE AROUND HERE, SHOULDN'T WE...
GO WANDERING AROUND IN THE DARK?
NOW, MAYBE IF I WAS YOUR AGE, BUT I'M GOING TO END UP WITH A BROKEN ANKLE IF I DO THAT.
AND IF I WAS YOUR AGE, I'D HAVE FOUND SOD ALL ANYWAY AND COME HOME WITH A COLD. LAST THING YOU WANT WHEN FIGHTING THE ETERNAL FORCES OF THE NIGHT IS SNIFFLES, DUNCAN.
PLUS...THEY'RE A HUMAN, NOT A STORY. HUMANS ARE TRICKIER THAN MONSTERS.
YOU DON'T GET ALL THE COLORS GOING STRANGE IF A HUMAN CREEPS UP ON YOU WITH A GUN.
YOU JUST GET A BULLET.
I GUESS YOU'RE THE EXPERT IN BULLETS.
OOH, THE CHEEK. MIND YOUR LIP, DUNCAN. YOU'RE GETTING THAT REAL UNLIKABLE BROODY HERO SARCASM, AND THAT GETS OLD QUICK.
LET'S GET OUT OF HERE. ROSE WILL NEED AN UPDATE.
I HOPE SHE HASN'T GONE TO BED.
HEY, IF WE HAVE TO TRAIPSE AROUND IN THE DARK, SHE CAN SLIP OUT OF THE DUVET ONCE IN A WHILE.

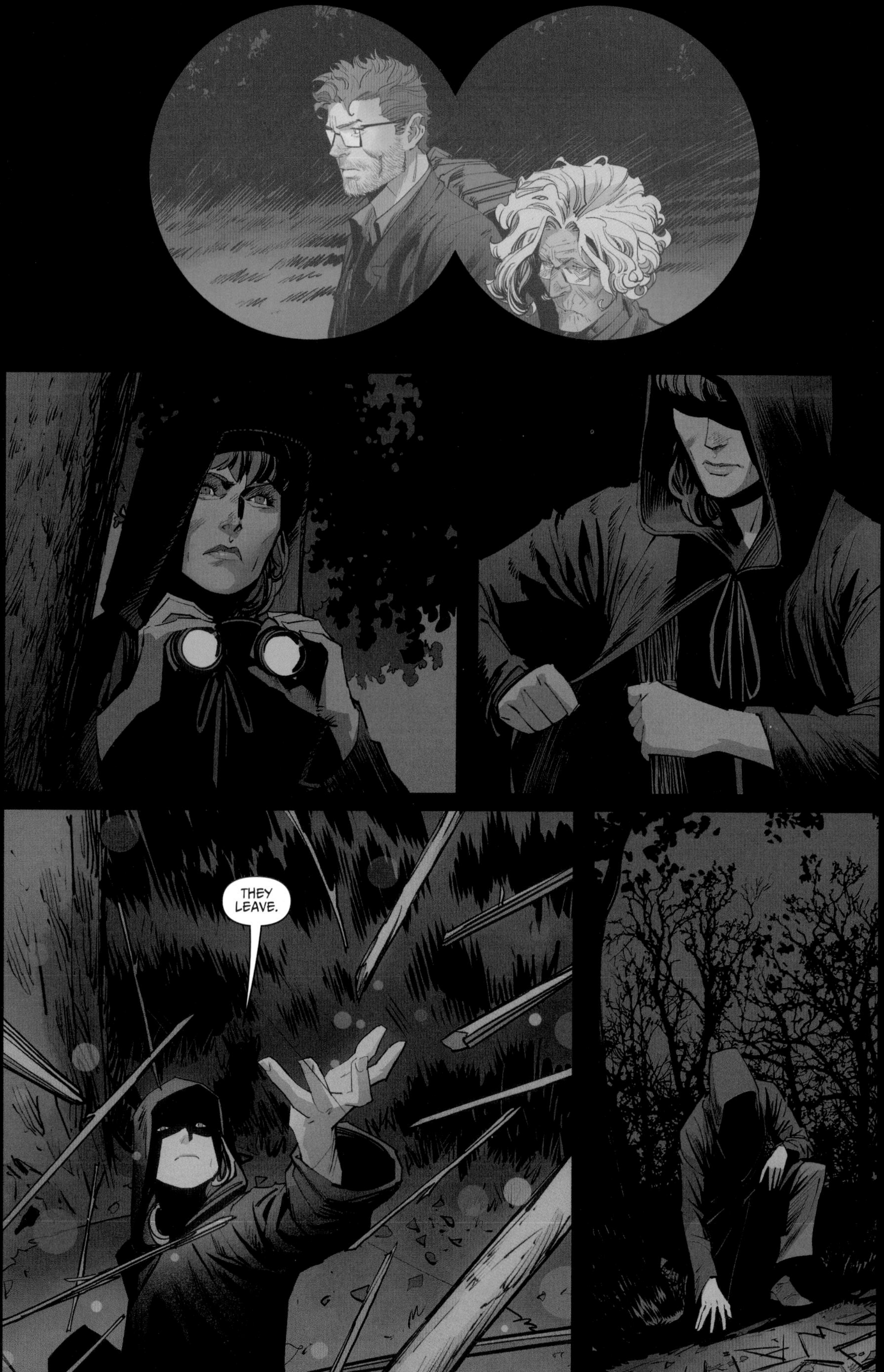
THEY LEAVE.

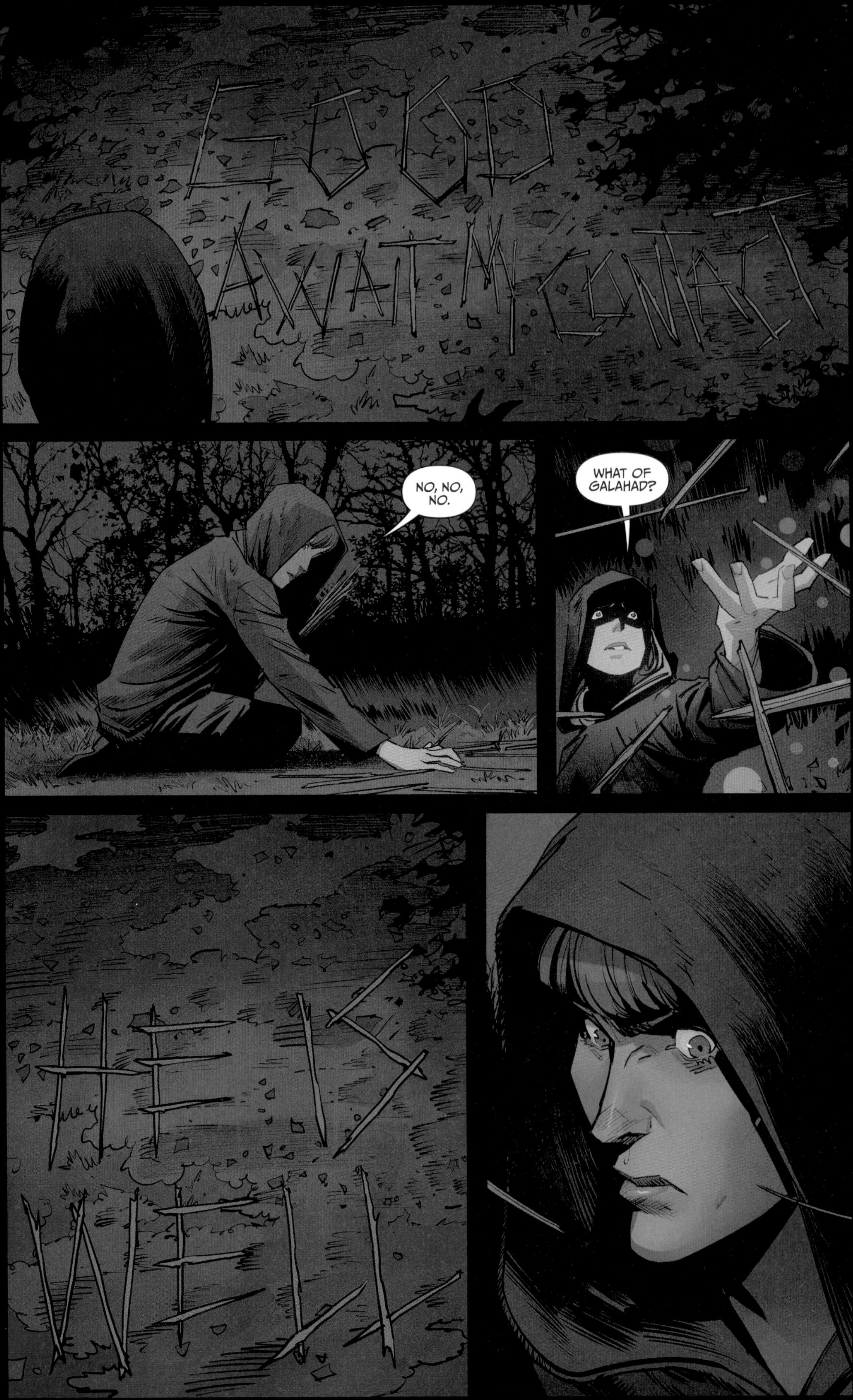
GOOD
AWAIT MY CONTACT
NO, NO, NO.
WHAT OF GALAHAD?
HE IS WELL

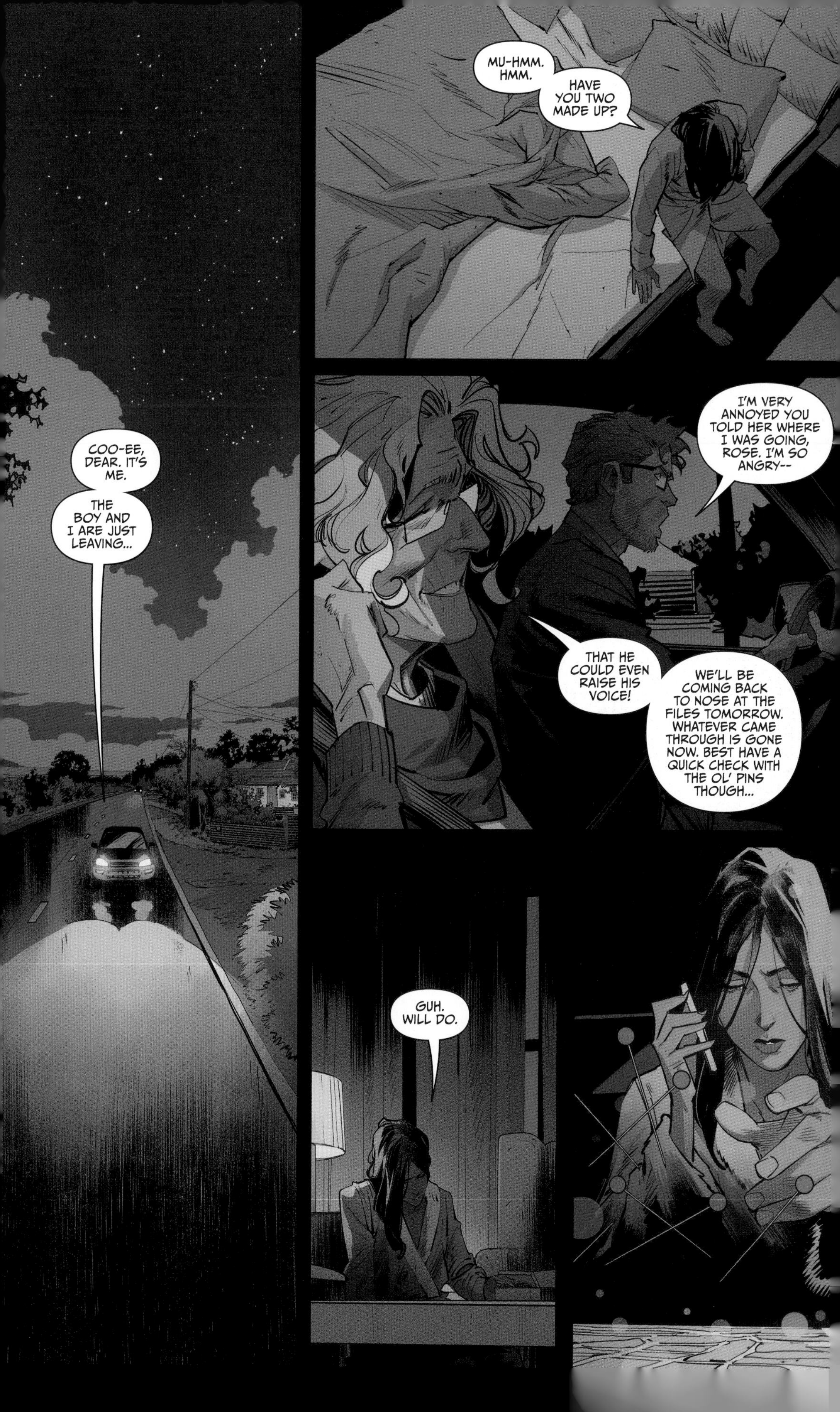
COO-EE, DEAR. IT'S ME.
THE BOY AND I ARE JUST LEAVING...
MU-HMM. HMM.
HAVE YOU TWO MADE UP?
I'M VERY ANNOYED YOU TOLD HER WHERE I WAS GOING, ROSE. I'M SO ANGRY--
THAT HE COULD EVEN RAISE HIS VOICE!
WE'LL BE COMING BACK TO NOSE AT THE FILES TOMORROW. WHATEVER CAME THROUGH IS GONE NOW. BEST HAVE A QUICK CHECK WITH THE OL' PINS THOUGH...
GUH. WILL DO.

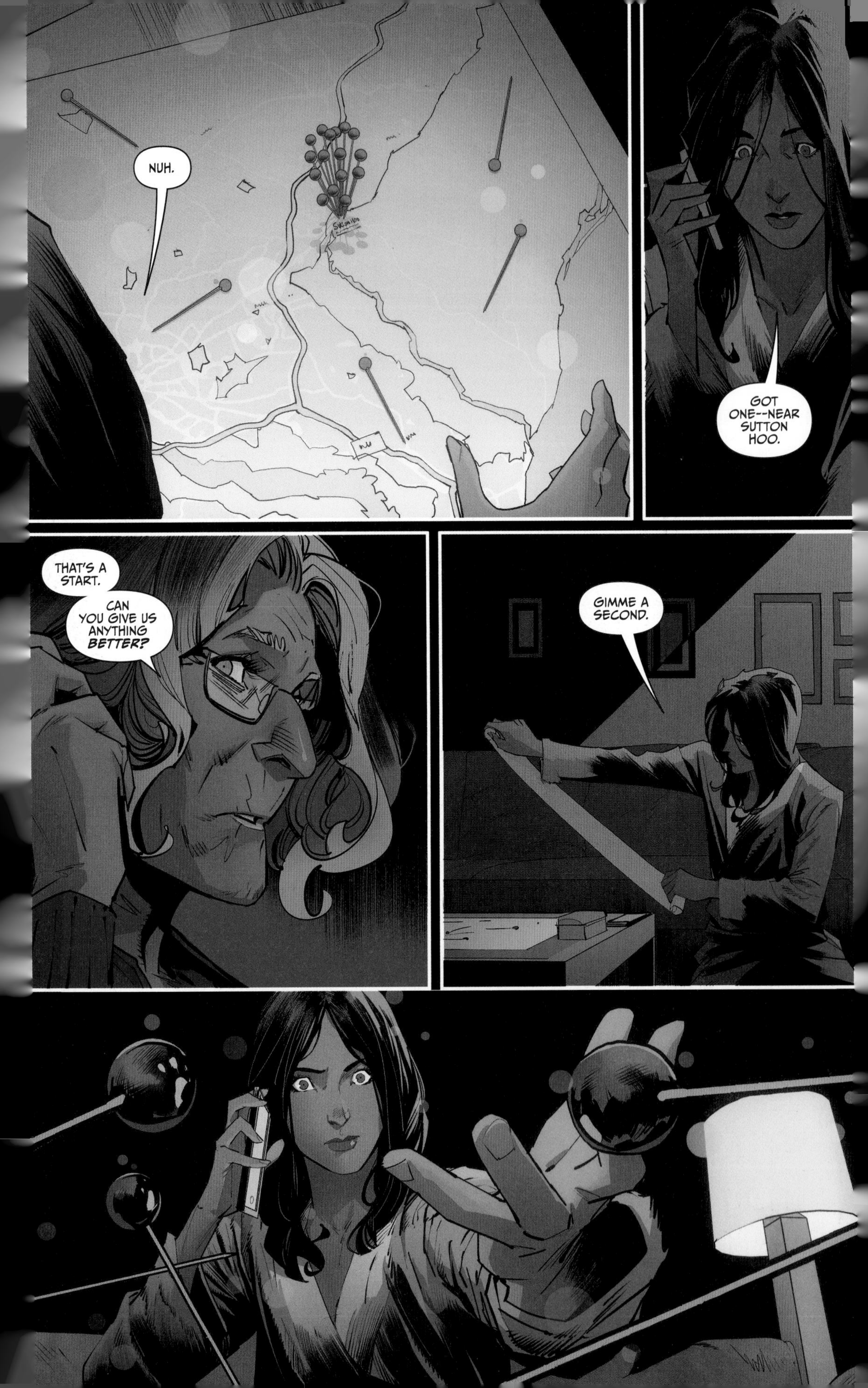
NUH.
GOT ONE--NEAR SUTTON HOO.
THAT'S A START.
CAN YOU GIVE US ANYTHING *BETTER?*
GIMME A SECOND.

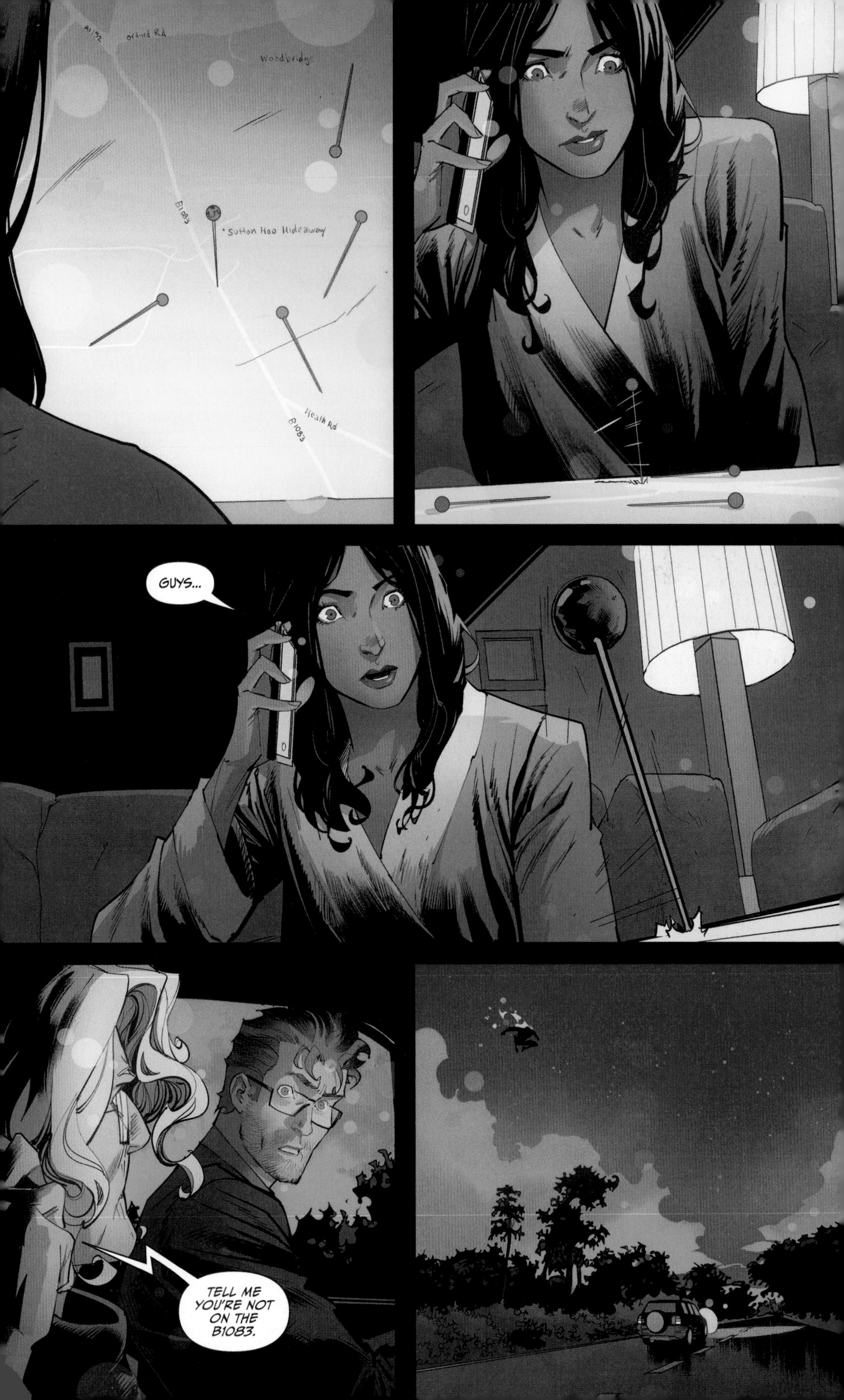
A1152
Orford Rd
Woodbridge
B1083
*Sutton Hoo Hideaway
Heath Rd
B1083
GUYS...
TELL ME YOU'RE NOT ON THE B1083.

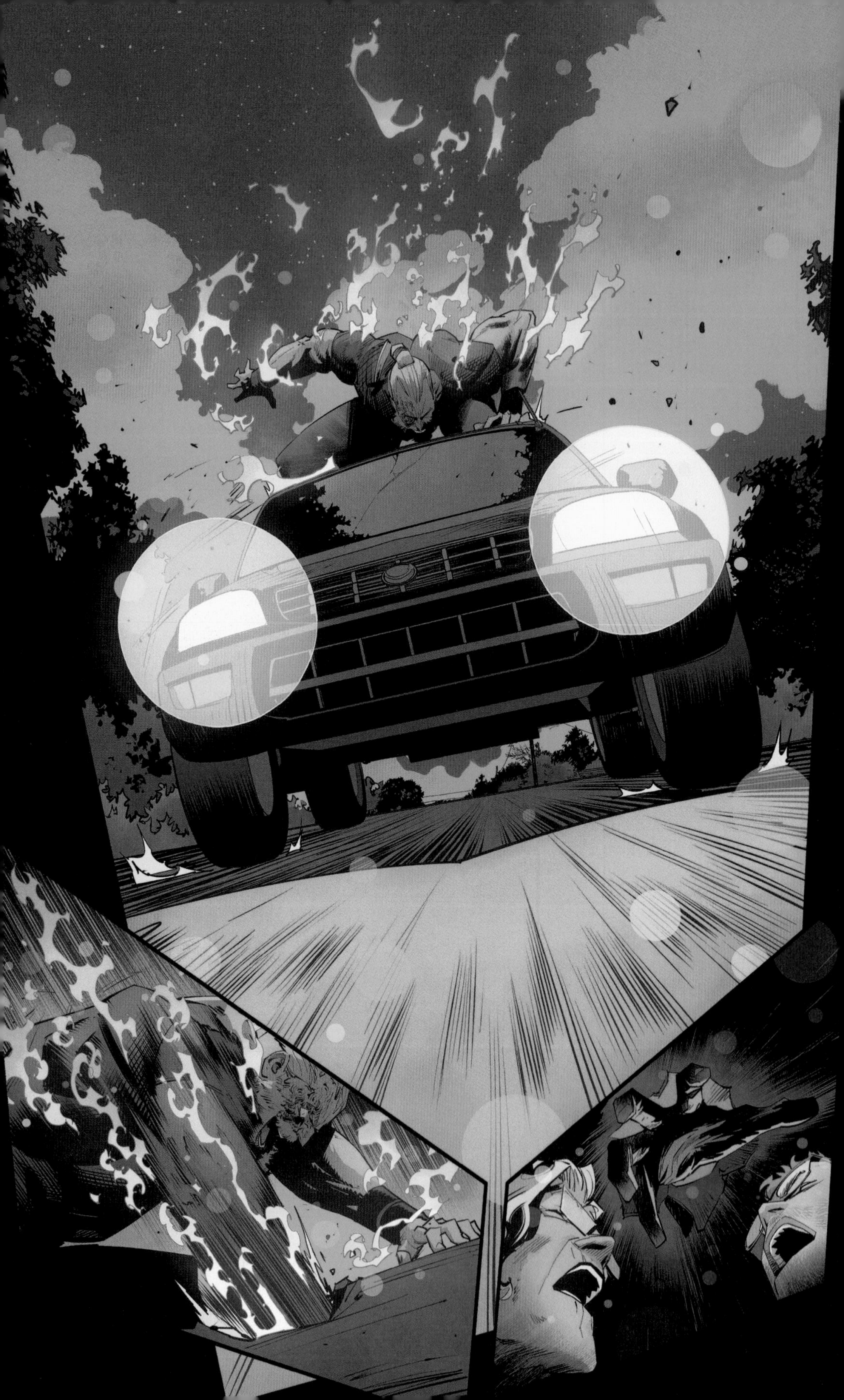

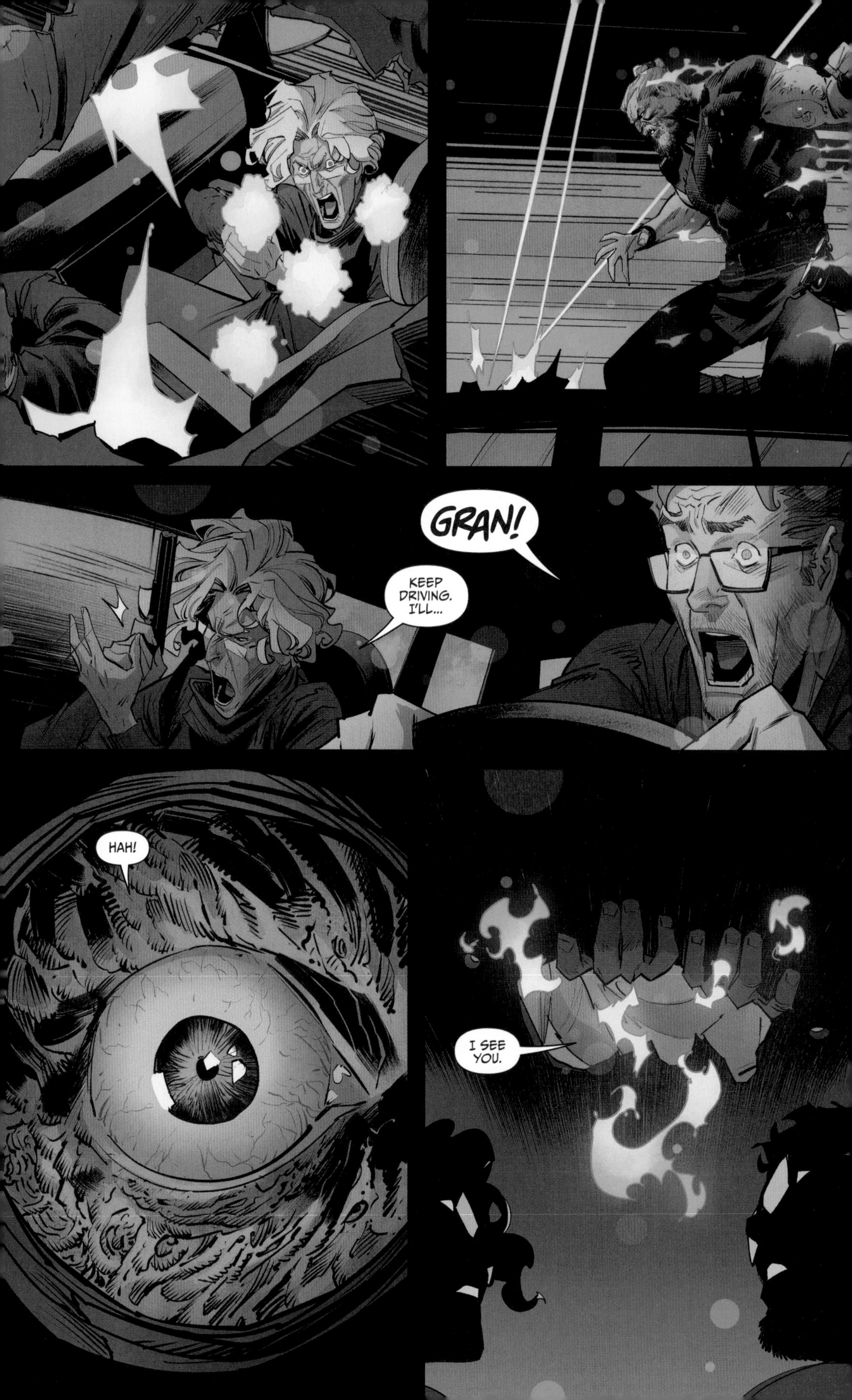
GRAN!
KEEP DRIVING. I'LL...
HAH!
I SEE YOU.

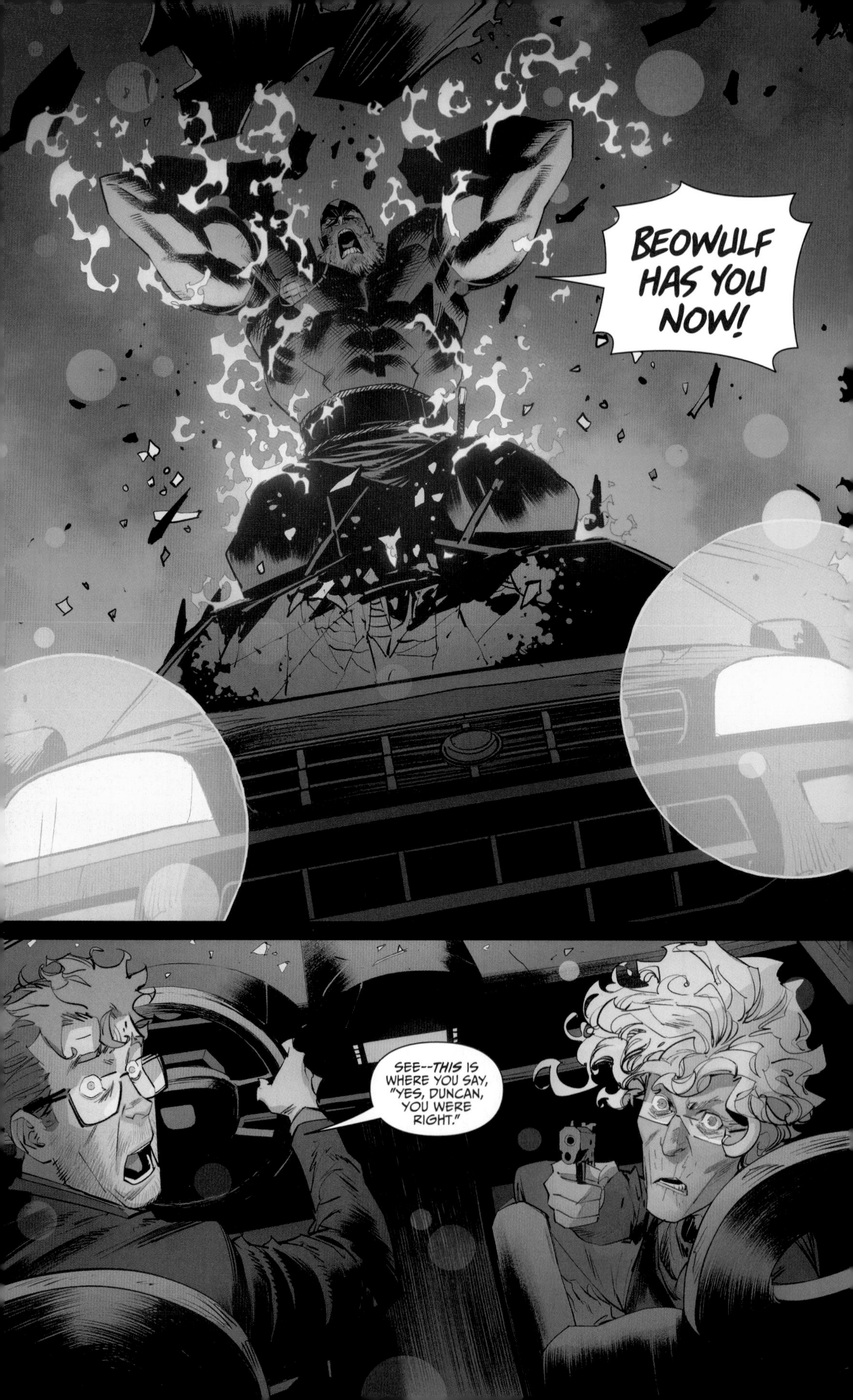
BEOWULF HAS YOU NOW!
SEE--THIS IS WHERE YOU SAY, "YES, DUNCAN, YOU WERE RIGHT."

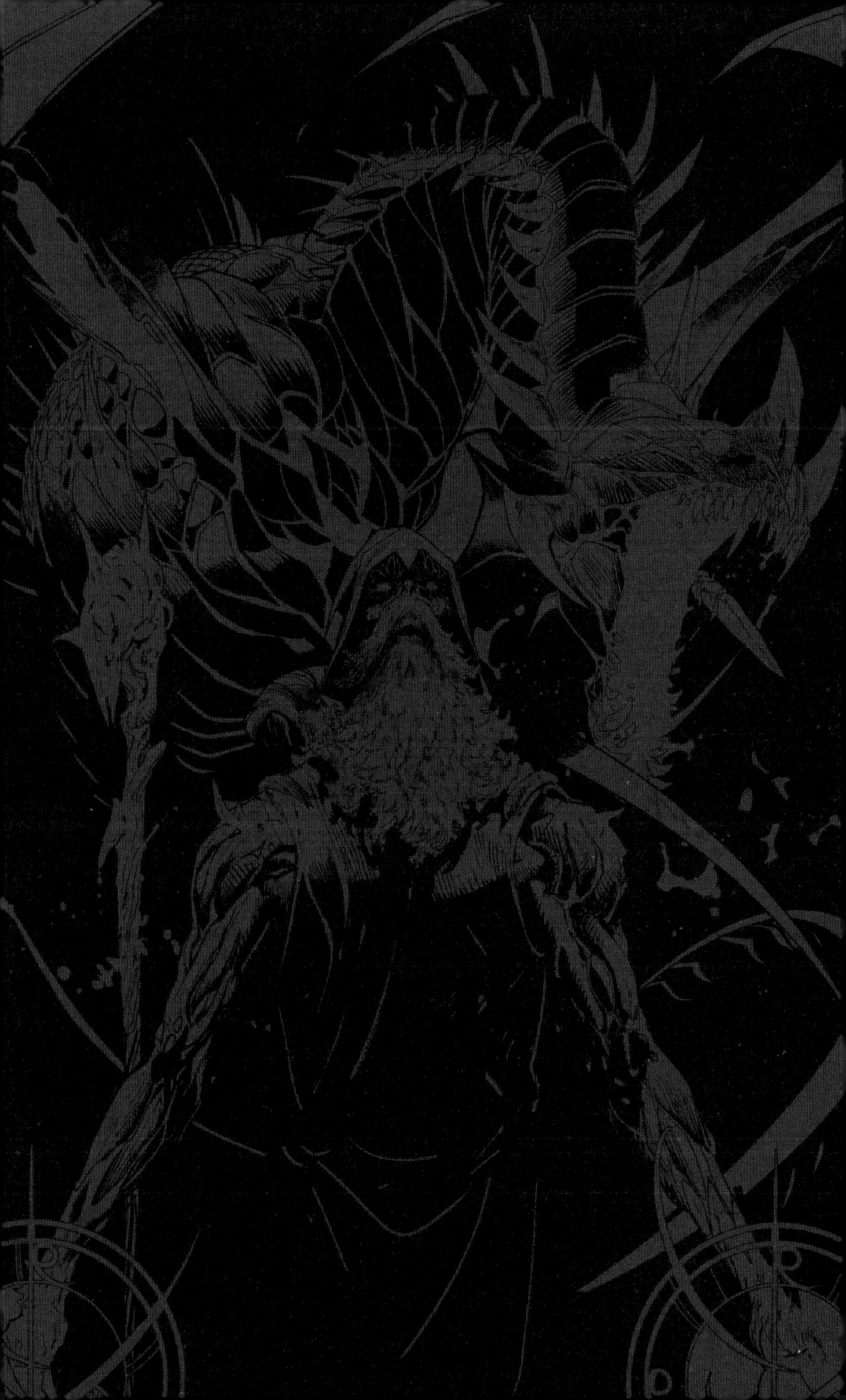

CHAPTER NINE

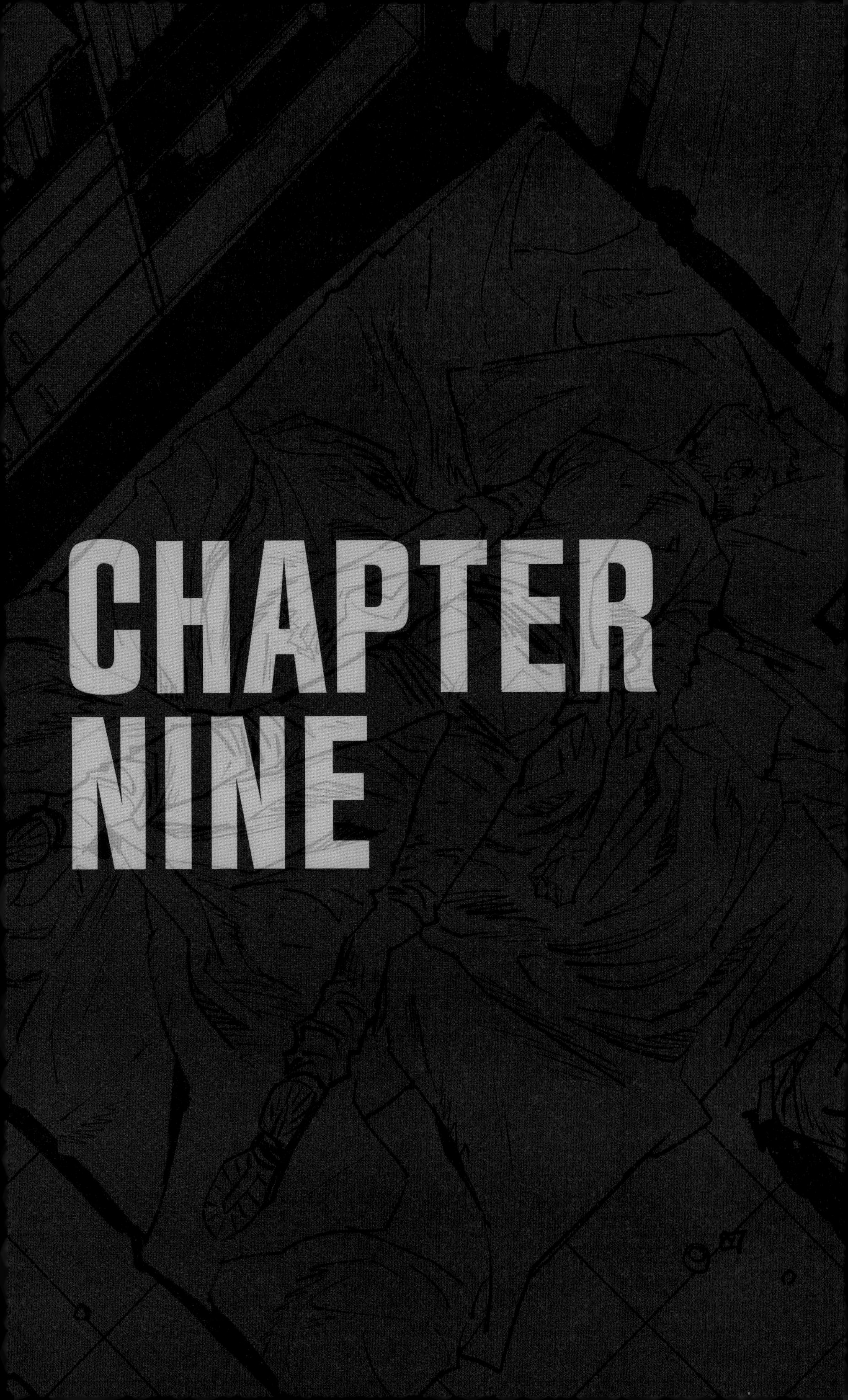

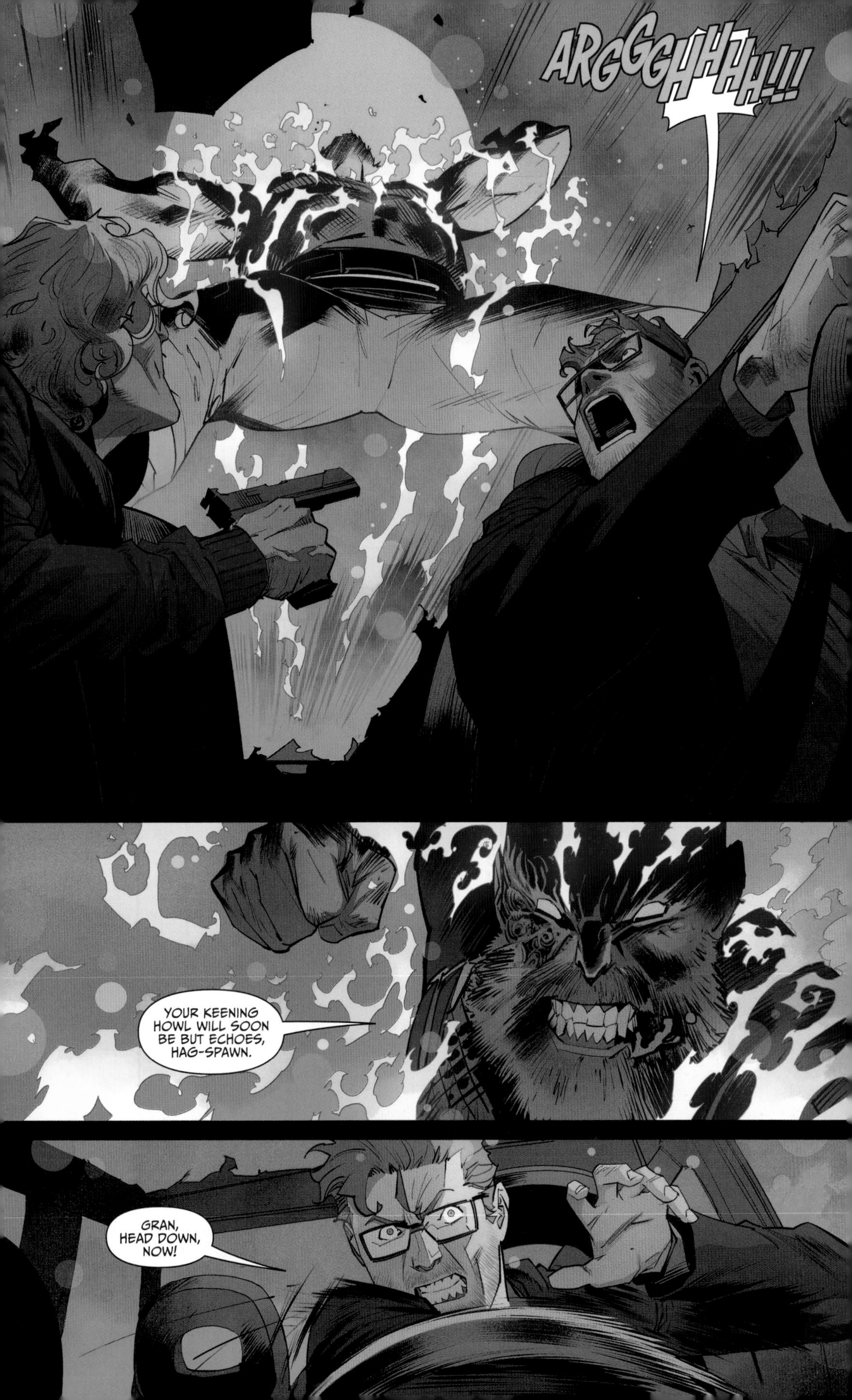
ARGGGHHHH!!!
YOUR KEENING HOWL WILL SOON BE BUT ECHOES, HAG-SPAWN.
GRAN, HEAD DOWN, NOW!

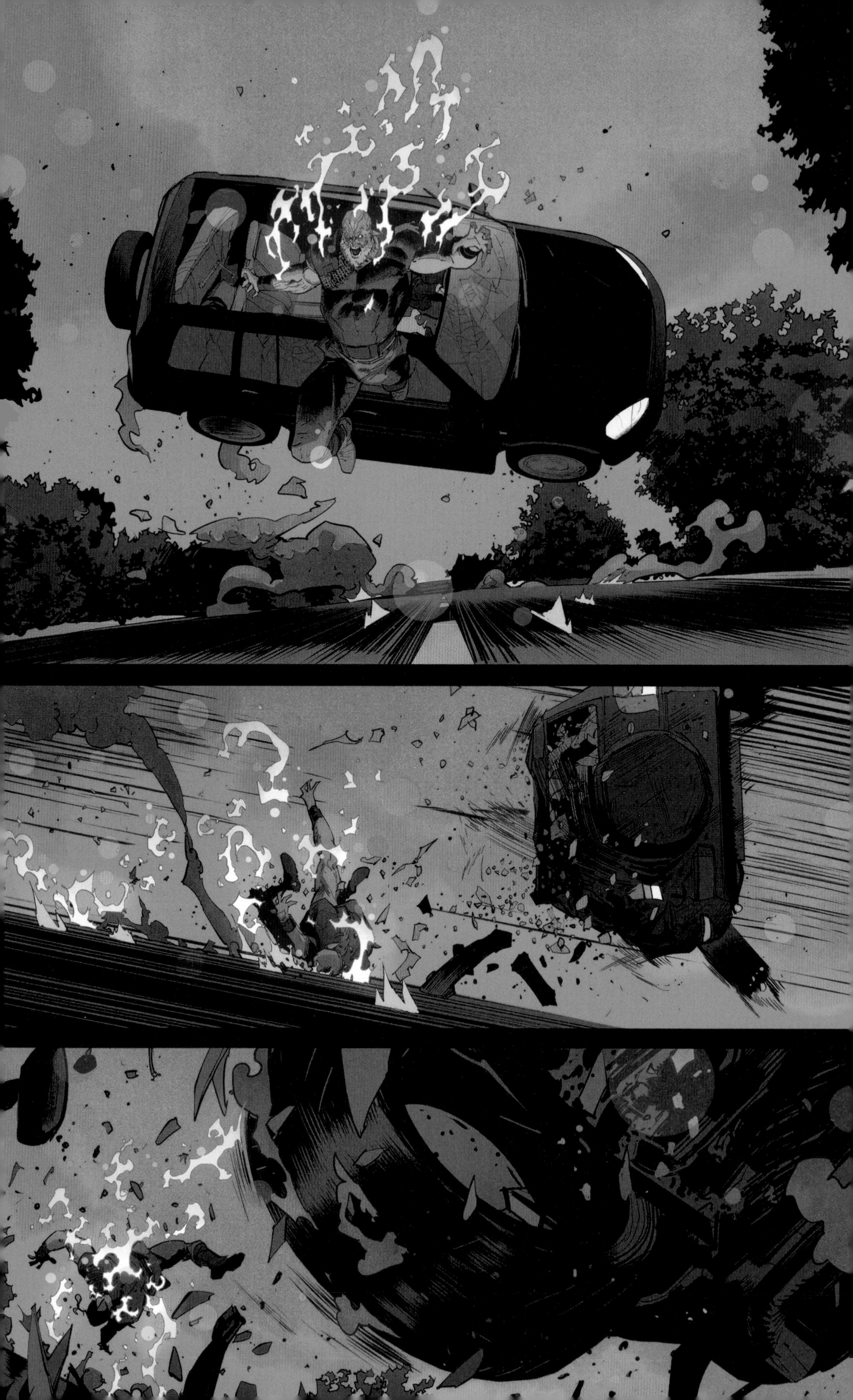

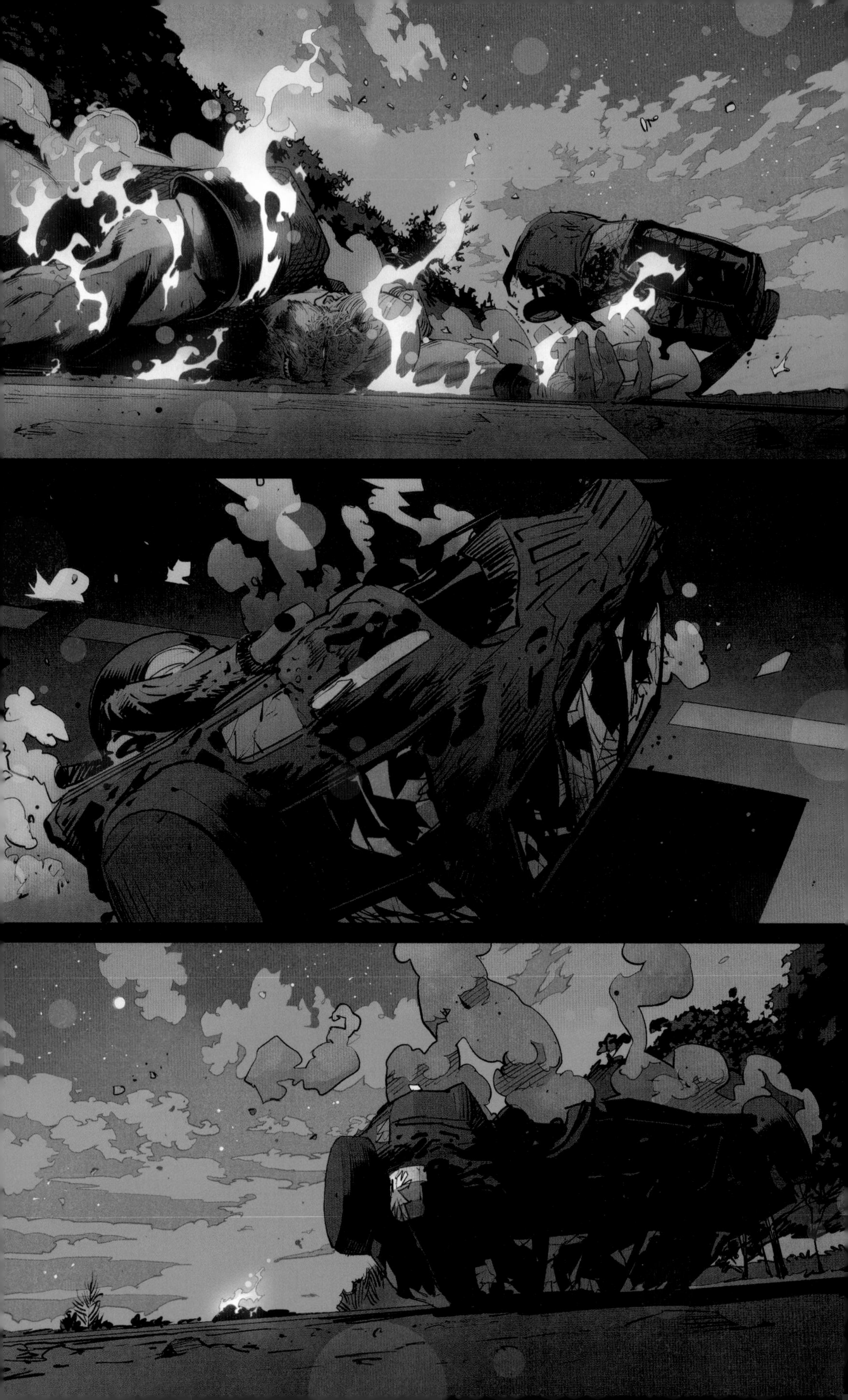

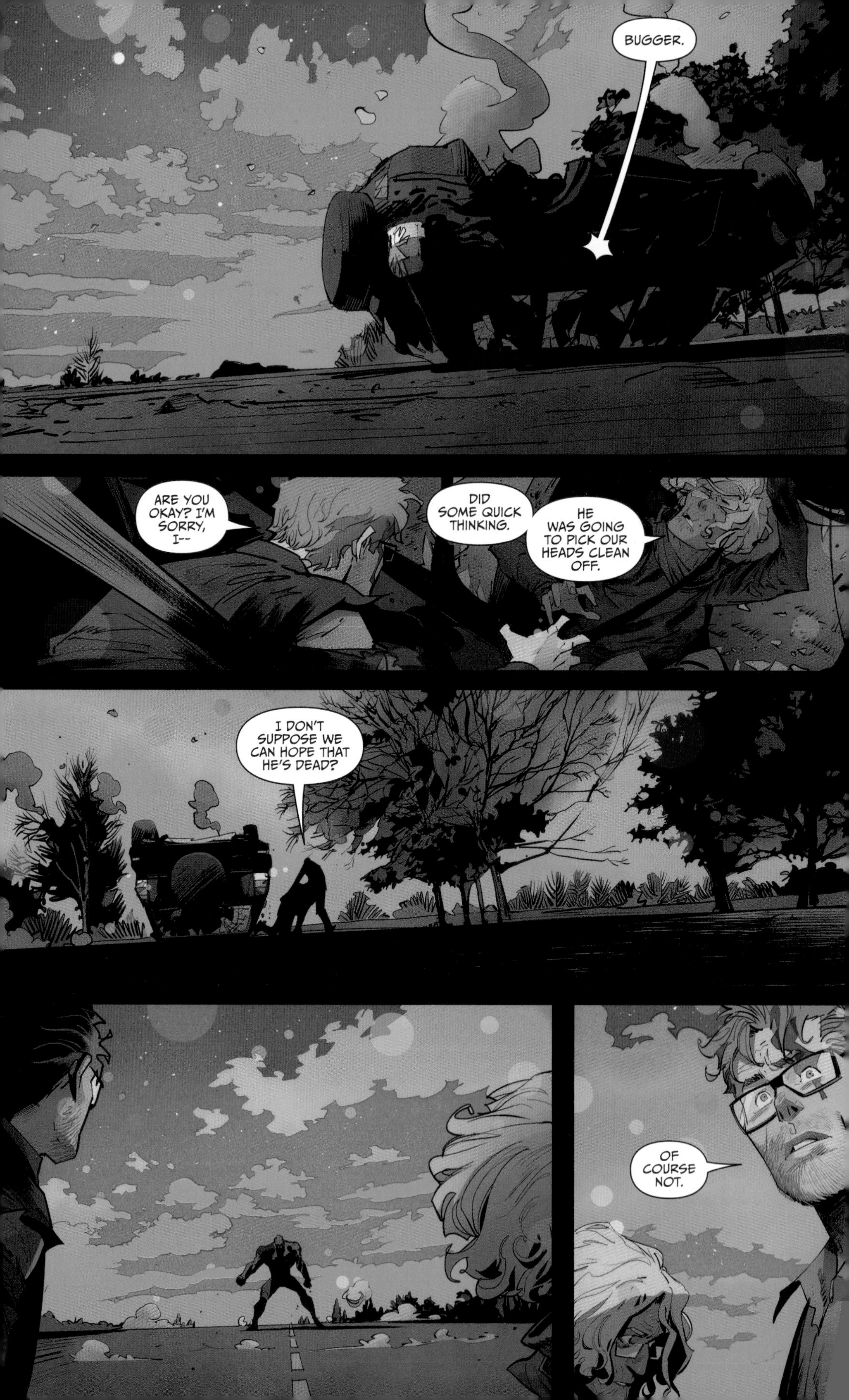
BUGGER.
ARE YOU OKAY? I'M SORRY, I--
DID SOME QUICK THINKING.
HE WAS GOING TO PICK OUR HEADS CLEAN OFF.
I DON'T SUPPOSE WE CAN HOPE THAT HE'S DEAD?
OF COURSE NOT.

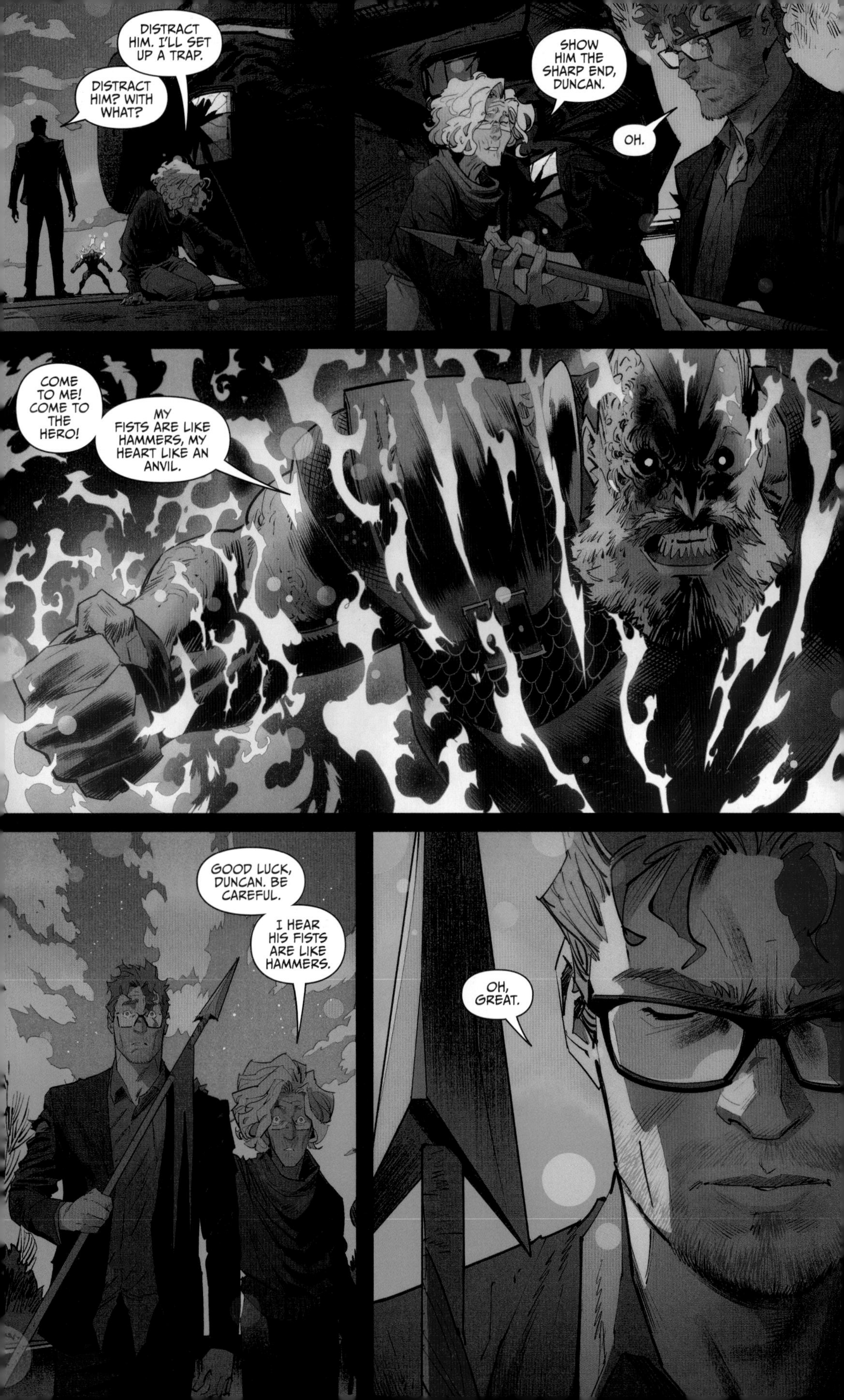
DISTRACT HIM. I'LL SET UP A TRAP.
DISTRACT HIM? WITH WHAT?
SHOW HIM THE SHARP END, DUNCAN.
OH.
COME TO ME! COME TO THE HERO!
MY FISTS ARE LIKE HAMMERS, MY HEART LIKE AN ANVIL.
GOOD LUCK, DUNCAN. BE CAREFUL.
I HEAR HIS FISTS ARE LIKE HAMMERS.
OH, GREAT.

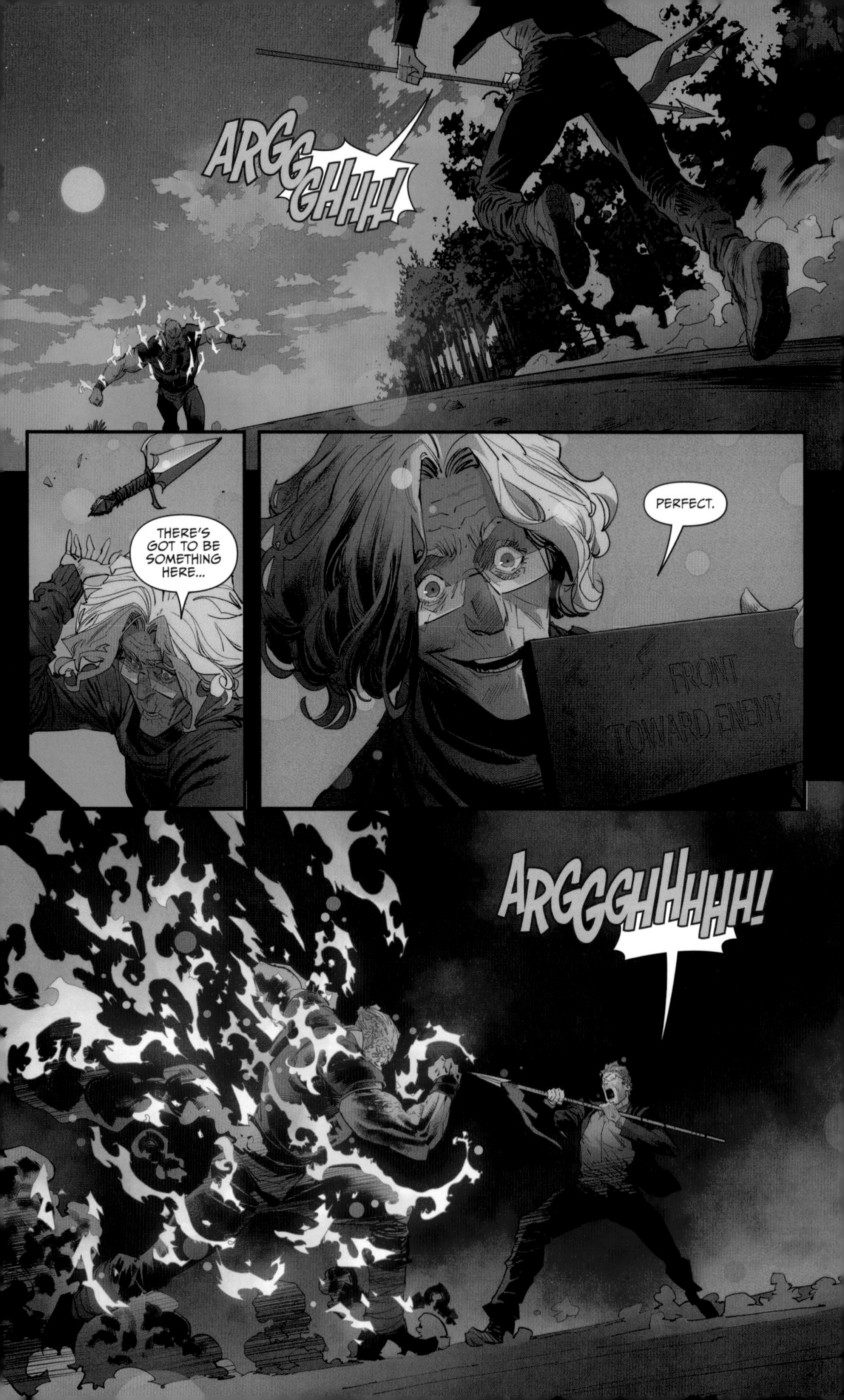

ARGGGHHH!
THERE'S GOT TO BE SOMETHING HERE...
PERFECT.
FRONT TOWARD ENEMY
ARGGGHHHHH!

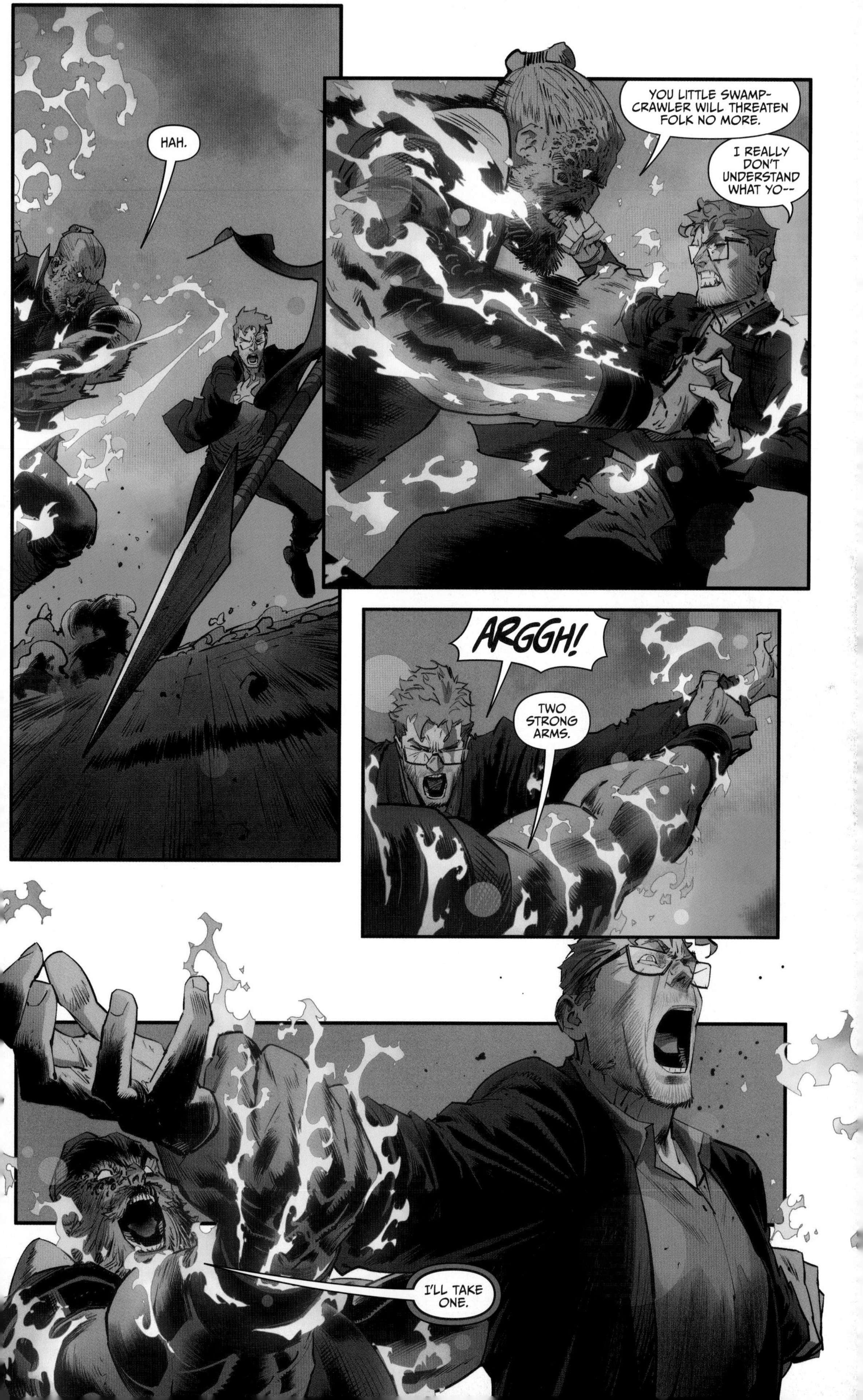
HAH.
YOU LITTLE SWAMP-CRAWLER WILL THREATEN FOLK NO MORE.
I REALLY DON'T UNDERSTAND WHAT YO--
ARGGH!
TWO STRONG ARMS.
I'LL TAKE ONE.

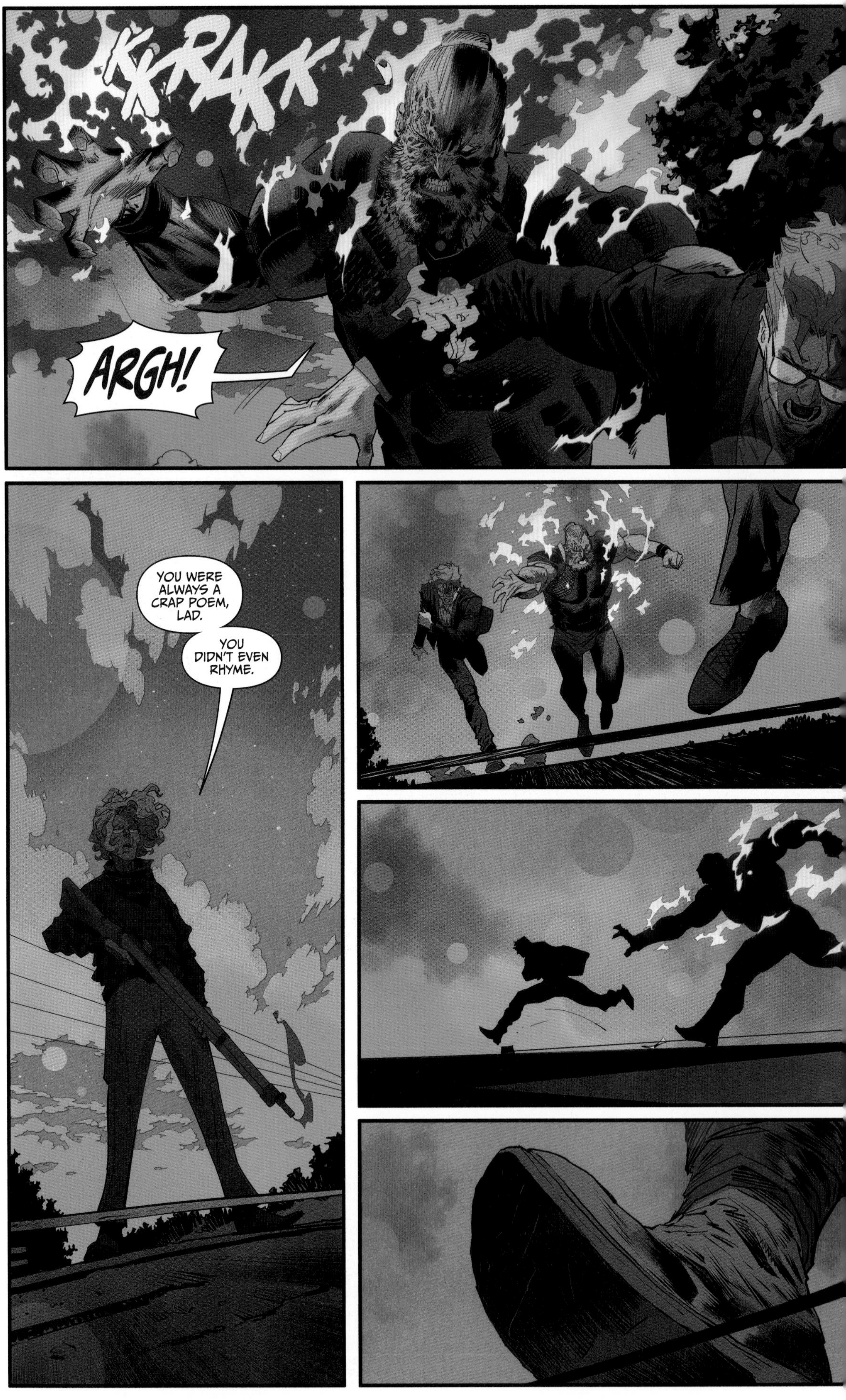
KKRAKK
ARGH!
YOU WERE ALWAYS A CRAP POEM, LAD.
YOU DIDN'T EVEN RHYME.

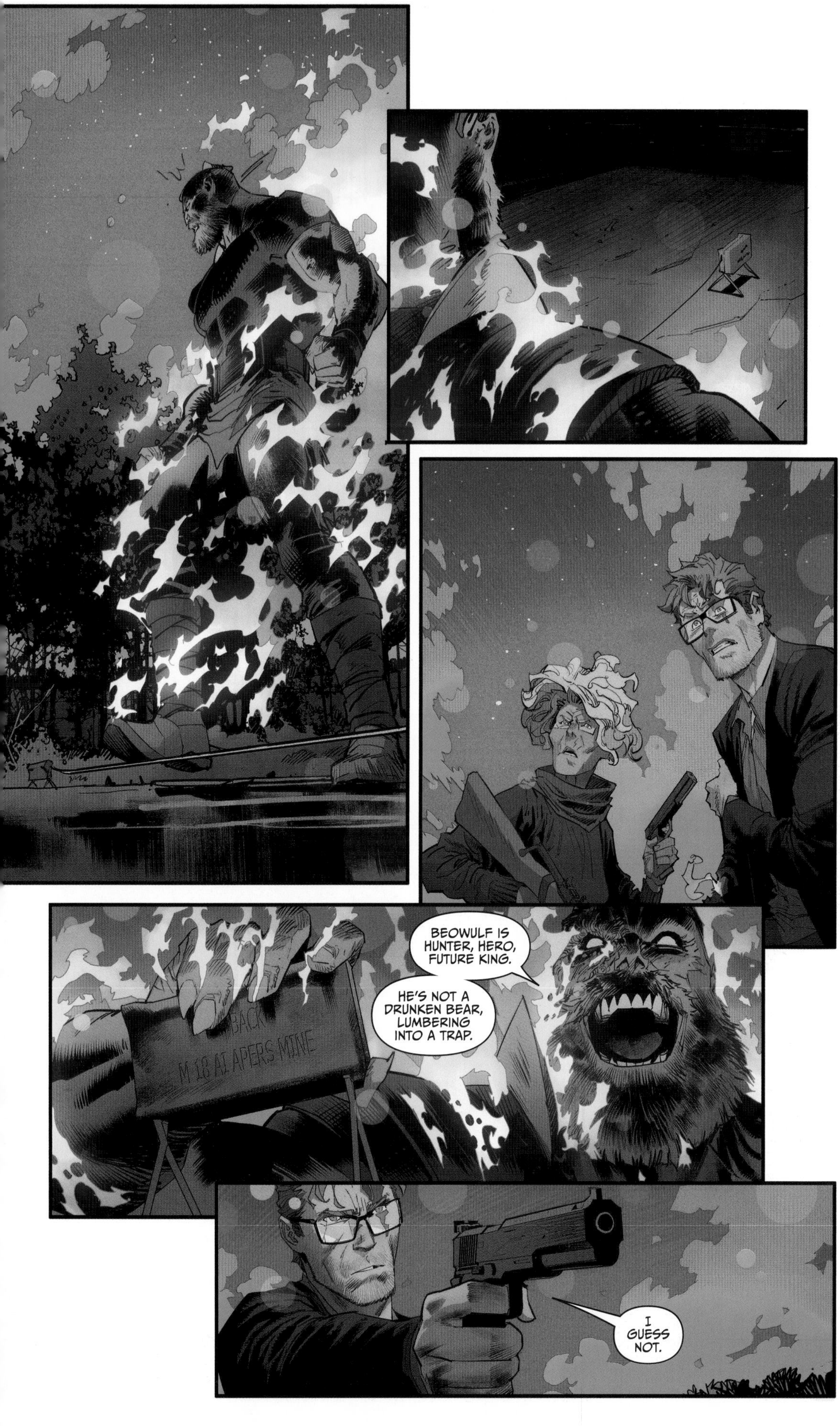
BACK
M 18 AT APERS MINE
BEOWULF IS HUNTER, HERO, FUTURE KING.
HE'S NOT A DRUNKEN BEAR, LUMBERING INTO A TRAP.
I GUESS NOT.

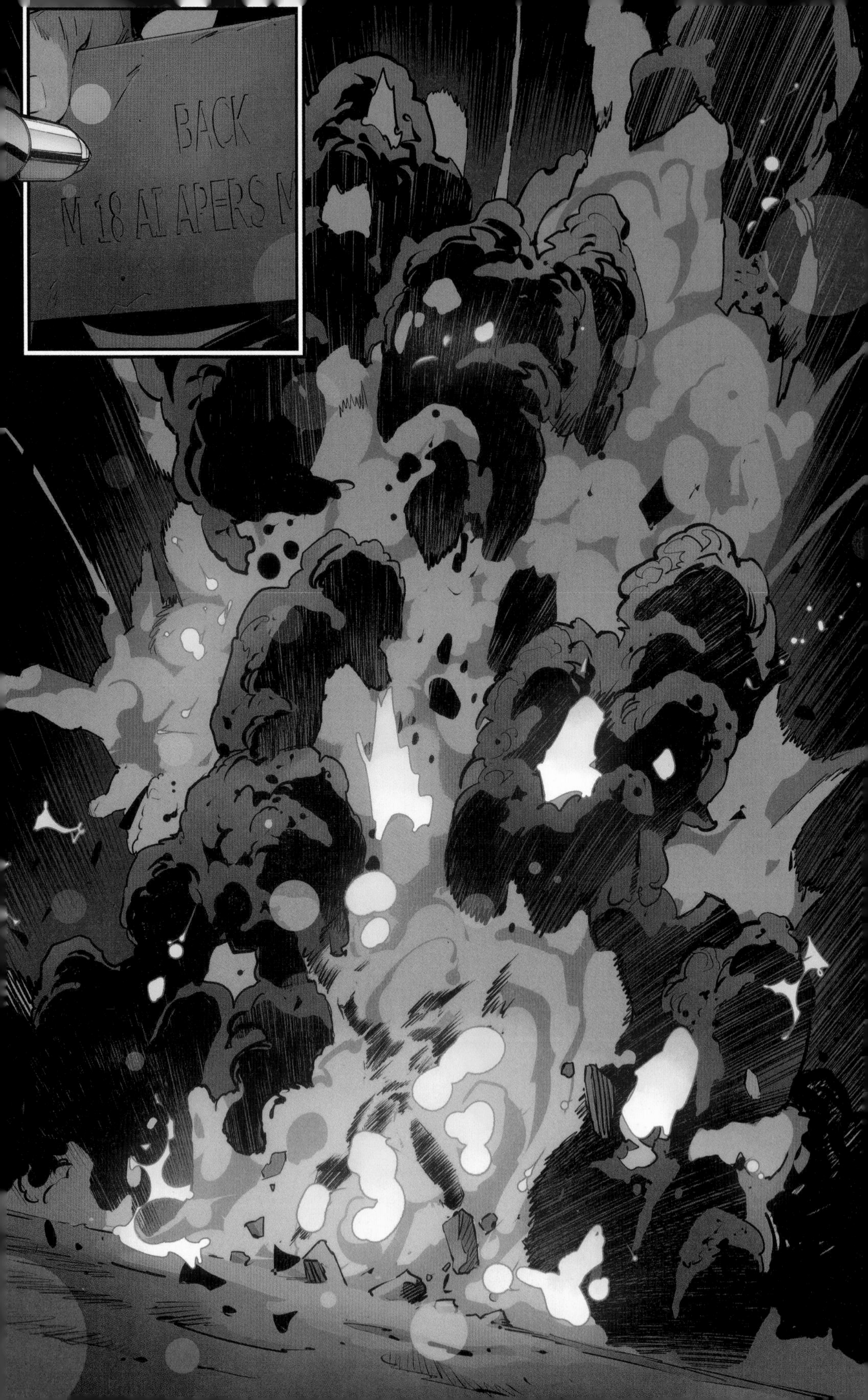
BACK
M 18 A1 APERS M

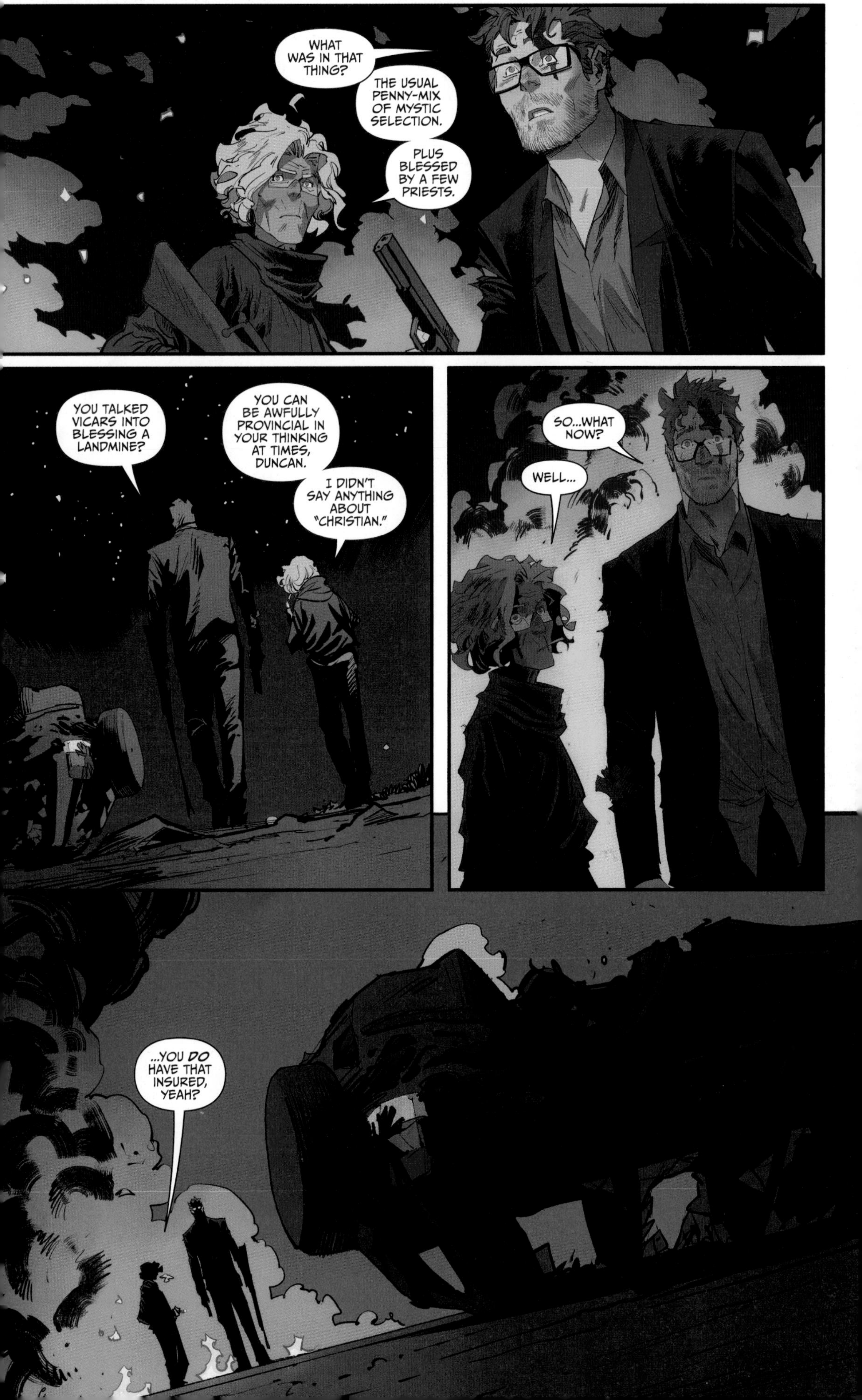
WHAT WAS IN THAT THING?
THE USUAL PENNY-MIX OF MYSTIC SELECTION.
PLUS BLESSED BY A FEW PRIESTS.
YOU TALKED VICARS INTO BLESSING A LANDMINE?
YOU CAN BE AWFULLY PROVINCIAL IN YOUR THINKING AT TIMES, DUNCAN.
I DIDN'T SAY ANYTHING ABOUT "CHRISTIAN."
SO...WHAT NOW?
WELL...
...YOU DO HAVE THAT INSURED, YEAH?

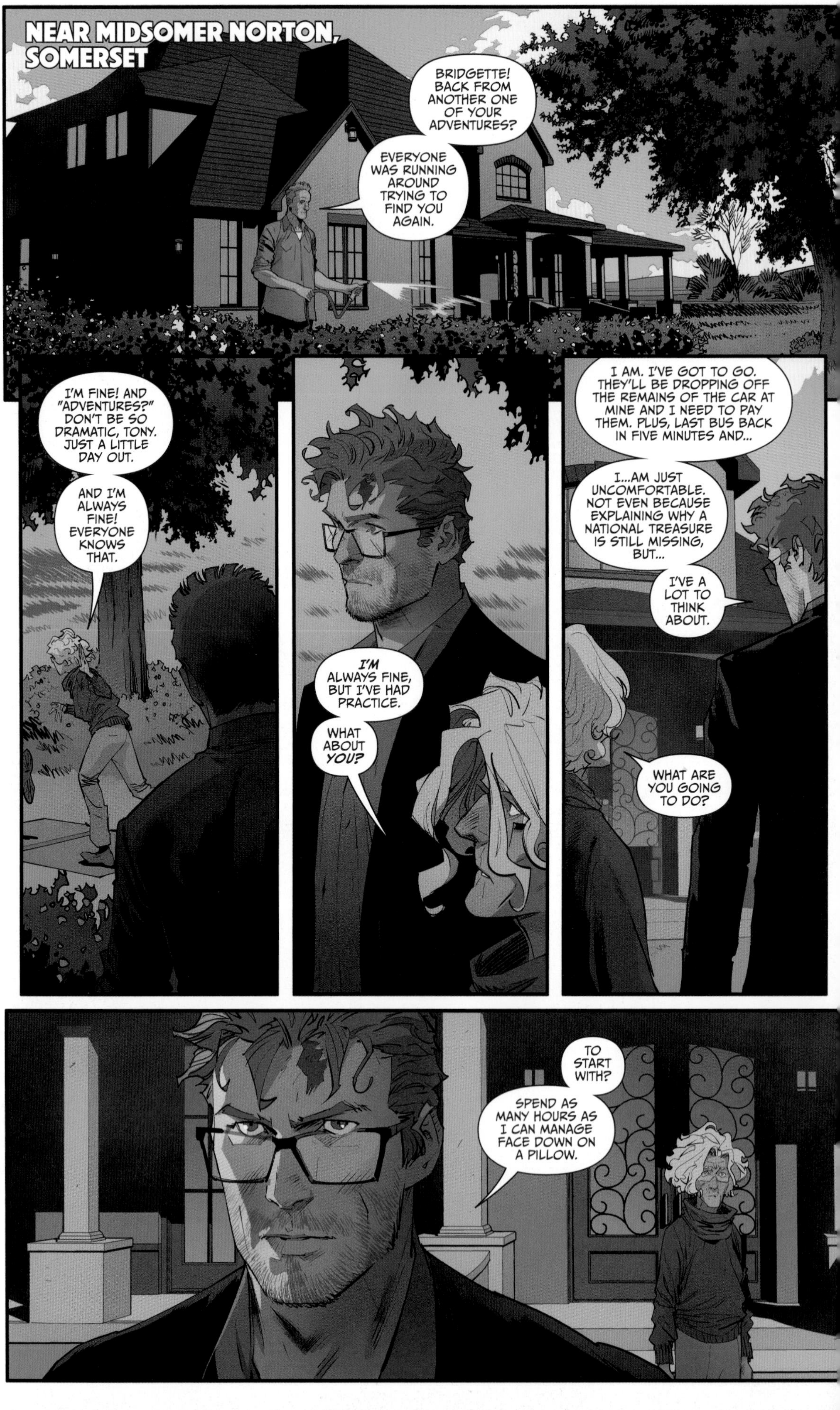
NEAR MIDSOMER NORTON, SOMERSET
BRIDGETTE! BACK FROM ANOTHER ONE OF YOUR ADVENTURES?
EVERYONE WAS RUNNING AROUND TRYING TO FIND YOU AGAIN.
I'M FINE! AND "ADVENTURES?" DON'T BE SO DRAMATIC, TONY. JUST A LITTLE DAY OUT.
AND I'M ALWAYS FINE! EVERYONE KNOWS THAT.
I'M ALWAYS FINE, BUT I'VE HAD PRACTICE.
WHAT ABOUT YOU?
I AM. I'VE GOT TO GO. THEY'LL BE DROPPING OFF THE REMAINS OF THE CAR AT MINE AND I NEED TO PAY THEM. PLUS, LAST BUS BACK IN FIVE MINUTES AND...
I...AM JUST UNCOMFORTABLE. NOT EVEN BECAUSE EXPLAINING WHY A NATIONAL TREASURE IS STILL MISSING, BUT...
I'VE A LOT TO THINK ABOUT.
WHAT ARE YOU GOING TO DO?
TO START WITH?
SPEND AS MANY HOURS AS I CAN MANAGE FACE DOWN ON A PILLOW.

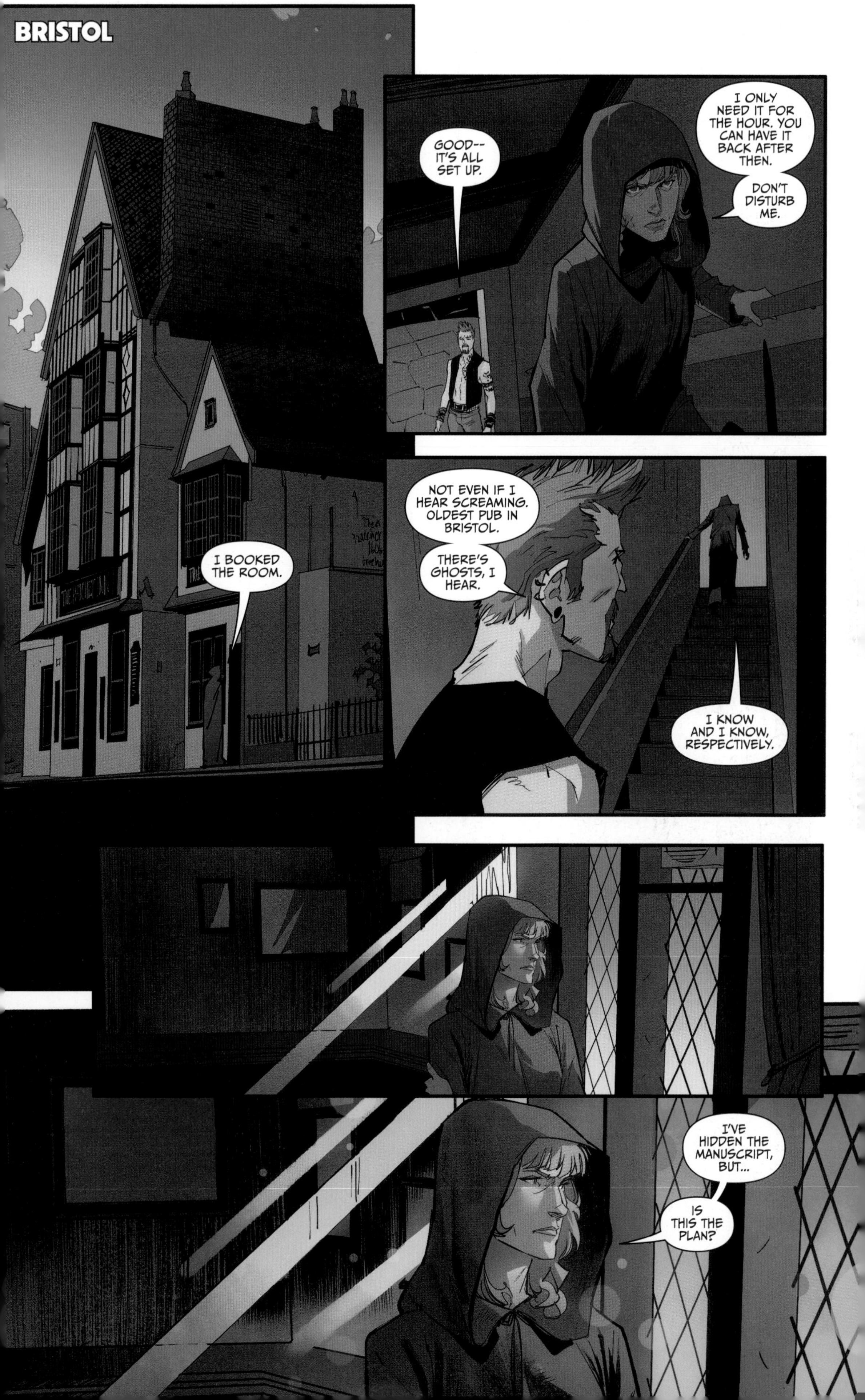
BRISTOL
I BOOKED THE ROOM.
GOOD-- IT'S ALL SET UP.
I ONLY NEED IT FOR THE HOUR. YOU CAN HAVE IT BACK AFTER THEN.
DON'T DISTURB ME.
NOT EVEN IF I HEAR SCREAMING. OLDEST PUB IN BRISTOL.
THERE'S GHOSTS, I HEAR.
I KNOW AND I KNOW, RESPECTIVELY.
I'VE HIDDEN THE MANUSCRIPT, BUT...
IS THIS THE PLAN?

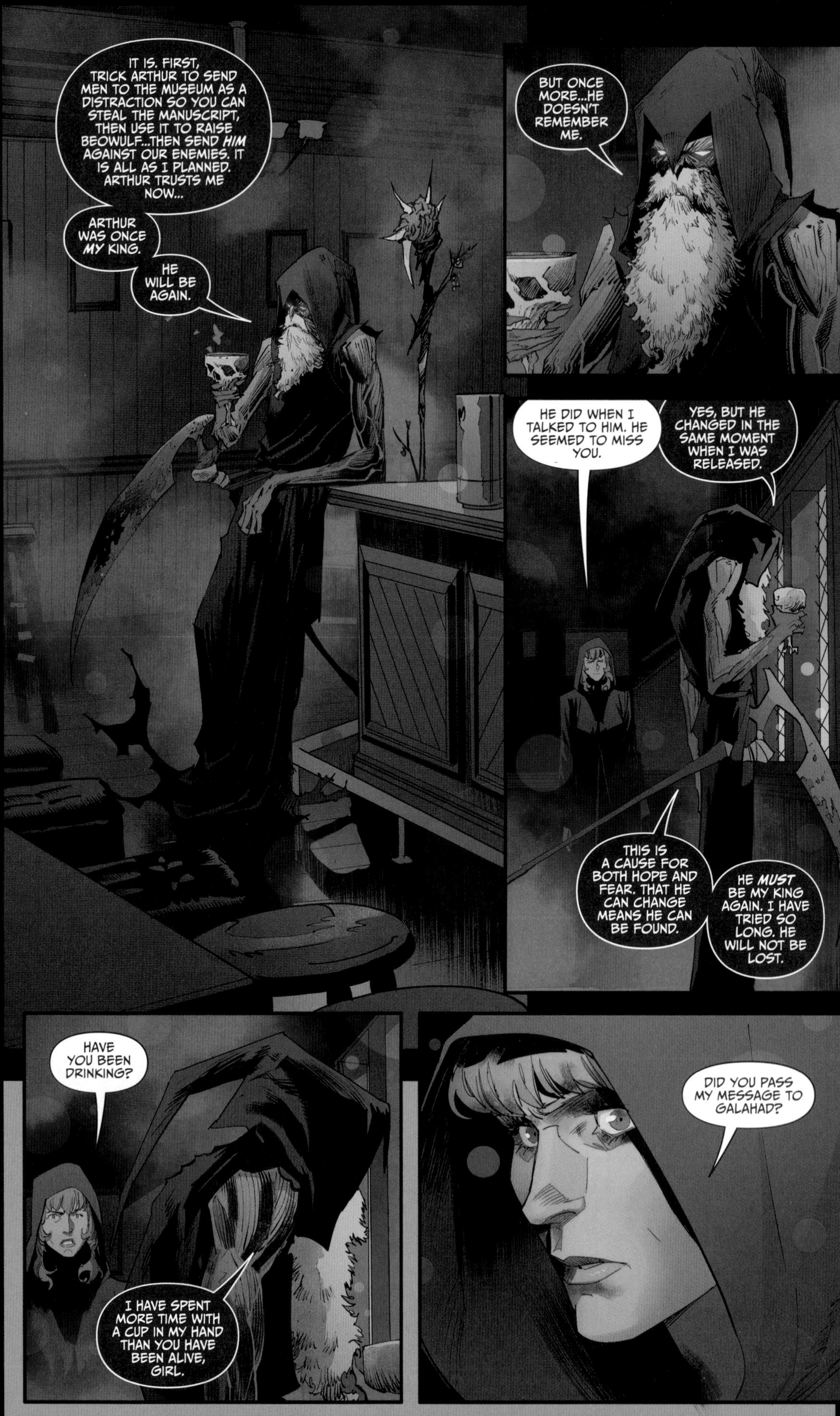

IT IS. FIRST, TRICK ARTHUR TO SEND MEN TO THE MUSEUM AS A DISTRACTION SO YOU CAN STEAL THE MANUSCRIPT, THEN USE IT TO RAISE BEOWULF...THEN SEND *HIM* AGAINST OUR ENEMIES. IT IS ALL AS I PLANNED. ARTHUR TRUSTS ME NOW...
ARTHUR WAS ONCE *MY* KING.
HE WILL BE AGAIN.
BUT ONCE MORE...HE DOESN'T REMEMBER ME.
HE DID WHEN I TALKED TO HIM. HE SEEMED TO MISS YOU.
YES, BUT HE CHANGED IN THE SAME MOMENT WHEN I WAS RELEASED.
THIS IS A CAUSE FOR BOTH HOPE AND FEAR. THAT HE CAN CHANGE MEANS HE CAN BE FOUND.
HE *MUST* BE MY KING AGAIN. I HAVE TRIED SO LONG. HE WILL NOT BE LOST.
HAVE YOU BEEN DRINKING?
I HAVE SPENT MORE TIME WITH A CUP IN MY HAND THAN YOU HAVE BEEN ALIVE, GIRL.
DID YOU PASS MY MESSAGE TO GALAHAD?

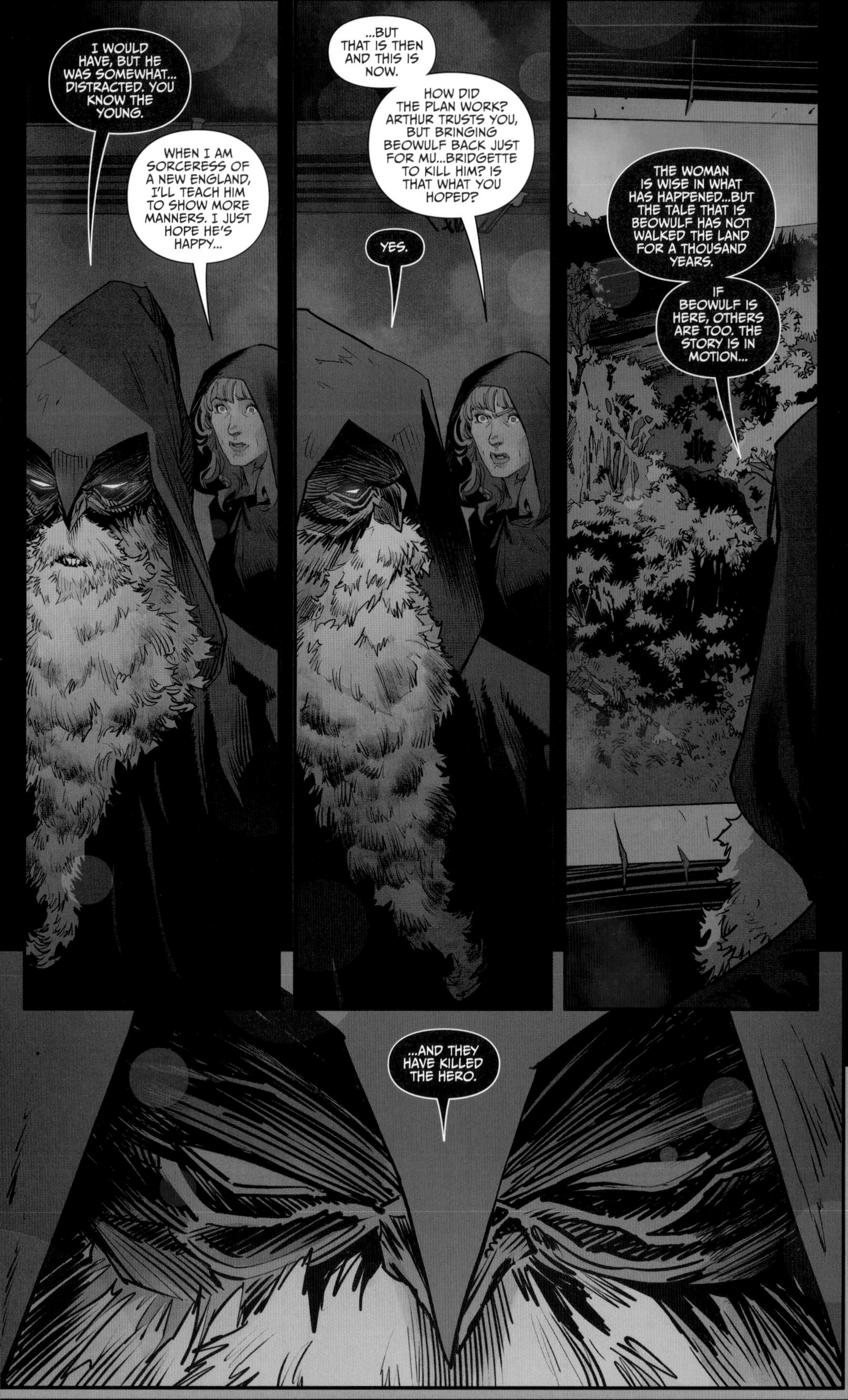
I WOULD HAVE, BUT HE WAS SOMEWHAT... DISTRACTED. YOU KNOW THE YOUNG.
WHEN I AM SORCERESS OF A NEW ENGLAND, I'LL TEACH HIM TO SHOW MORE MANNERS. I JUST HOPE HE'S HAPPY...
...BUT THAT IS THEN AND THIS IS NOW.
HOW DID THE PLAN WORK? ARTHUR TRUSTS YOU, BUT BRINGING BEOWULF BACK JUST FOR MU...BRIDGETTE TO KILL HIM? IS THAT WHAT YOU HOPED?
YES.
THE WOMAN IS WISE IN WHAT HAS HAPPENED...BUT THE TALE THAT IS BEOWULF HAS NOT WALKED THE LAND FOR A THOUSAND YEARS.
IF BEOWULF IS HERE, OTHERS ARE TOO. THE STORY IS IN MOTION...
...AND THEY HAVE KILLED THE HERO.

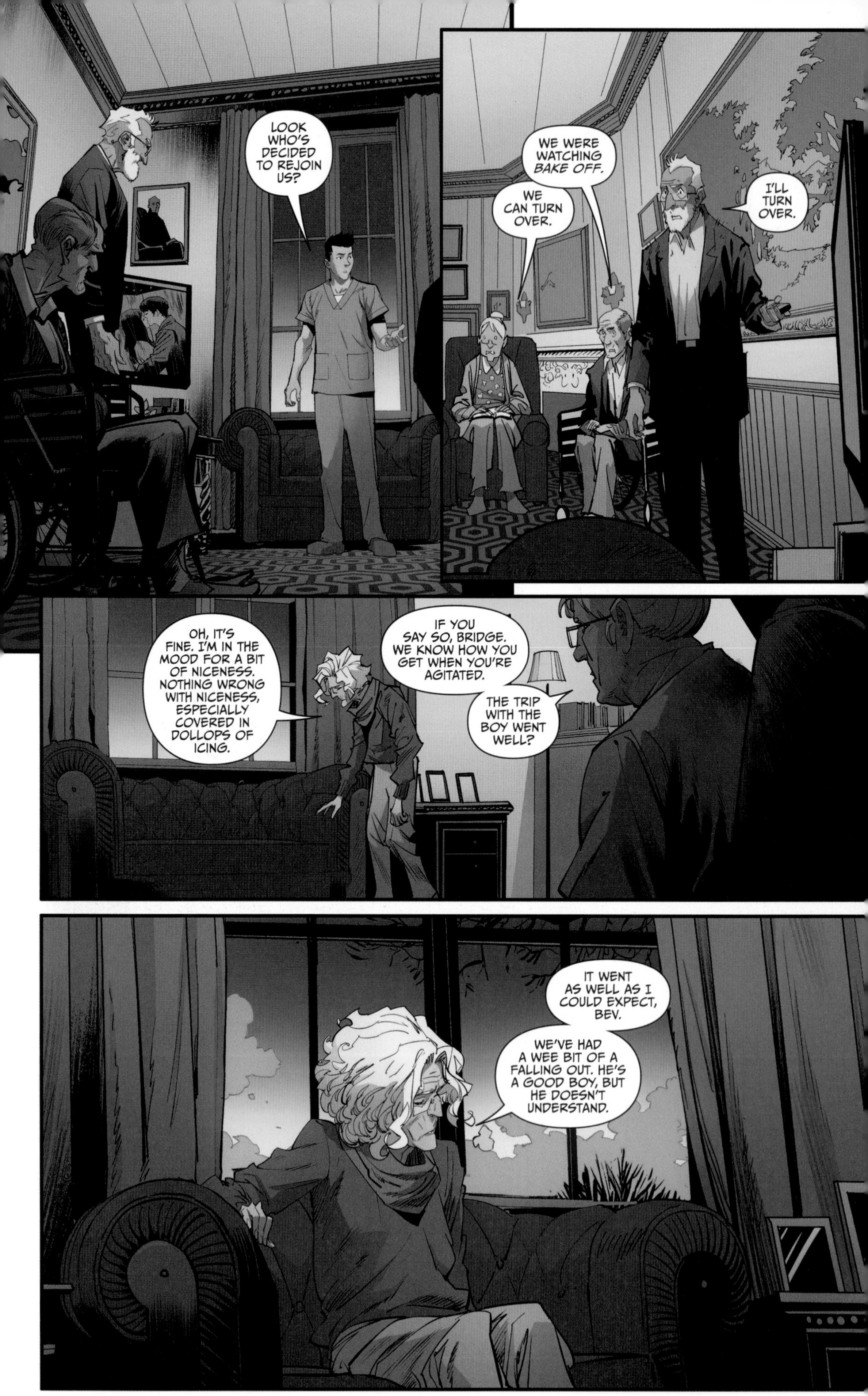
LOOK WHO'S DECIDED TO REJOIN US?
WE WERE WATCHING *BAKE OFF*.
WE CAN TURN OVER.
I'LL TURN OVER.
OH, IT'S FINE. I'M IN THE MOOD FOR A BIT OF NICENESS. NOTHING WRONG WITH NICENESS, ESPECIALLY COVERED IN DOLLOPS OF ICING.
IF YOU SAY SO, BRIDGE. WE KNOW HOW YOU GET WHEN YOU'RE AGITATED.
THE TRIP WITH THE BOY WENT WELL?
IT WENT AS WELL AS I COULD EXPECT, BEV.
WE'VE HAD A WEE BIT OF A FALLING OUT. HE'S A GOOD BOY, BUT HE DOESN'T UNDERSTAND.

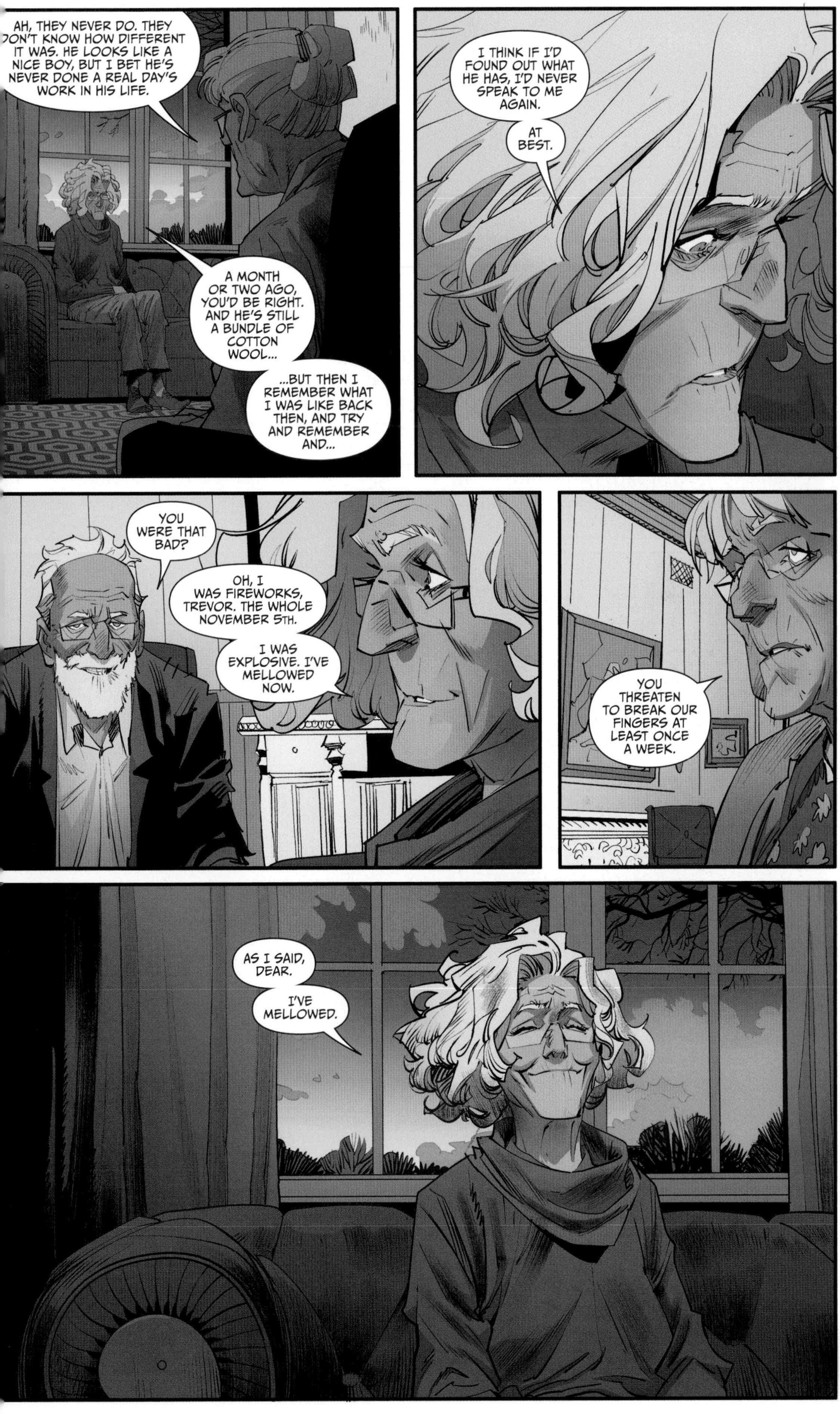
AH, THEY NEVER DO. THEY DON'T KNOW HOW DIFFERENT IT WAS. HE LOOKS LIKE A NICE BOY, BUT I BET HE'S NEVER DONE A REAL DAY'S WORK IN HIS LIFE.
A MONTH OR TWO AGO, YOU'D BE RIGHT. AND HE'S STILL A BUNDLE OF COTTON WOOL...
...BUT THEN I REMEMBER WHAT I WAS LIKE BACK THEN, AND TRY AND REMEMBER AND...
I THINK IF I'D FOUND OUT WHAT HE HAS, I'D NEVER SPEAK TO ME AGAIN.
AT BEST.
YOU WERE THAT BAD?
OH, I WAS FIREWORKS, TREVOR. THE WHOLE NOVEMBER 5TH.
I WAS EXPLOSIVE. I'VE MELLOWED NOW.
YOU THREATEN TO BREAK OUR FINGERS AT LEAST ONCE A WEEK.
AS I SAID, DEAR.
I'VE MELLOWED.

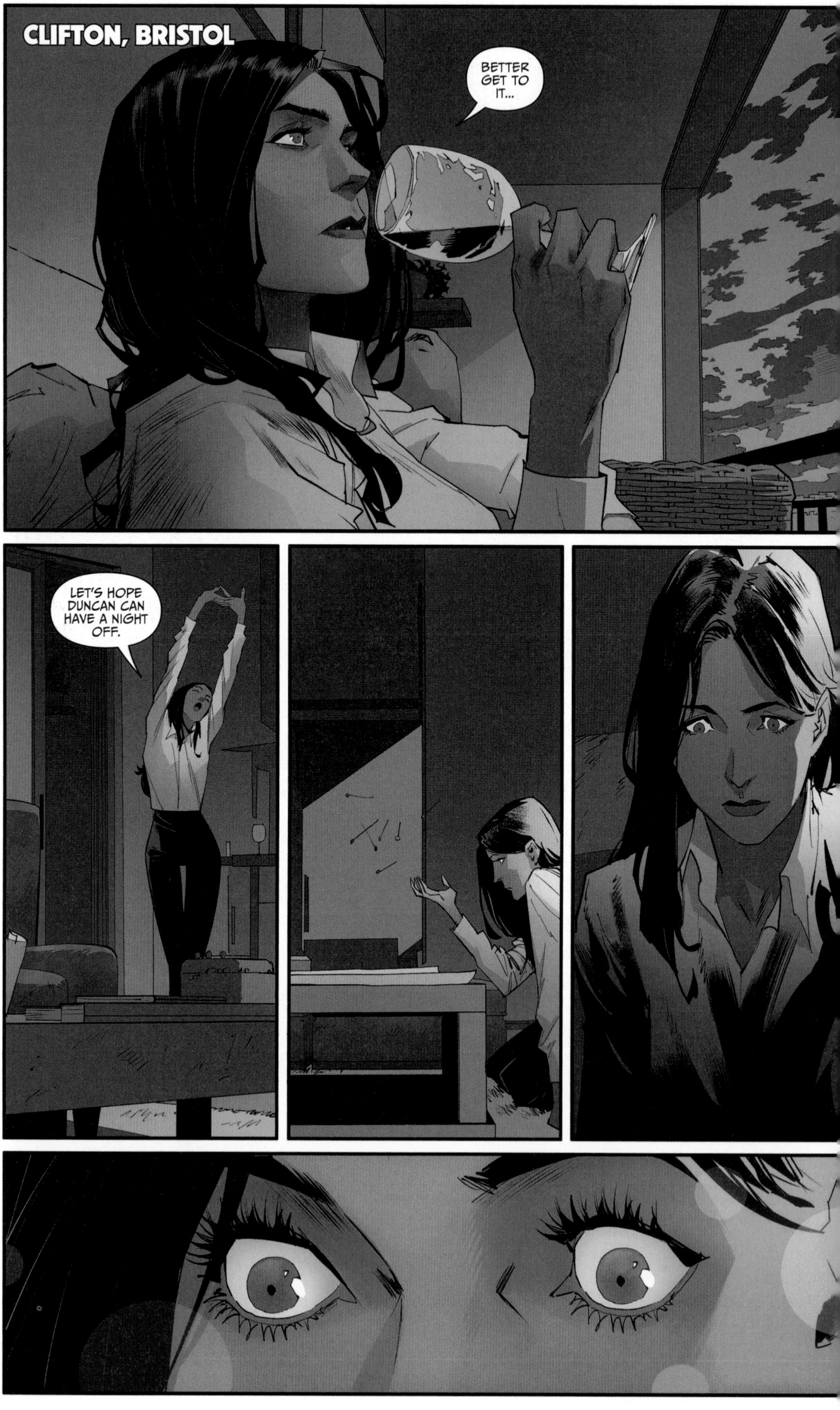
CLIFTON, BRISTOL
BETTER GET TO IT...
LET'S HOPE DUNCAN CAN HAVE A NIGHT OFF.

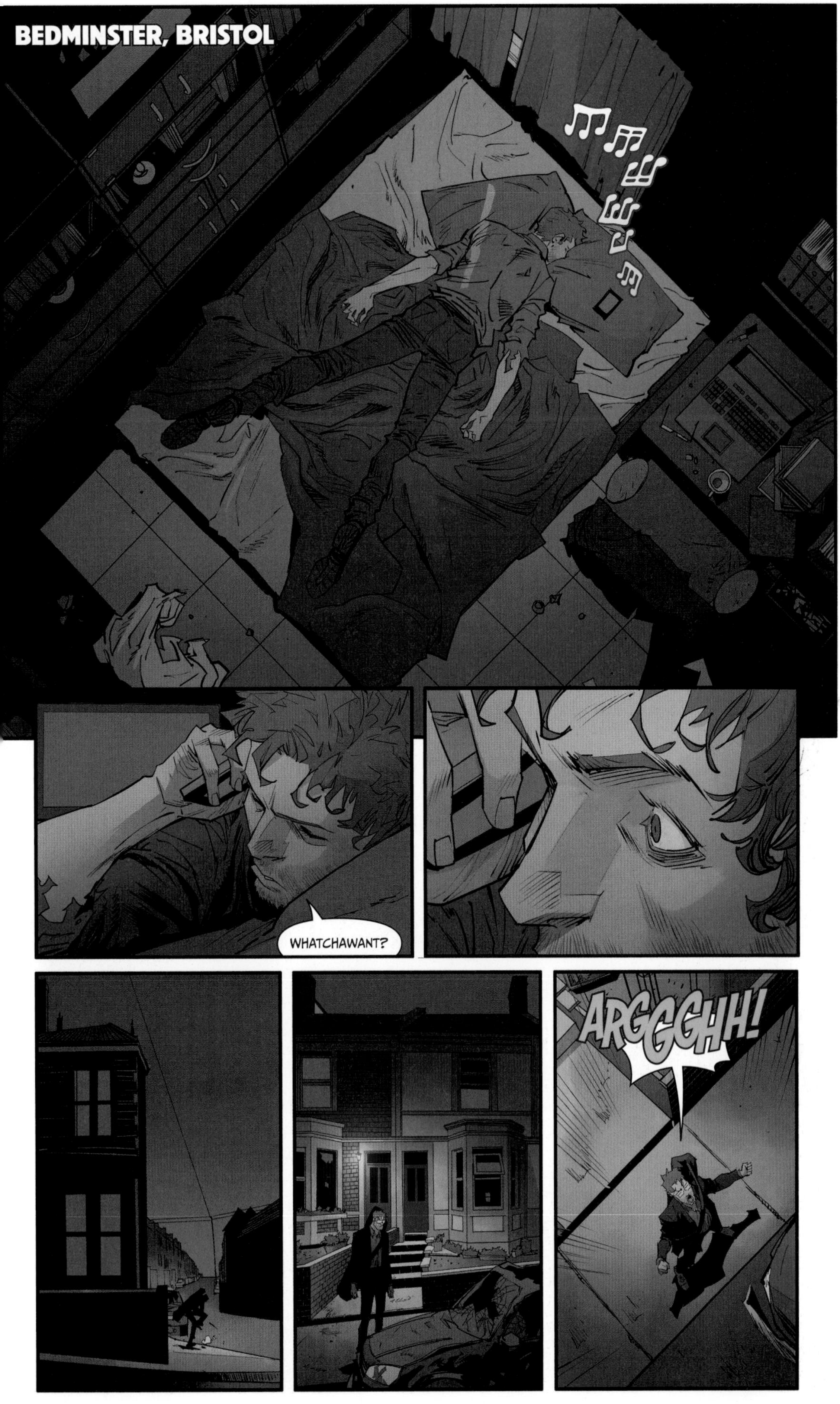
BEDMINSTER, BRISTOL
WHATCHAWANT?
ARGGGHH!

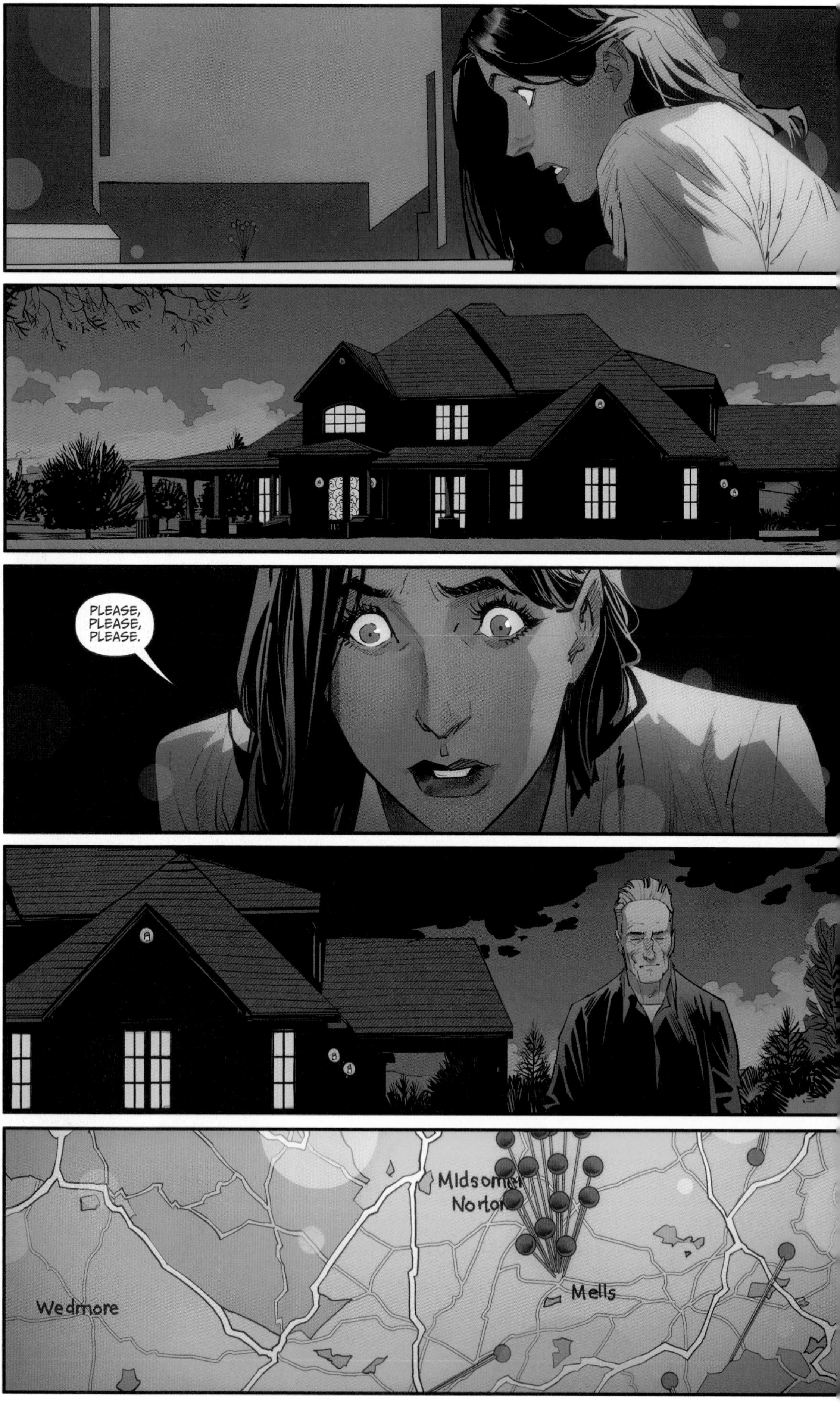

PLEASE, PLEASE, PLEASE.
Mells
Wedmore

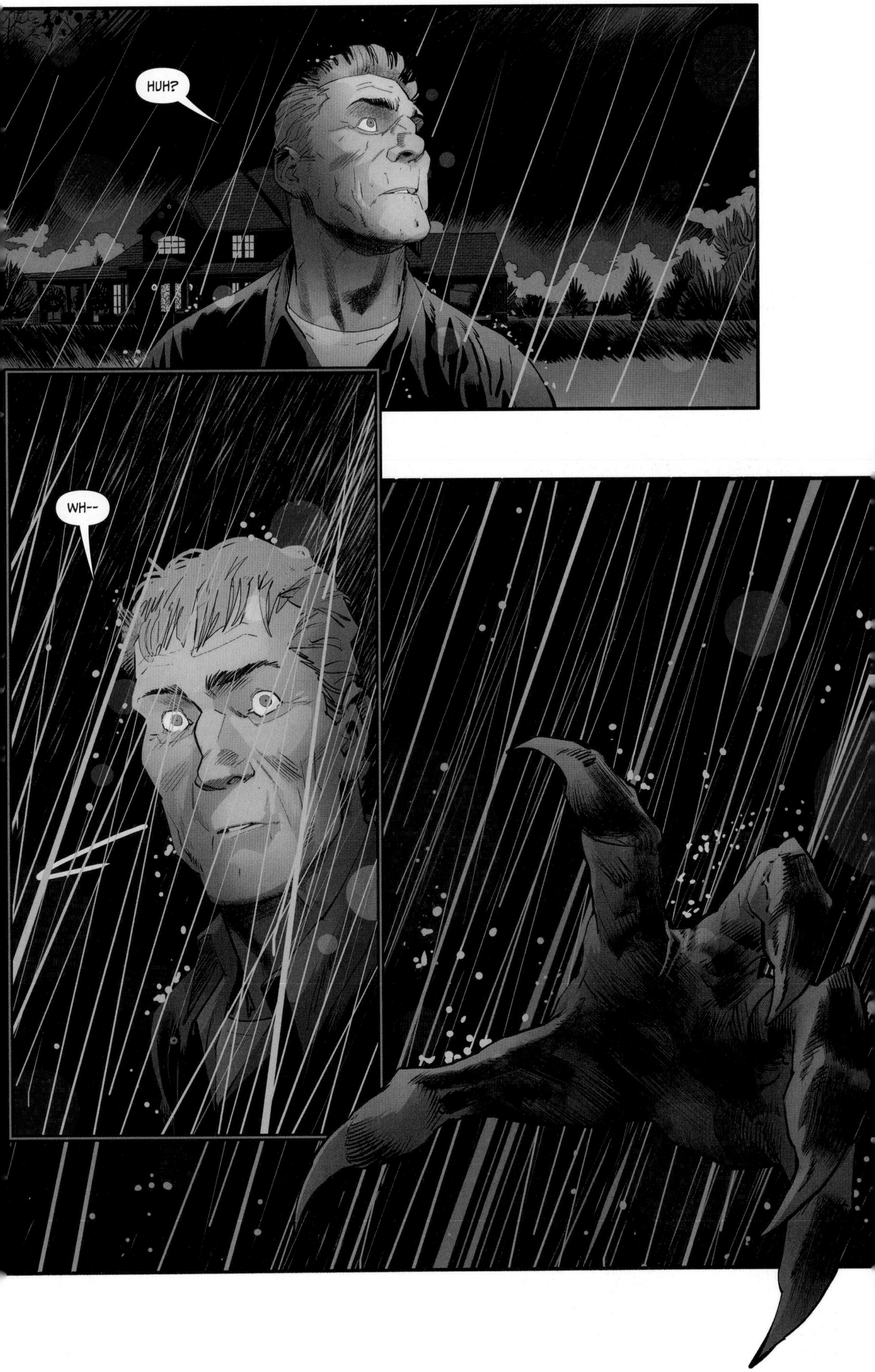
HUH?
WH--

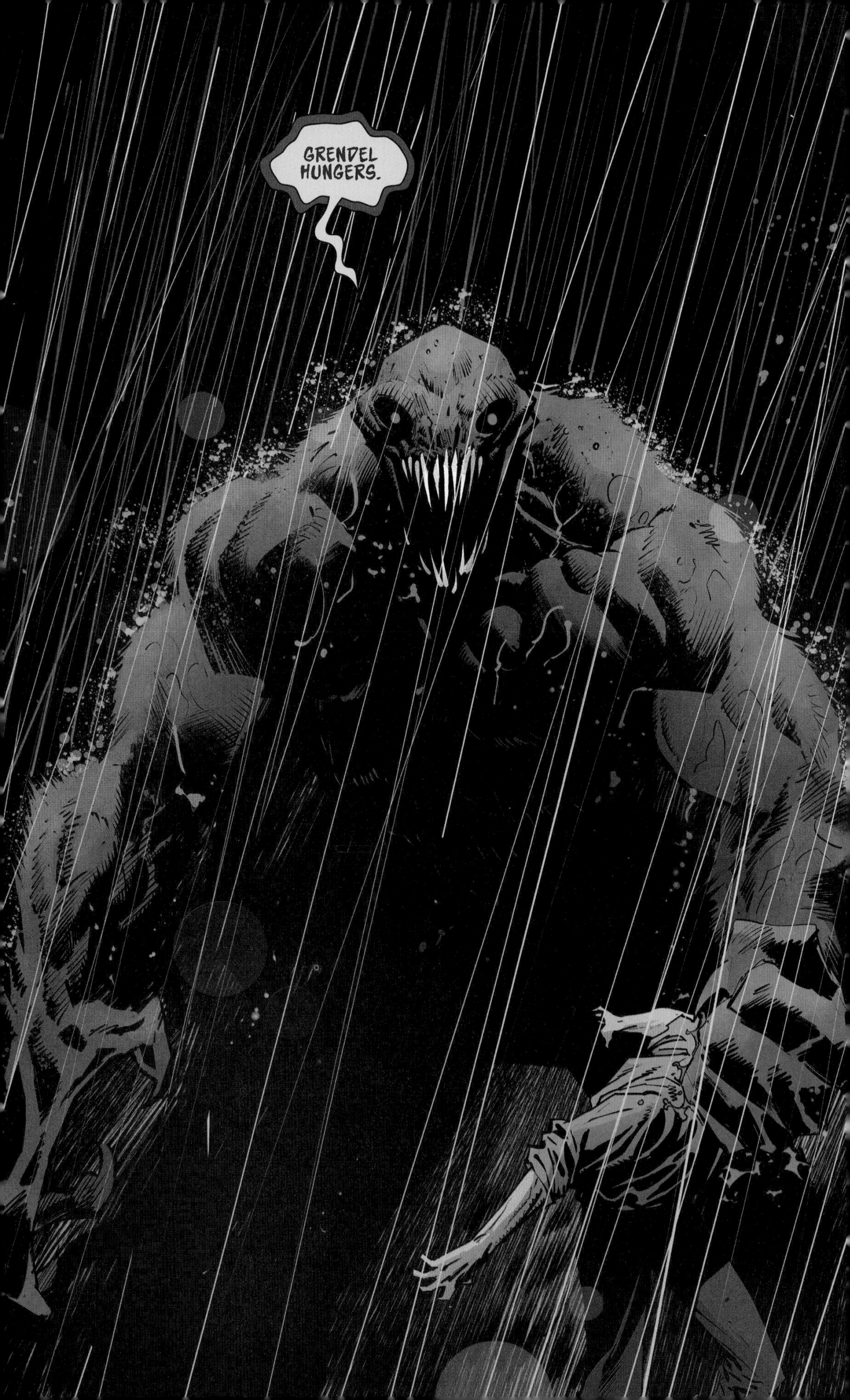
GRENDEL HUNGERS.

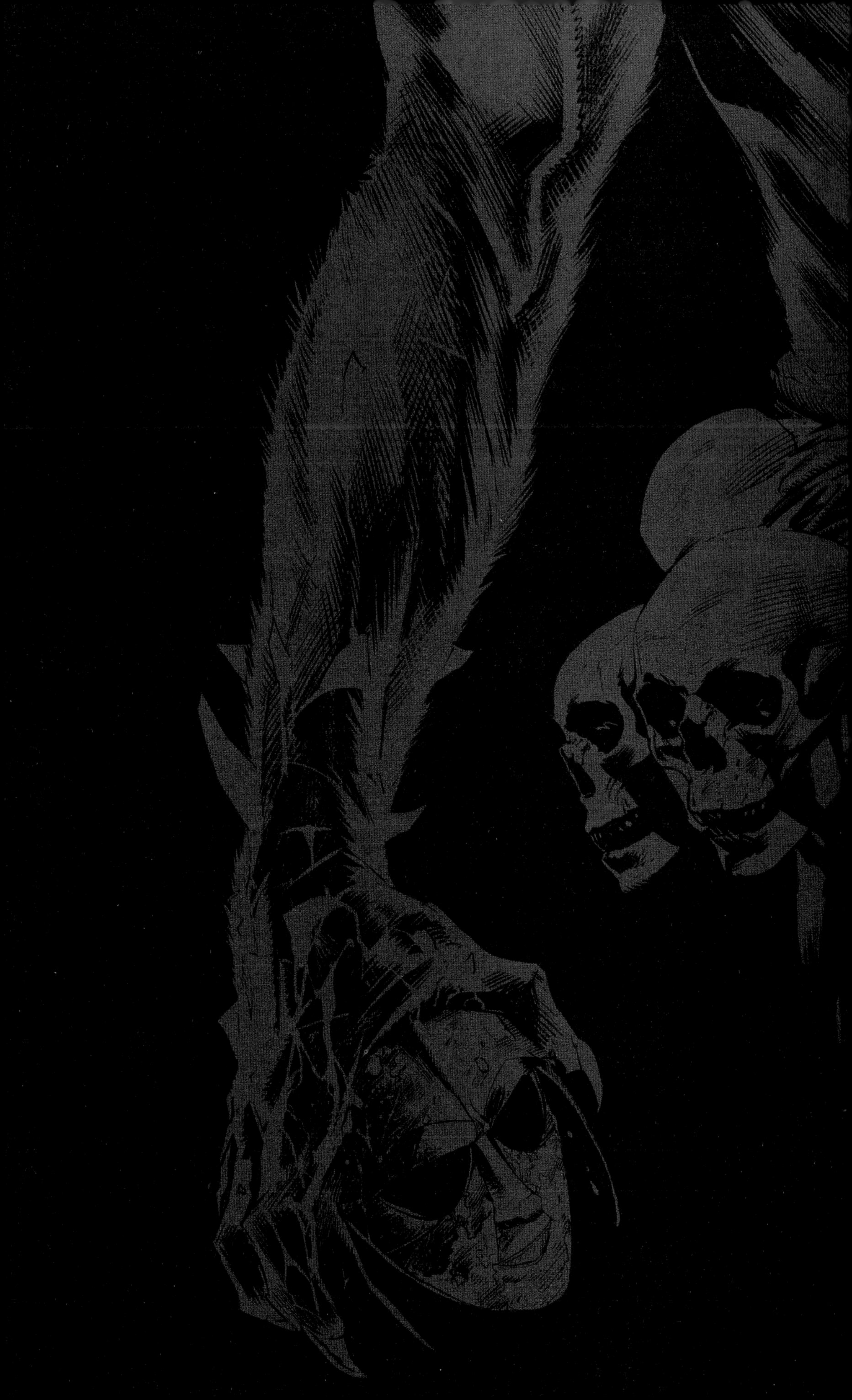

CHAPTER TEN

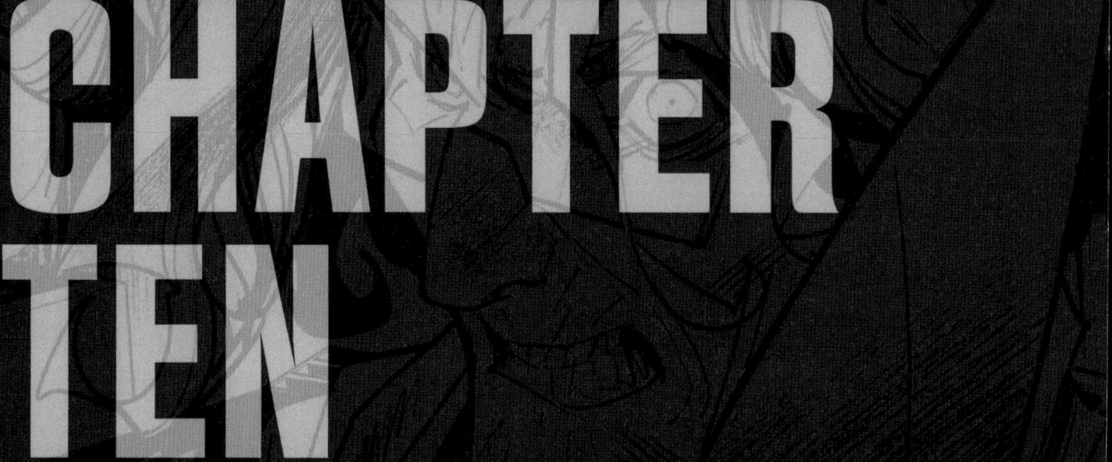

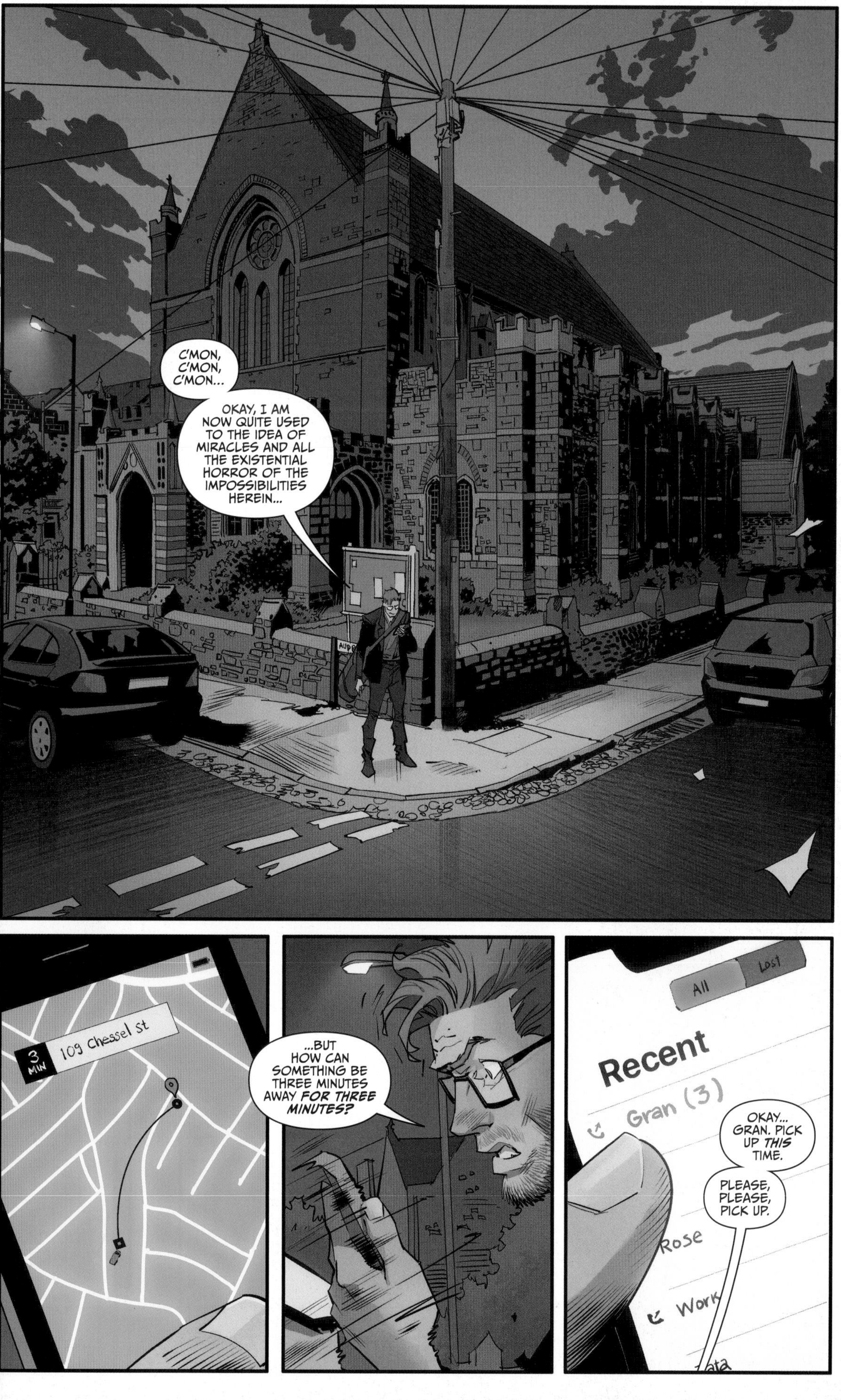
C'MON, C'MON, C'MON...
OKAY, I AM NOW QUITE USED TO THE IDEA OF MIRACLES AND ALL THE EXISTENTIAL HORROR OF THE IMPOSSIBILITIES HEREIN...
3 MIN
109 Chessel St
...BUT HOW CAN SOMETHING BE THREE MINUTES AWAY *FOR THREE MINUTES?*
All
Lost
Recent
Gran (3)
Rose
Work
OKAY... GRAN. PICK UP *THIS* TIME.
PLEASE, PLEASE, PICK UP.

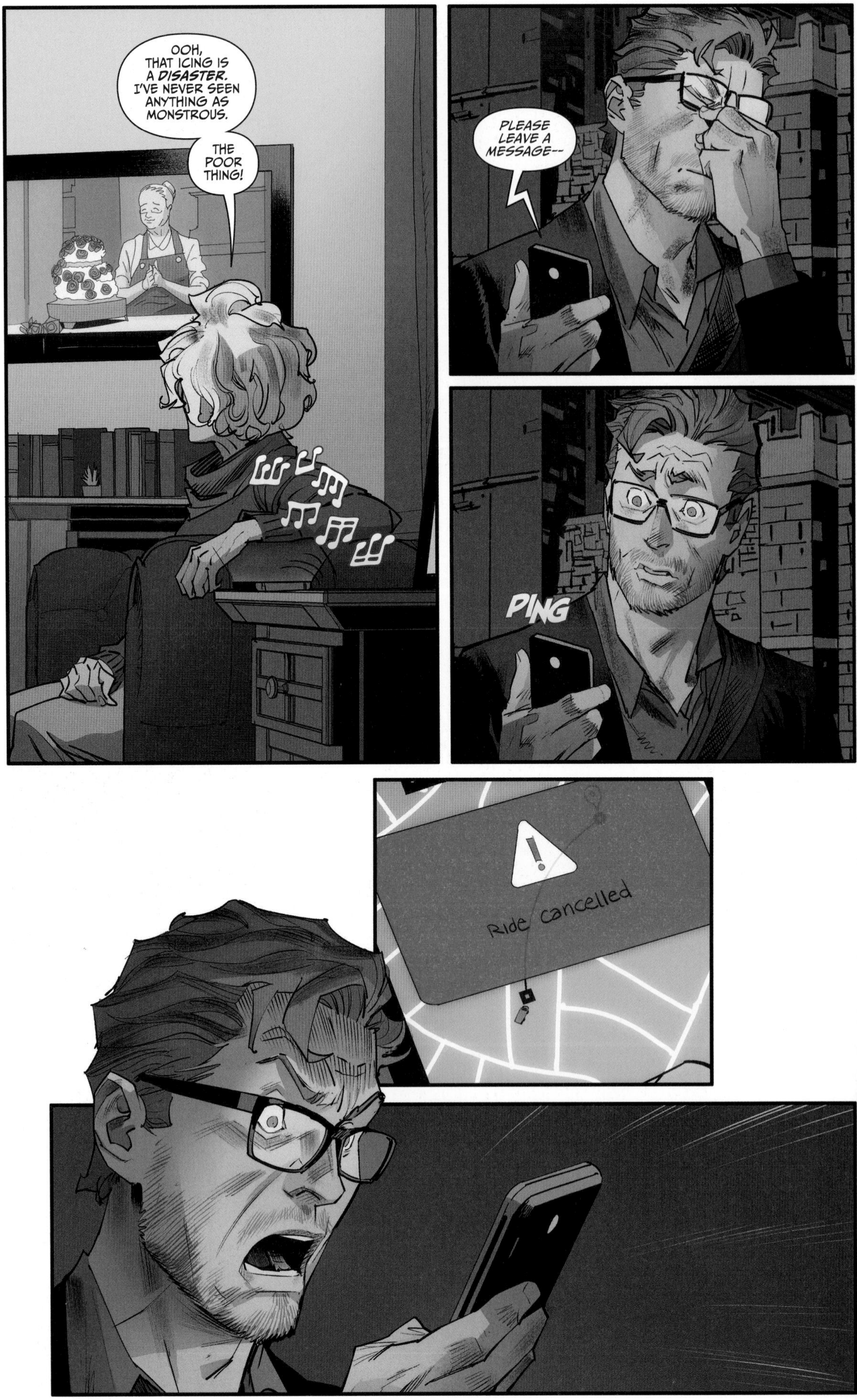
OOH, THAT ICING IS A **DISASTER**. I'VE NEVER SEEN ANYTHING AS MONSTROUS.
THE POOR THING!
PLEASE LEAVE A MESSAGE--
PING
Ride Cancelled

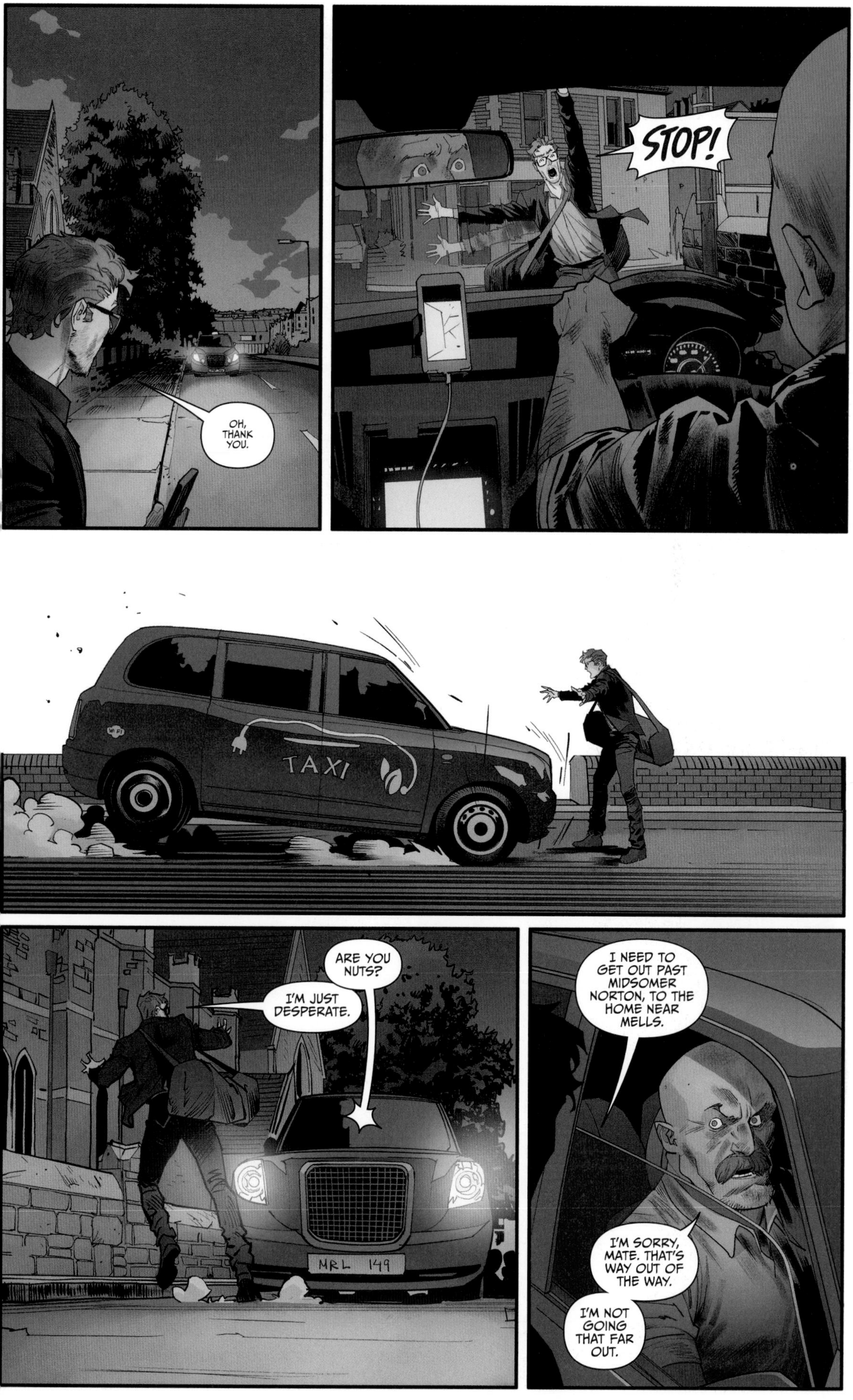
OH, THANK YOU.
STOP!
TAXI
ARE YOU NUTS?
I'M JUST DESPERATE.
MRL 149
I NEED TO GET OUT PAST MIDSOMER NORTON, TO THE HOME NEAR MELLS.
I'M SORRY, MATE. THAT'S WAY OUT OF THE WAY.
I'M NOT GOING THAT FAR OUT.

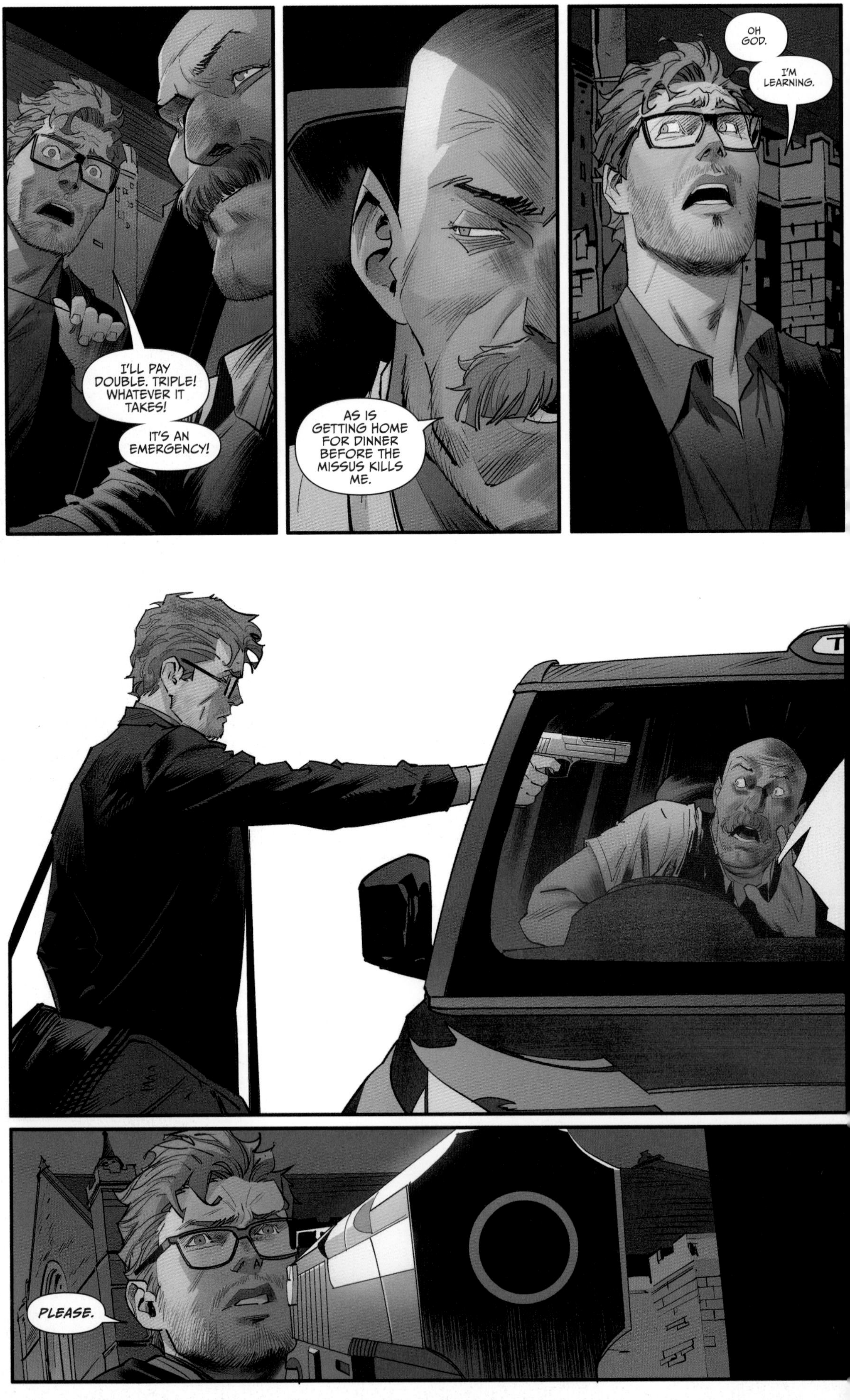
I'LL PAY DOUBLE. TRIPLE! WHATEVER IT TAKES!
IT'S AN EMERGENCY!
AS IS GETTING HOME FOR DINNER BEFORE THE MISSUS KILLS ME.
OH GOD.
I'M LEARNING.
PLEASE.

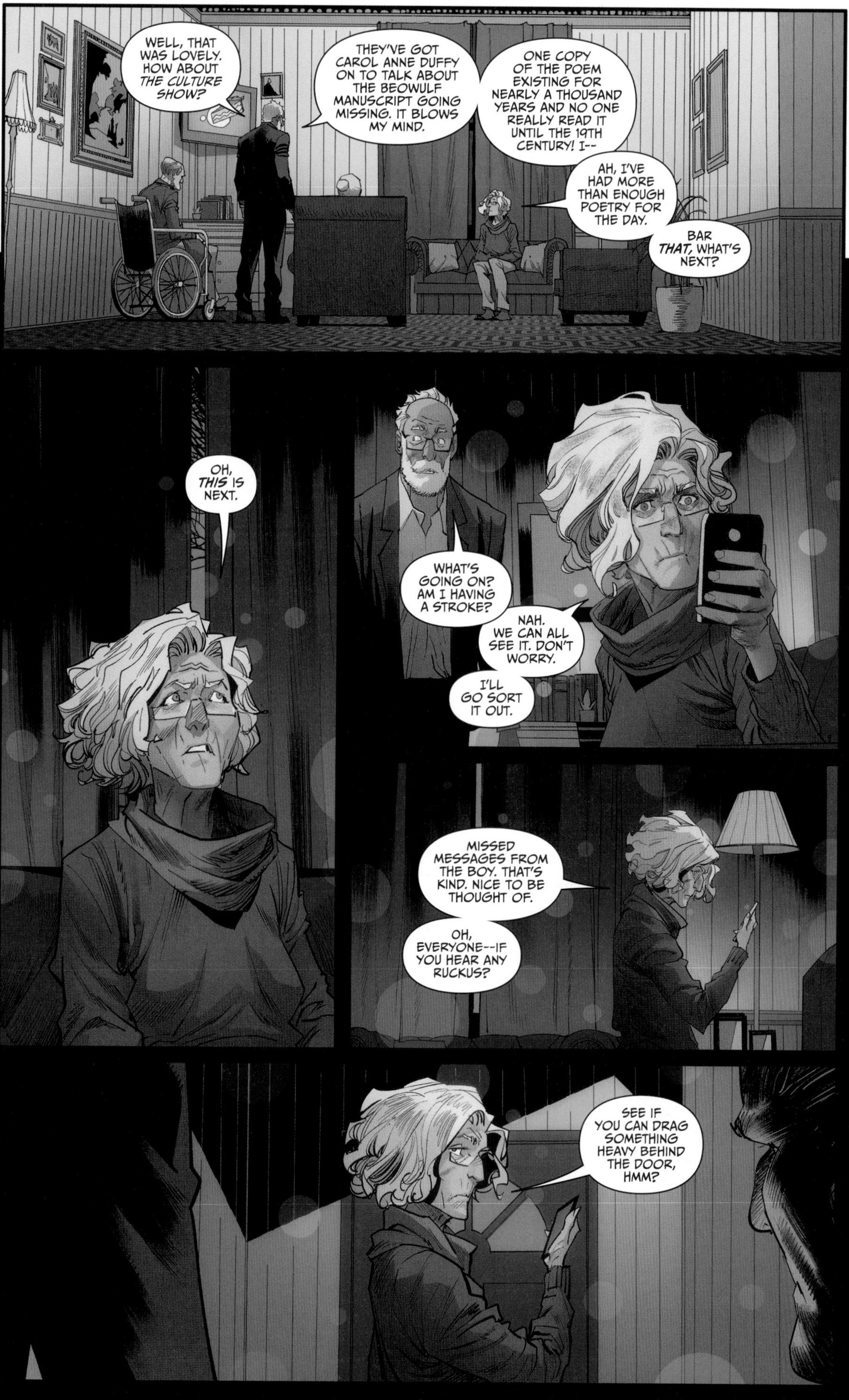

WELL, THAT WAS LOVELY. HOW ABOUT *THE CULTURE SHOW?*
THEY'VE GOT CAROL ANNE DUFFY ON TO TALK ABOUT THE BEOWULF MANUSCRIPT GOING MISSING. IT BLOWS MY MIND.
ONE COPY OF THE POEM EXISTING FOR NEARLY A THOUSAND YEARS AND NO ONE REALLY READ IT UNTIL THE 19TH CENTURY! I--
AH, I'VE HAD MORE THAN ENOUGH POETRY FOR THE DAY.
BAR *THAT,* WHAT'S NEXT?
OH, *THIS* IS NEXT.
WHAT'S GOING ON? AM I HAVING A STROKE?
NAH. WE CAN ALL SEE IT. DON'T WORRY.
I'LL GO SORT IT OUT.
MISSED MESSAGES FROM THE BOY. THAT'S KIND. NICE TO BE THOUGHT OF.
OH, EVERYONE--IF YOU HEAR ANY RUCKUS?
SEE IF YOU CAN DRAG SOMETHING HEAVY BEHIND THE DOOR, HMM?

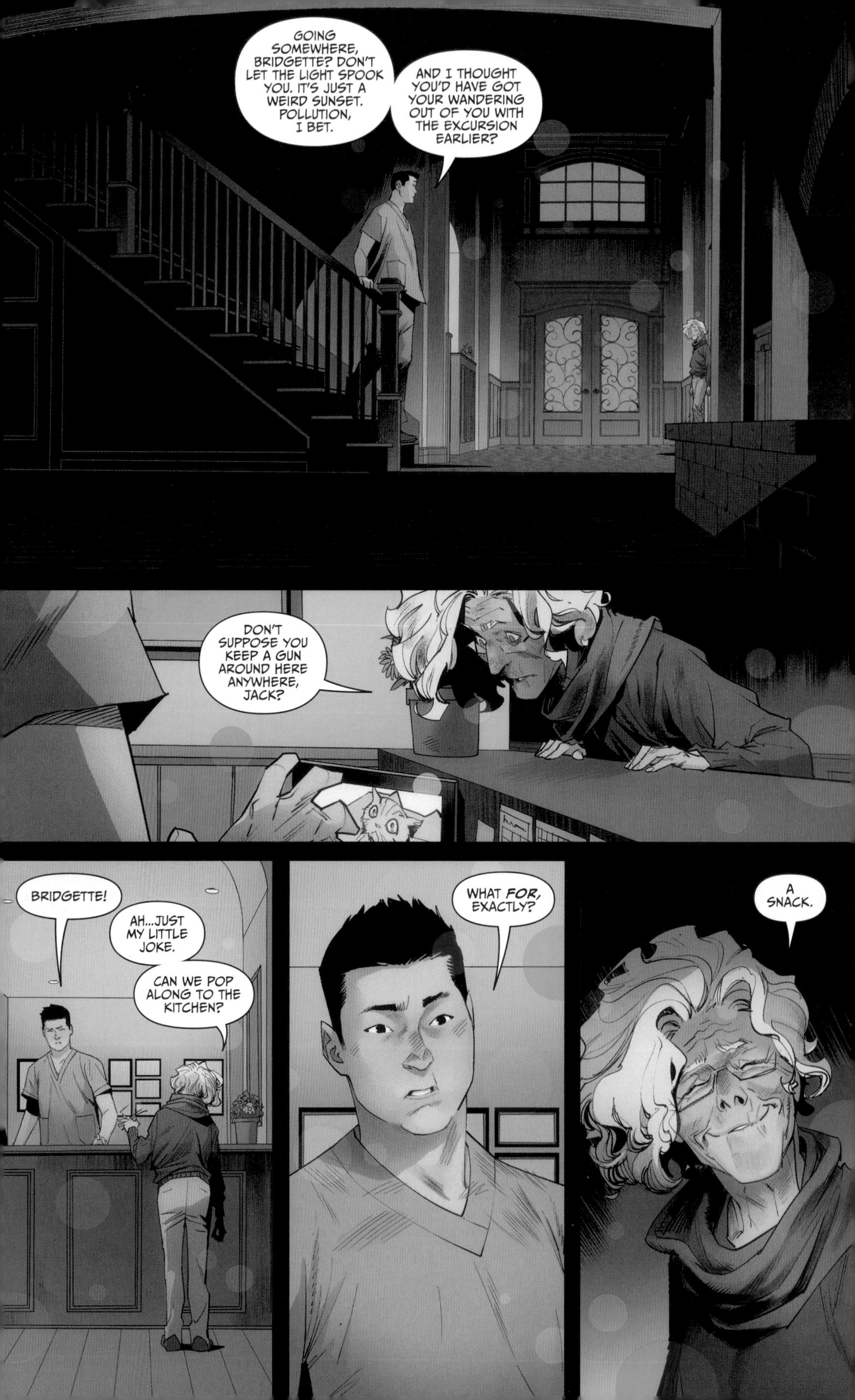
GOING SOMEWHERE, BRIDGETTE? DON'T LET THE LIGHT SPOOK YOU. IT'S JUST A WEIRD SUNSET. POLLUTION, I BET.
AND I THOUGHT YOU'D HAVE GOT YOUR WANDERING OUT OF YOU WITH THE EXCURSION EARLIER?
DON'T SUPPOSE YOU KEEP A GUN AROUND HERE ANYWHERE, JACK?
BRIDGETTE!
AH...JUST MY LITTLE JOKE.
CAN WE POP ALONG TO THE KITCHEN?
WHAT *FOR,* EXACTLY?
A SNACK.

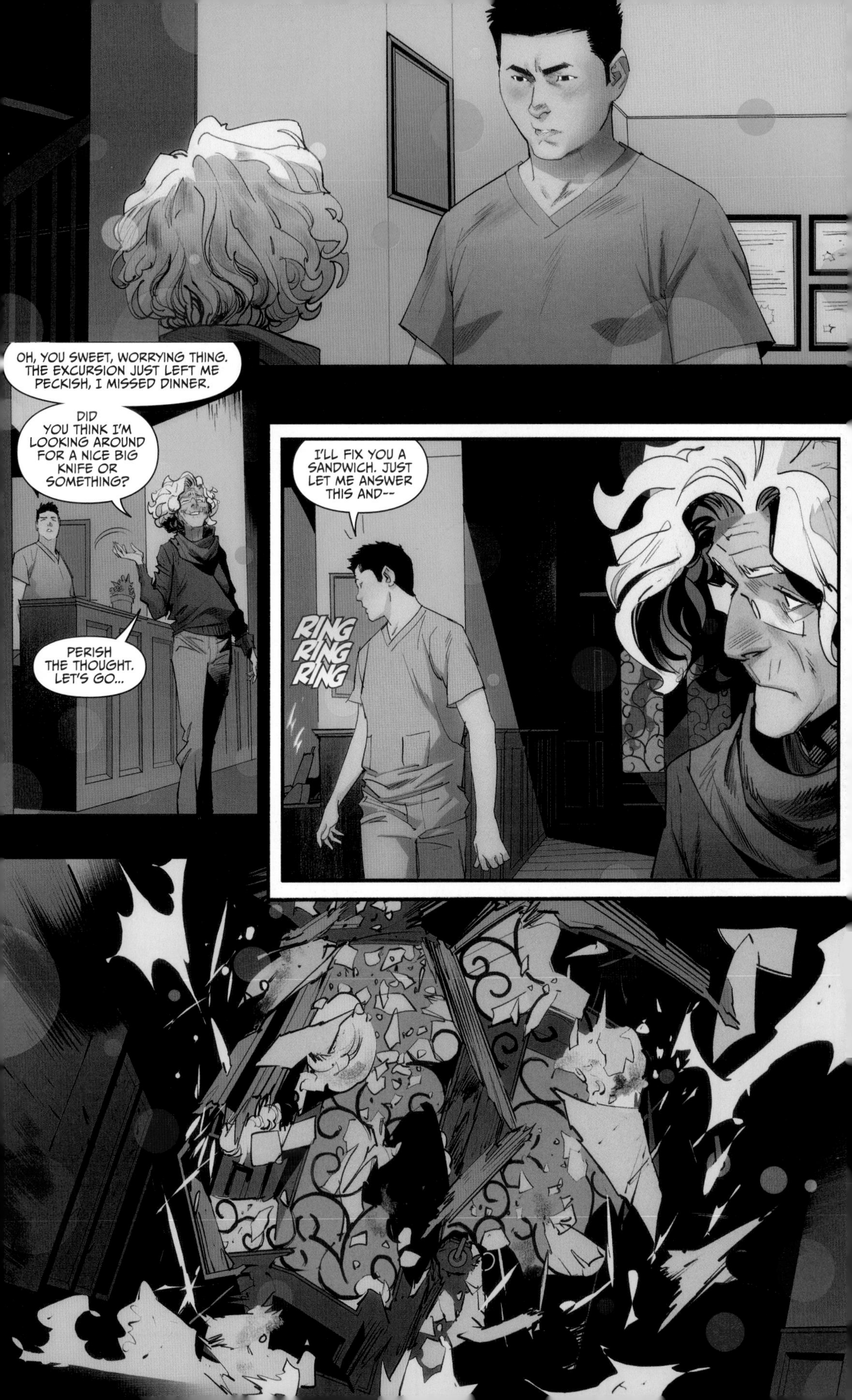
OH, YOU SWEET, WORRYING THING. THE EXCURSION JUST LEFT ME PECKISH, I MISSED DINNER.
DID YOU THINK I'M LOOKING AROUND FOR A NICE BIG KNIFE OR SOMETHING?
PERISH THE THOUGHT. LET'S GO...
I'LL FIX YOU A SANDWICH. JUST LET ME ANSWER THIS AND--
RING RING RING

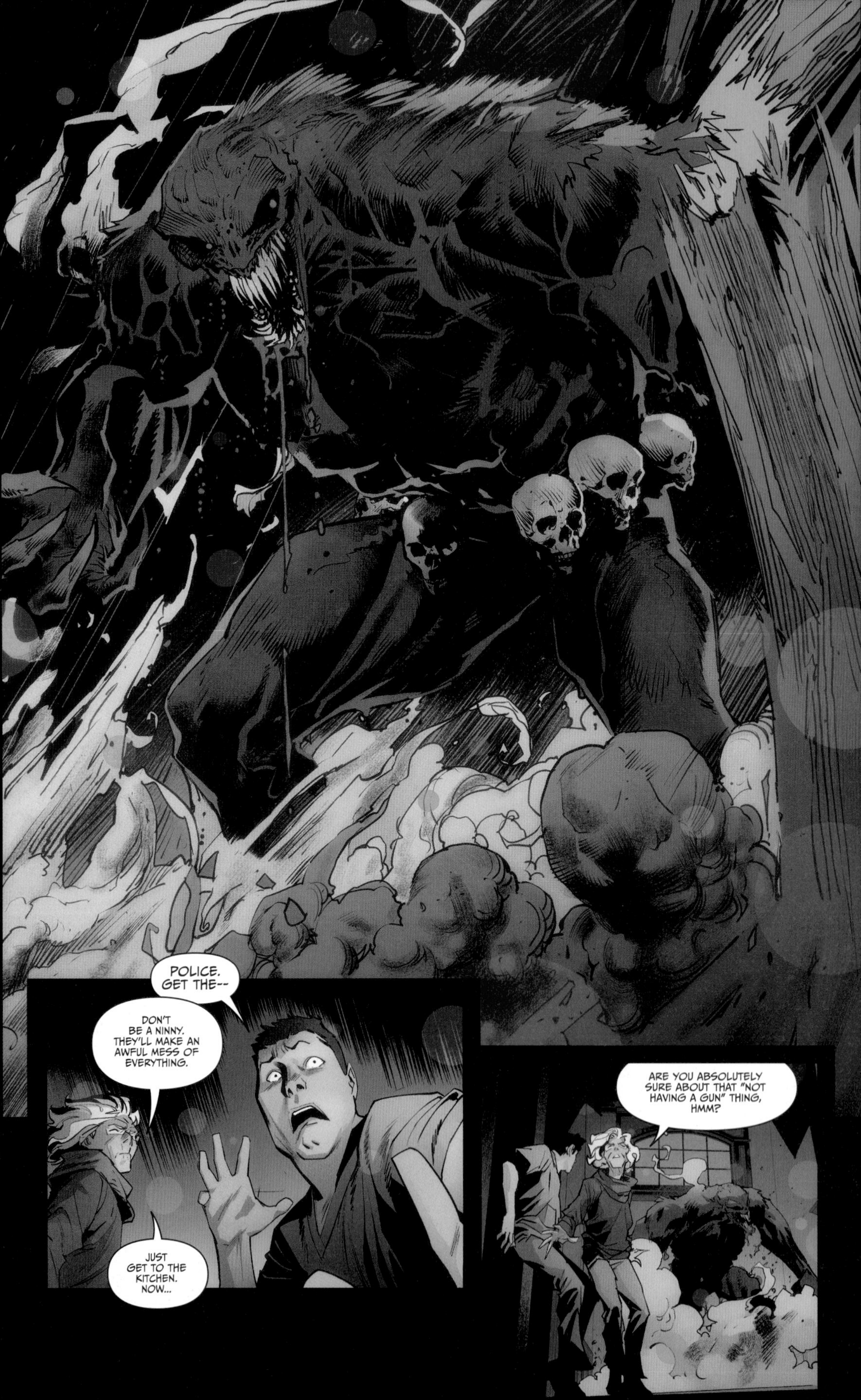
POLICE. GET THE--
DON'T BE A NINNY. THEY'LL MAKE AN AWFUL MESS OF EVERYTHING.
JUST GET TO THE KITCHEN. NOW...
ARE YOU ABSOLUTELY SURE ABOUT THAT "NOT HAVING A GUN" THING, HMM?

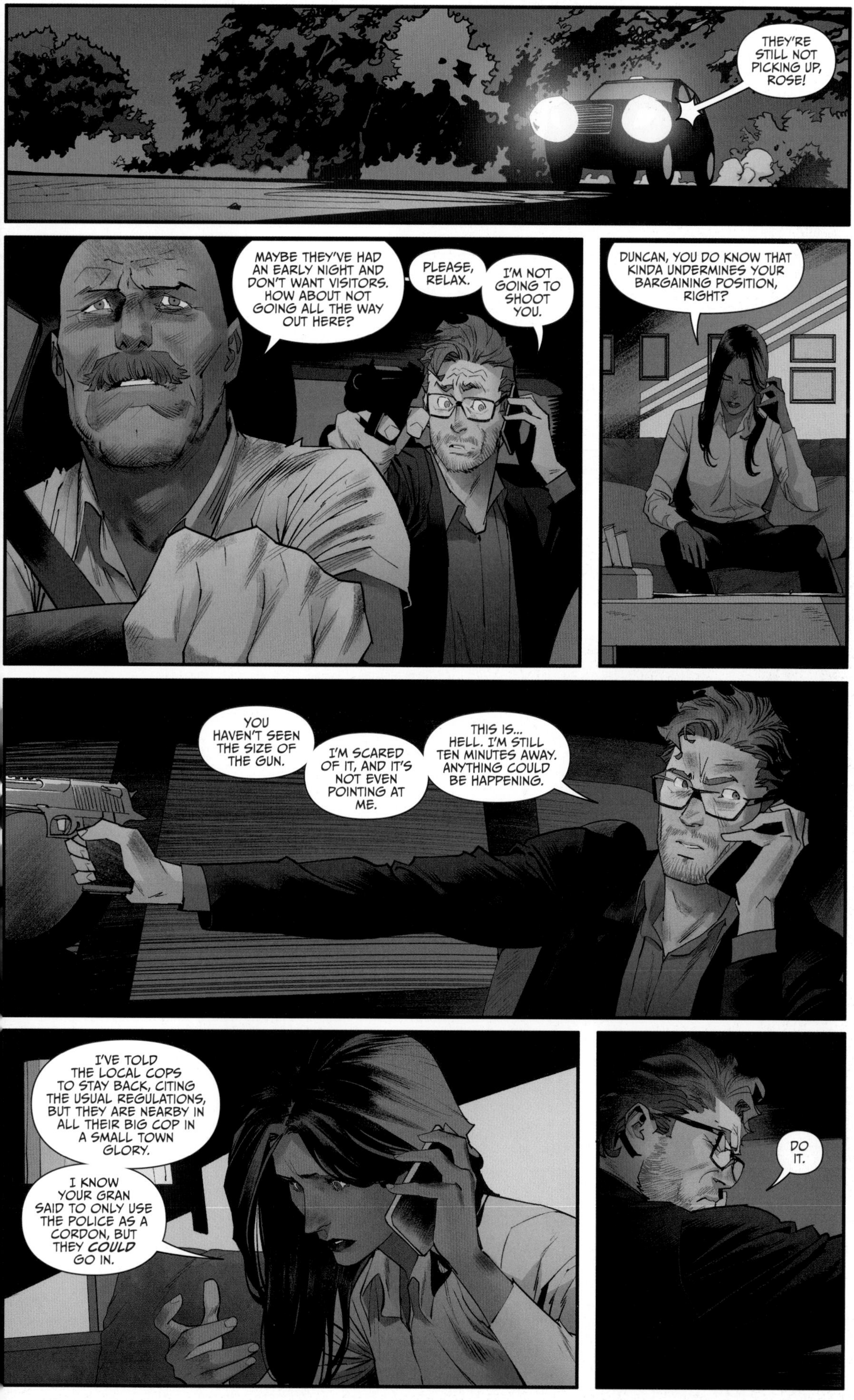
THEY'RE STILL NOT PICKING UP, ROSE!
MAYBE THEY'VE HAD AN EARLY NIGHT AND DON'T WANT VISITORS. HOW ABOUT NOT GOING ALL THE WAY OUT HERE?
PLEASE, RELAX.
I'M NOT GOING TO SHOOT YOU.
DUNCAN, YOU DO KNOW THAT KINDA UNDERMINES YOUR BARGAINING POSITION, RIGHT?
YOU HAVEN'T SEEN THE SIZE OF THE GUN.
I'M SCARED OF IT, AND IT'S NOT EVEN POINTING AT ME.
THIS IS... HELL. I'M STILL TEN MINUTES AWAY. ANYTHING COULD BE HAPPENING.
I'VE TOLD THE LOCAL COPS TO STAY BACK, CITING THE USUAL REGULATIONS, BUT THEY ARE NEARBY IN ALL THEIR BIG COP IN A SMALL TOWN GLORY.
I KNOW YOUR GRAN SAID TO ONLY USE THE POLICE AS A CORDON, BUT THEY ***COULD*** GO IN.
DO IT.

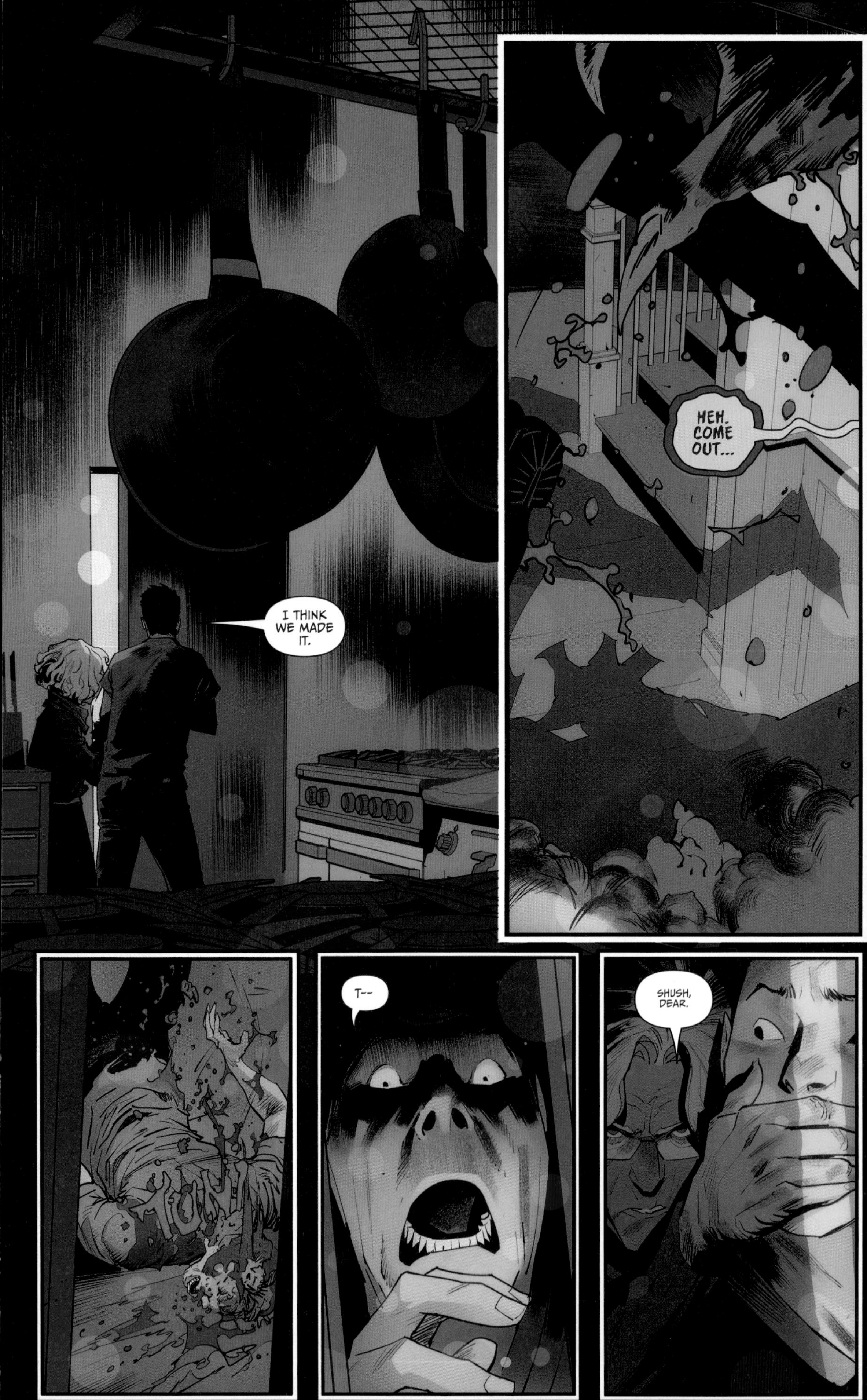
I THINK WE MADE IT.
HEH. COME OUT...
T--
SHUSH, DEAR.

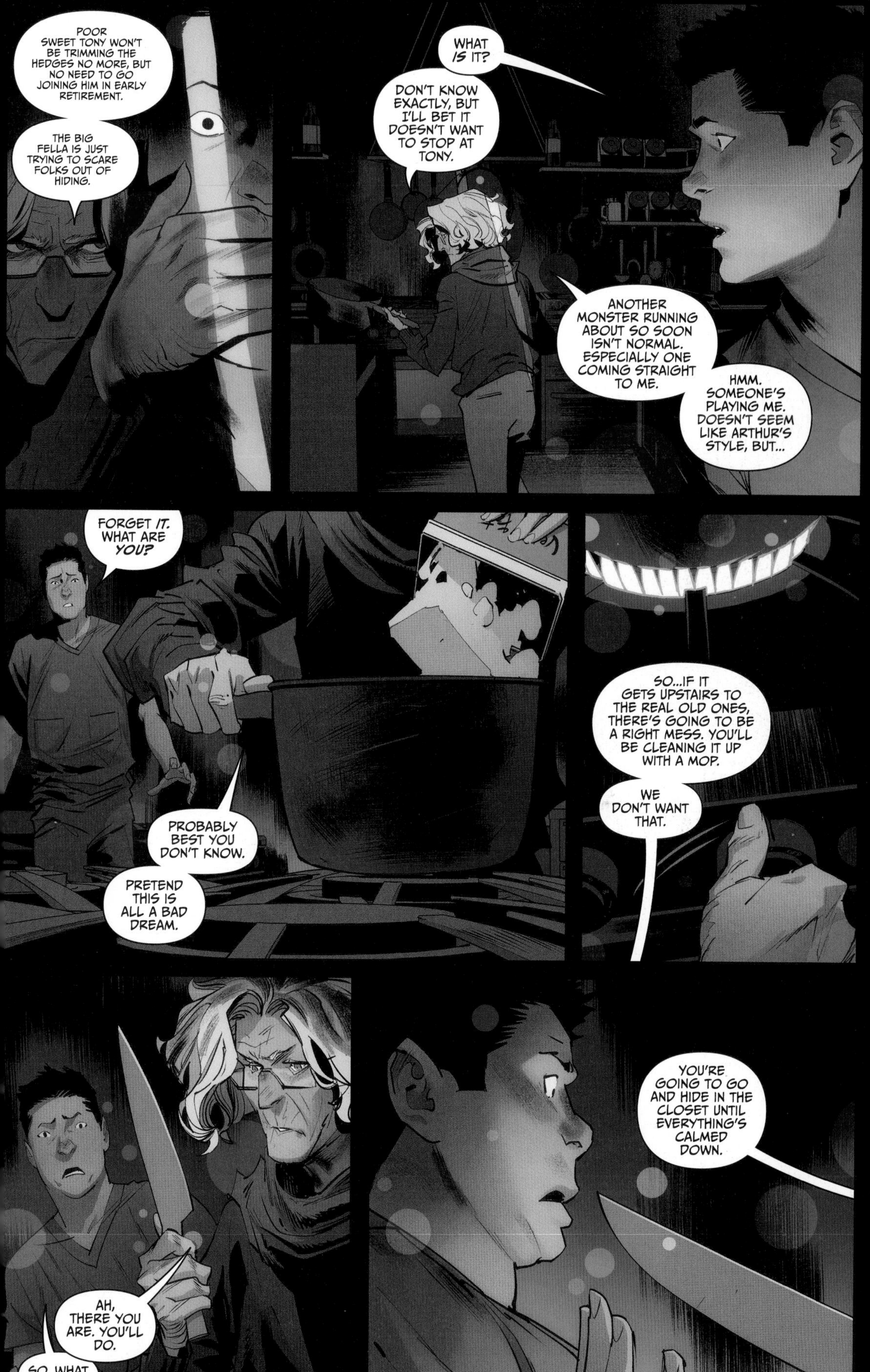
POOR SWEET TONY WON'T BE TRIMMING THE HEDGES NO MORE, BUT NO NEED TO GO JOINING HIM IN EARLY RETIREMENT.
THE BIG FELLA IS JUST TRYING TO SCARE FOLKS OUT OF HIDING.
WHAT *IS* IT?
DON'T KNOW EXACTLY, BUT I'LL BET IT DOESN'T WANT TO STOP AT TONY.
ANOTHER MONSTER RUNNING ABOUT SO SOON ISN'T NORMAL. ESPECIALLY ONE COMING STRAIGHT TO ME.
HMM. SOMEONE'S PLAYING ME. DOESN'T SEEM LIKE ARTHUR'S STYLE, BUT...
FORGET *IT*. WHAT ARE *YOU?*
PROBABLY BEST YOU DON'T KNOW.
PRETEND THIS IS ALL A BAD DREAM.
SO...IF IT GETS UPSTAIRS TO THE REAL OLD ONES, THERE'S GOING TO BE A RIGHT MESS. YOU'LL BE CLEANING IT UP WITH A MOP.
WE DON'T WANT THAT.
AH, THERE YOU ARE. YOU'LL DO.
SO, WHAT NOW?
YOU'RE GOING TO GO AND HIDE IN THE CLOSET UNTIL EVERYTHING'S CALMED DOWN.

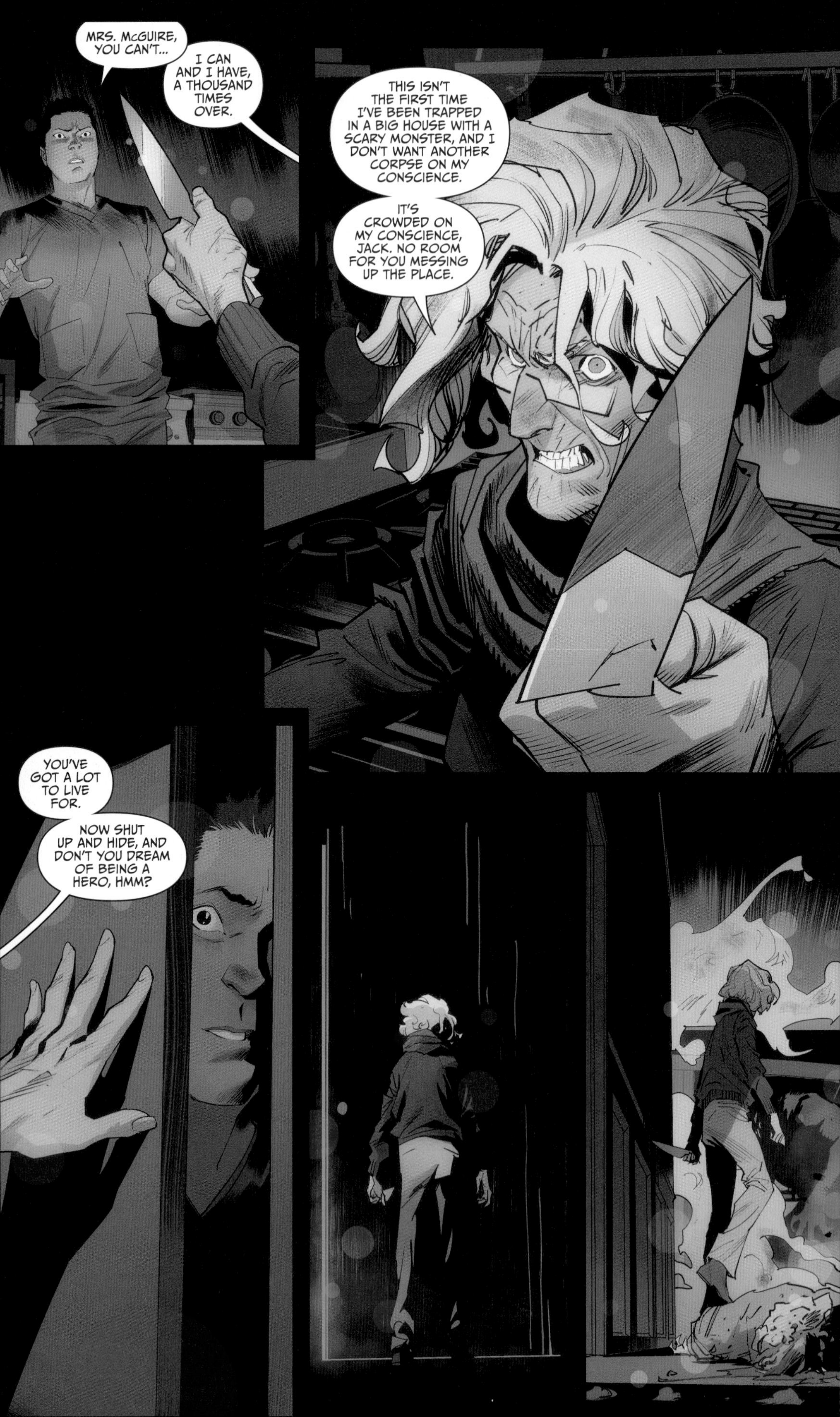
MRS. McGUIRE, YOU CAN'T...
I CAN AND I HAVE, A THOUSAND TIMES OVER.
THIS ISN'T THE FIRST TIME I'VE BEEN TRAPPED IN A BIG HOUSE WITH A SCARY MONSTER, AND I DON'T WANT ANOTHER CORPSE ON MY CONSCIENCE.
IT'S CROWDED ON MY CONSCIENCE, JACK. NO ROOM FOR YOU MESSING UP THE PLACE.
YOU'VE GOT A LOT TO LIVE FOR.
NOW SHUT UP AND HIDE, AND DON'T YOU DREAM OF BEING A HERO, HMM?

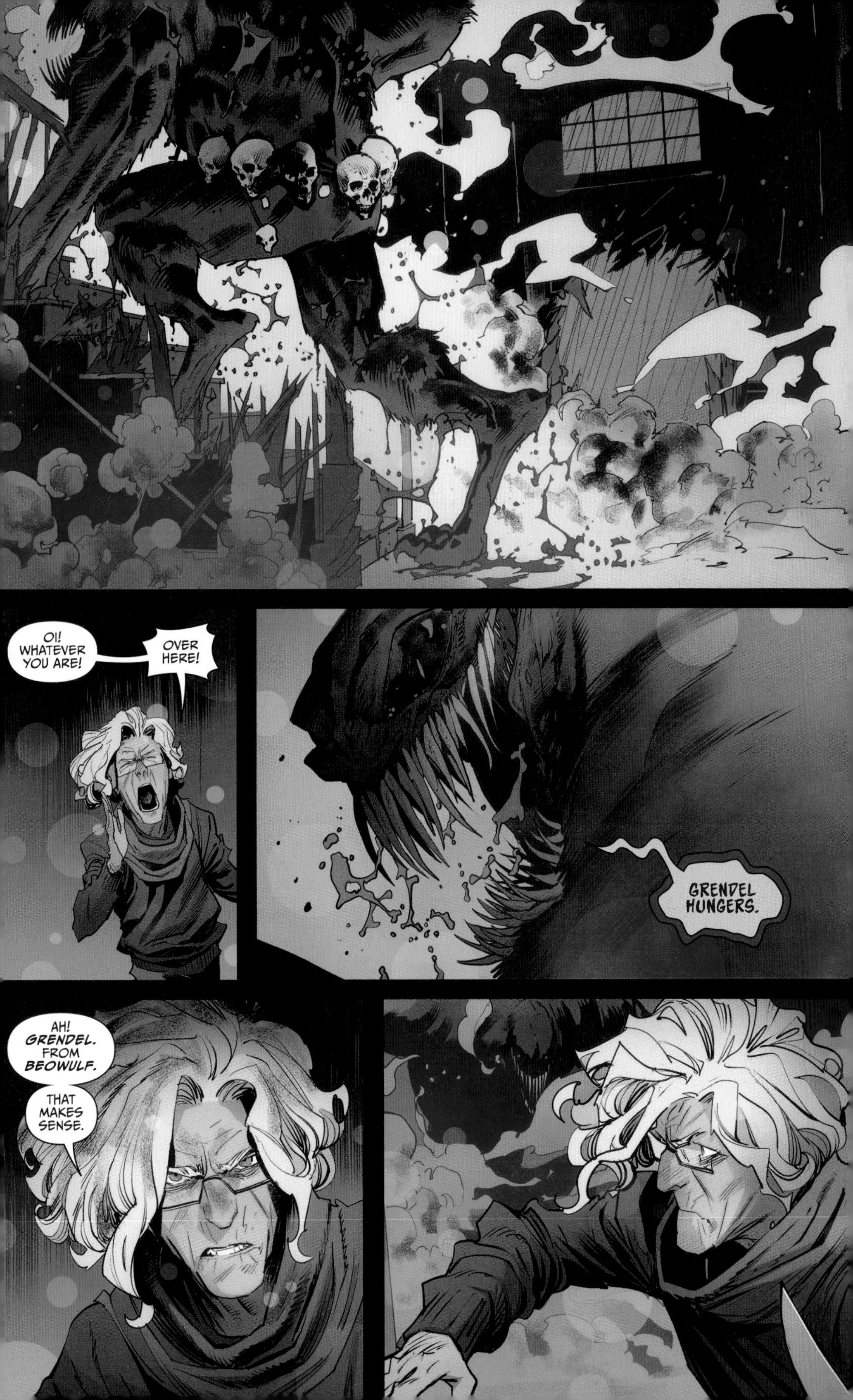
OI! WHATEVER YOU ARE!
OVER HERE!
GRENDEL HUNGERS.
AH! *GRENDEL.* FROM *BEOWULF.*
THAT MAKES SENSE.

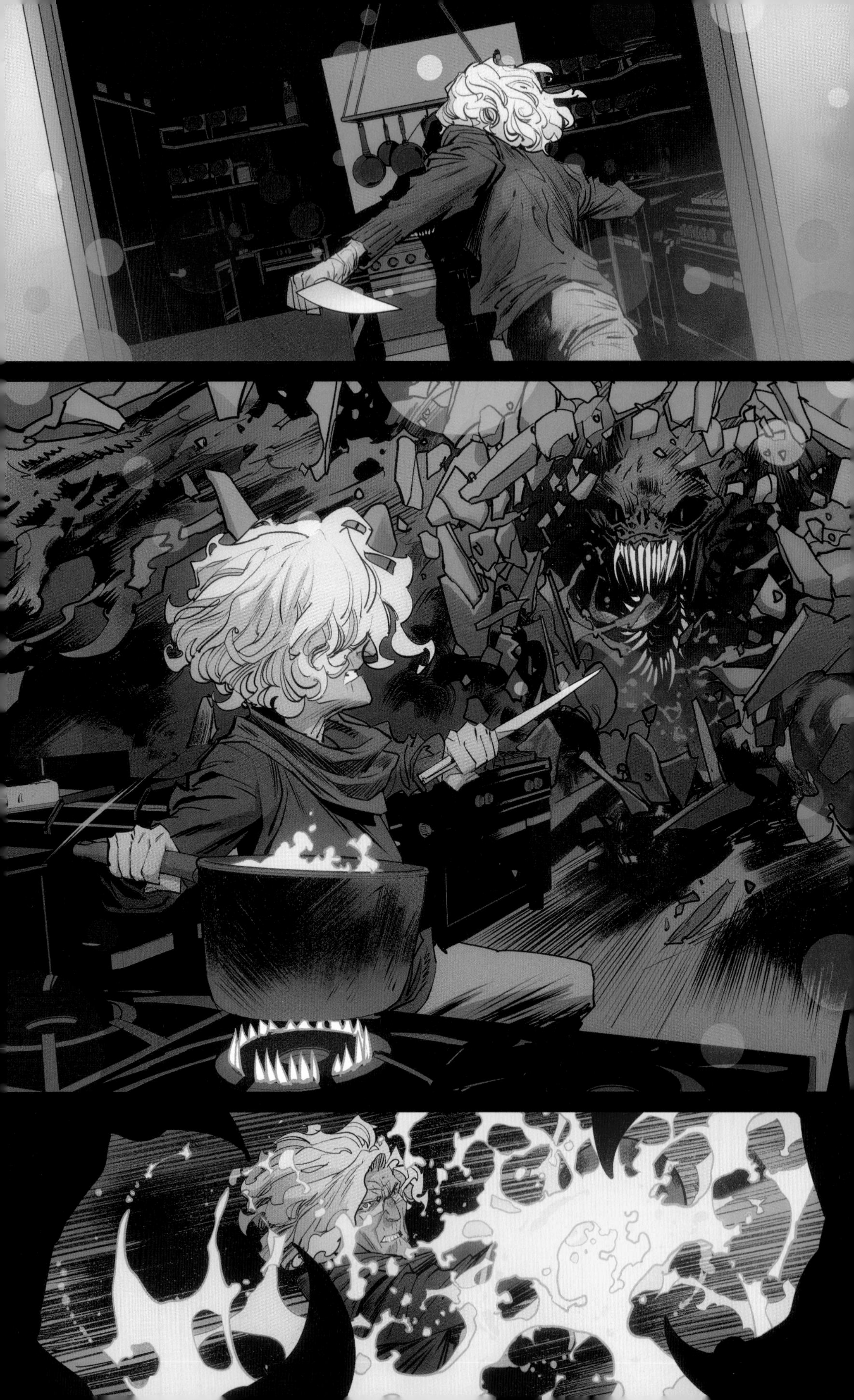

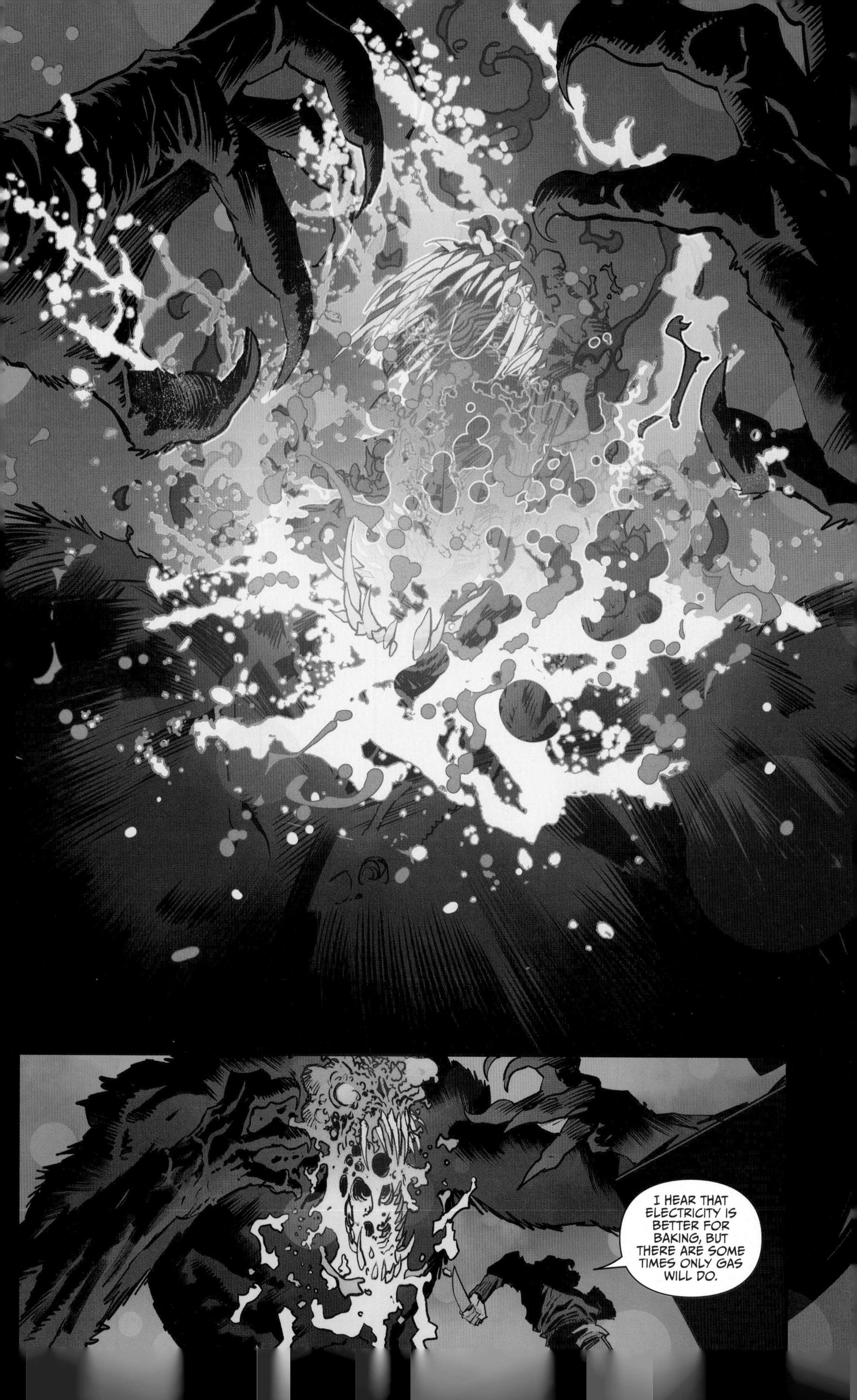
I HEAR THAT ELECTRICITY IS BETTER FOR BAKING, BUT THERE ARE SOME TIMES ONLY GAS WILL DO.

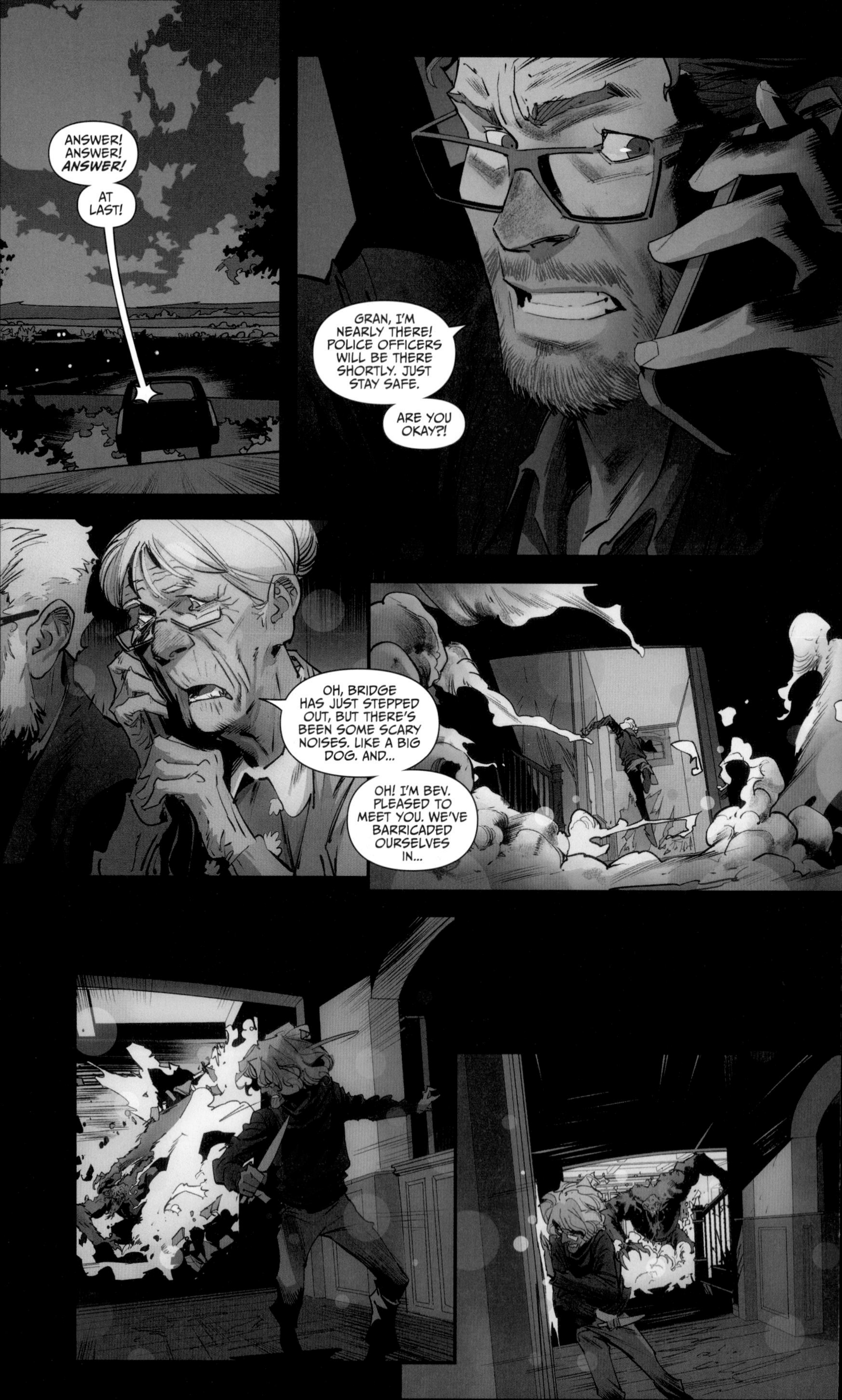
ANSWER! ANSWER! ANSWER!
AT LAST!
GRAN, I'M NEARLY THERE! POLICE OFFICERS WILL BE THERE SHORTLY. JUST STAY SAFE.
ARE YOU OKAY?!
OH, BRIDGE HAS JUST STEPPED OUT, BUT THERE'S BEEN SOME SCARY NOISES. LIKE A BIG DOG. AND...
OH! I'M BEV. PLEASED TO MEET YOU. WE'VE BARRICADED OURSELVES IN...

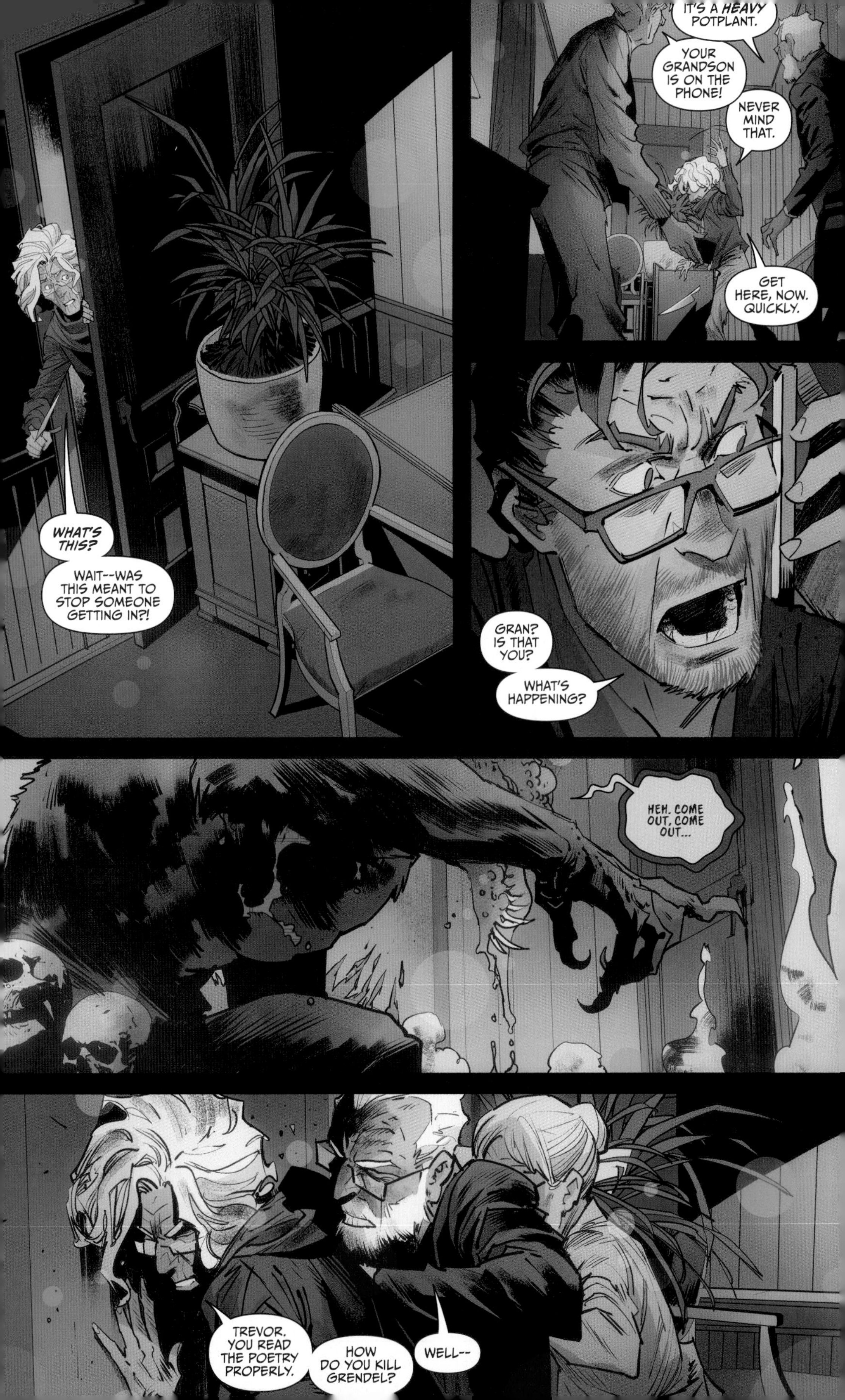

WHAT'S THIS?
WAIT--WAS THIS MEANT TO STOP SOMEONE GETTING IN?!
IT'S A HEAVY POTPLANT.
YOUR GRANDSON IS ON THE PHONE!
NEVER MIND THAT.
GET HERE, NOW. QUICKLY.
GRAN? IS THAT YOU?
WHAT'S HAPPENING?
HEH. COME OUT, COME OUT...
TREVOR. YOU READ THE POETRY PROPERLY.
HOW DO YOU KILL GRENDEL?
WELL--

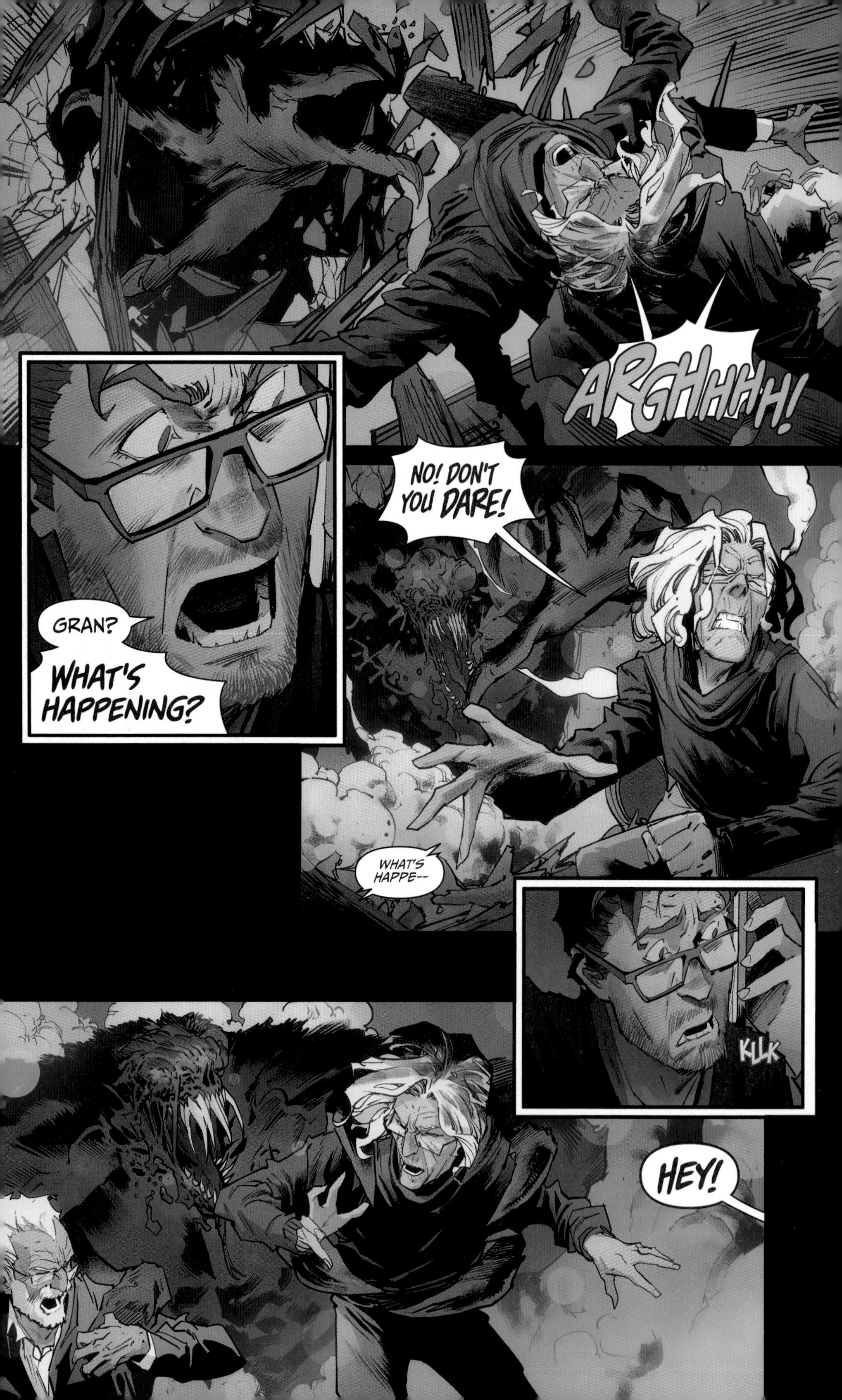
ARGHHHH!
GRAN?
WHAT'S HAPPENING?
NO! DON'T YOU DARE!
WHAT'S HAPPE--
KLIK
HEY!

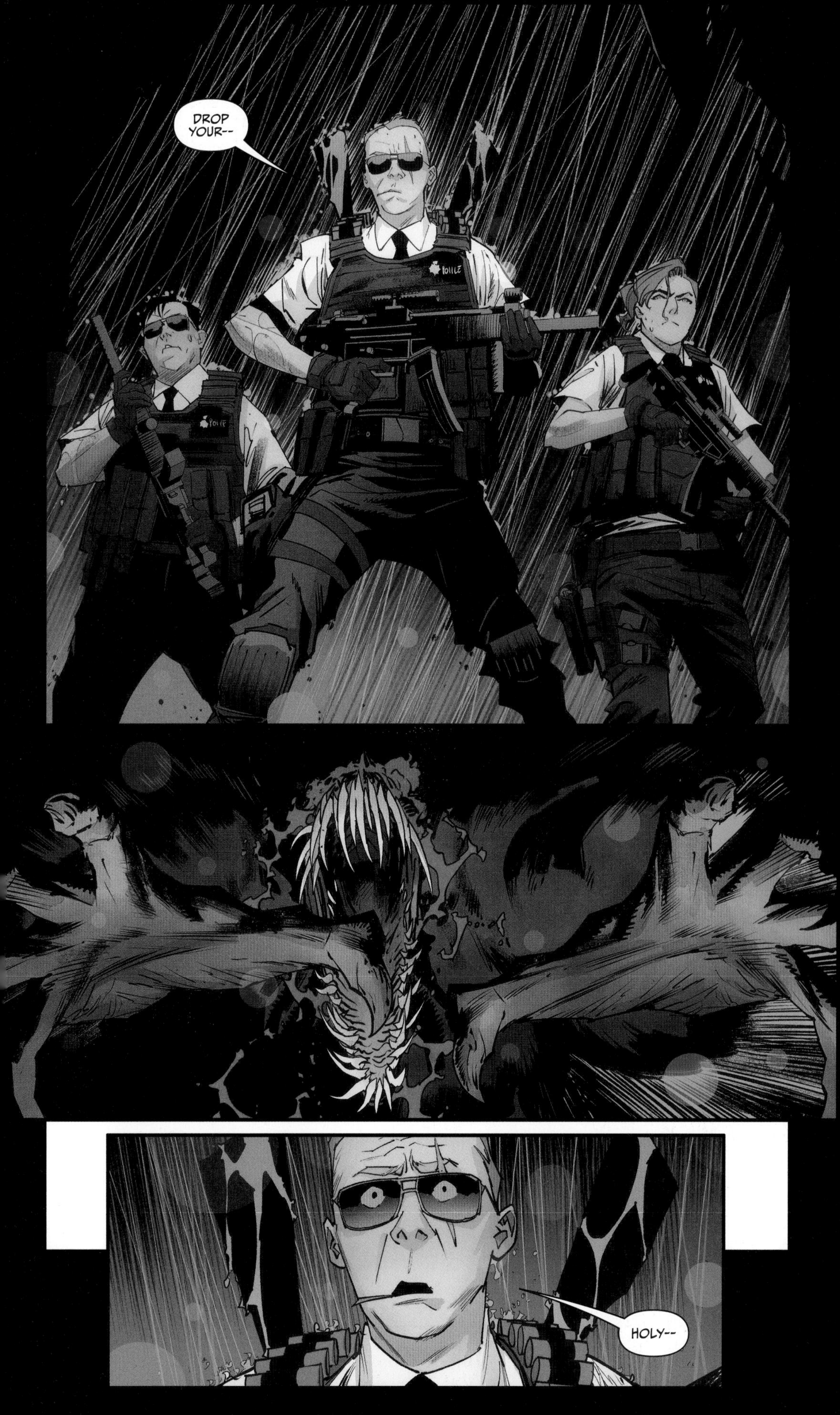
DROP YOUR--
HOLY--

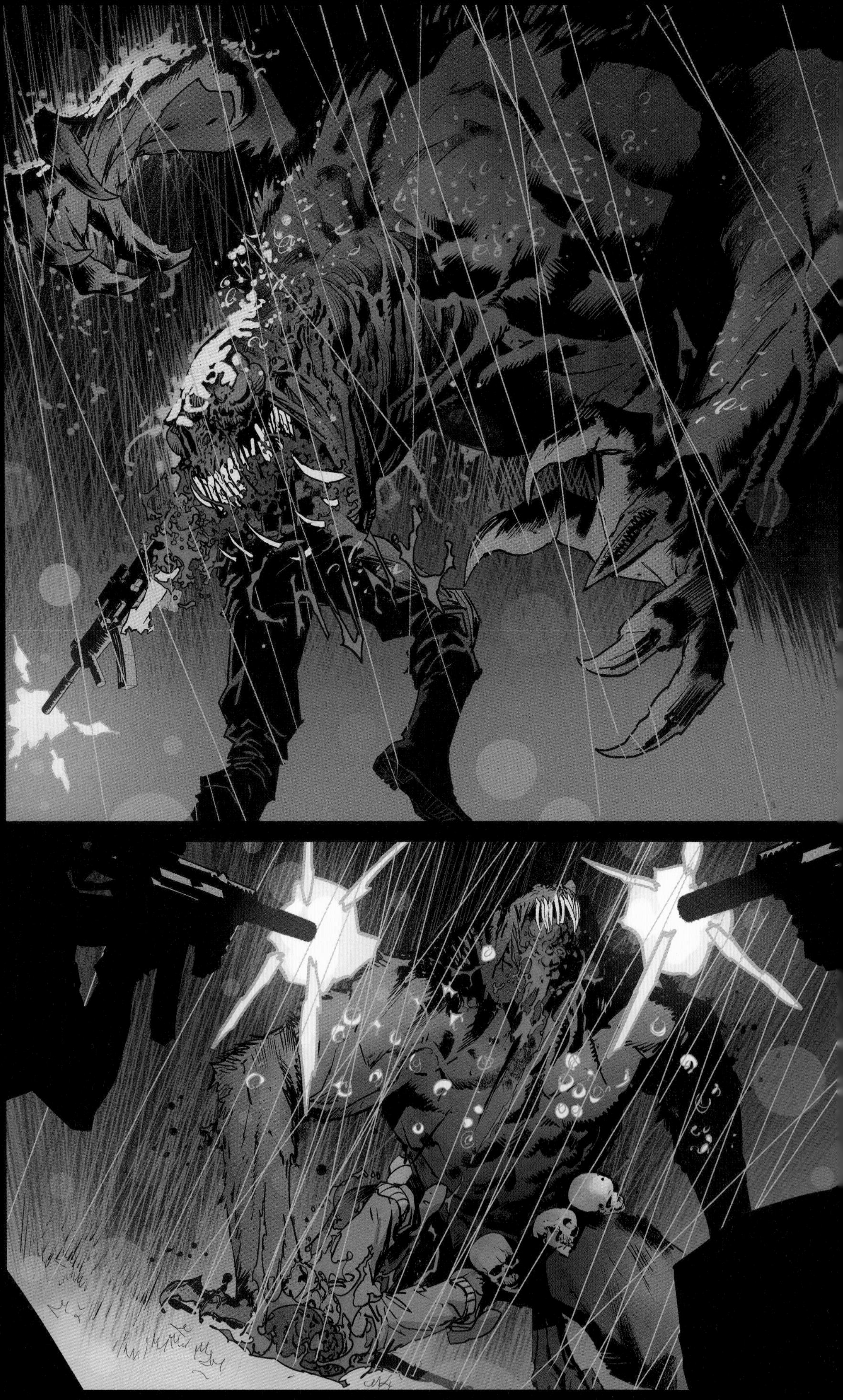

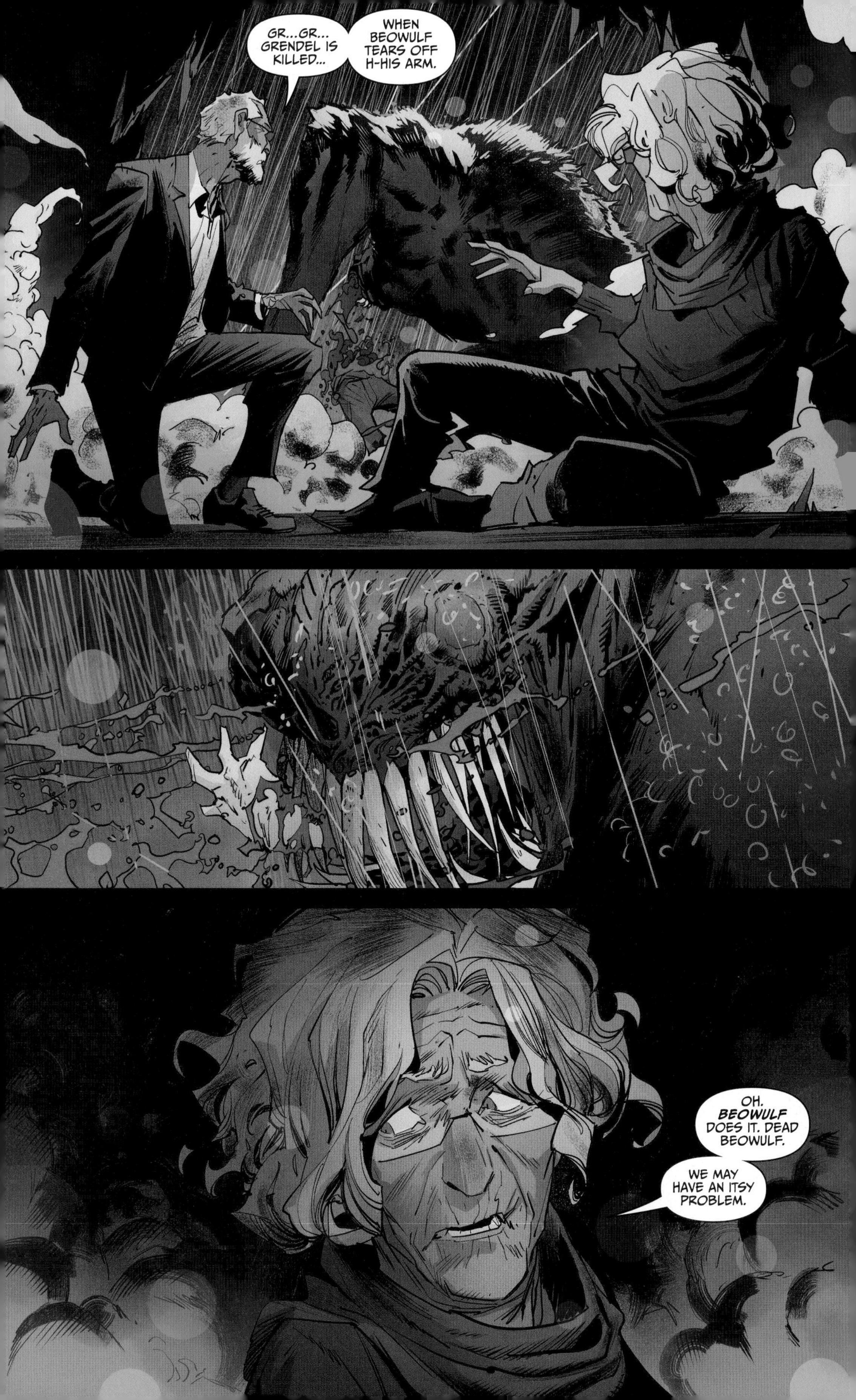
GR...GR... GRENDEL IS KILLED...
WHEN BEOWULF TEARS OFF H-HIS ARM.
OH. BEOWULF DOES IT. DEAD BEOWULF.
WE MAY HAVE AN ITSY PROBLEM.

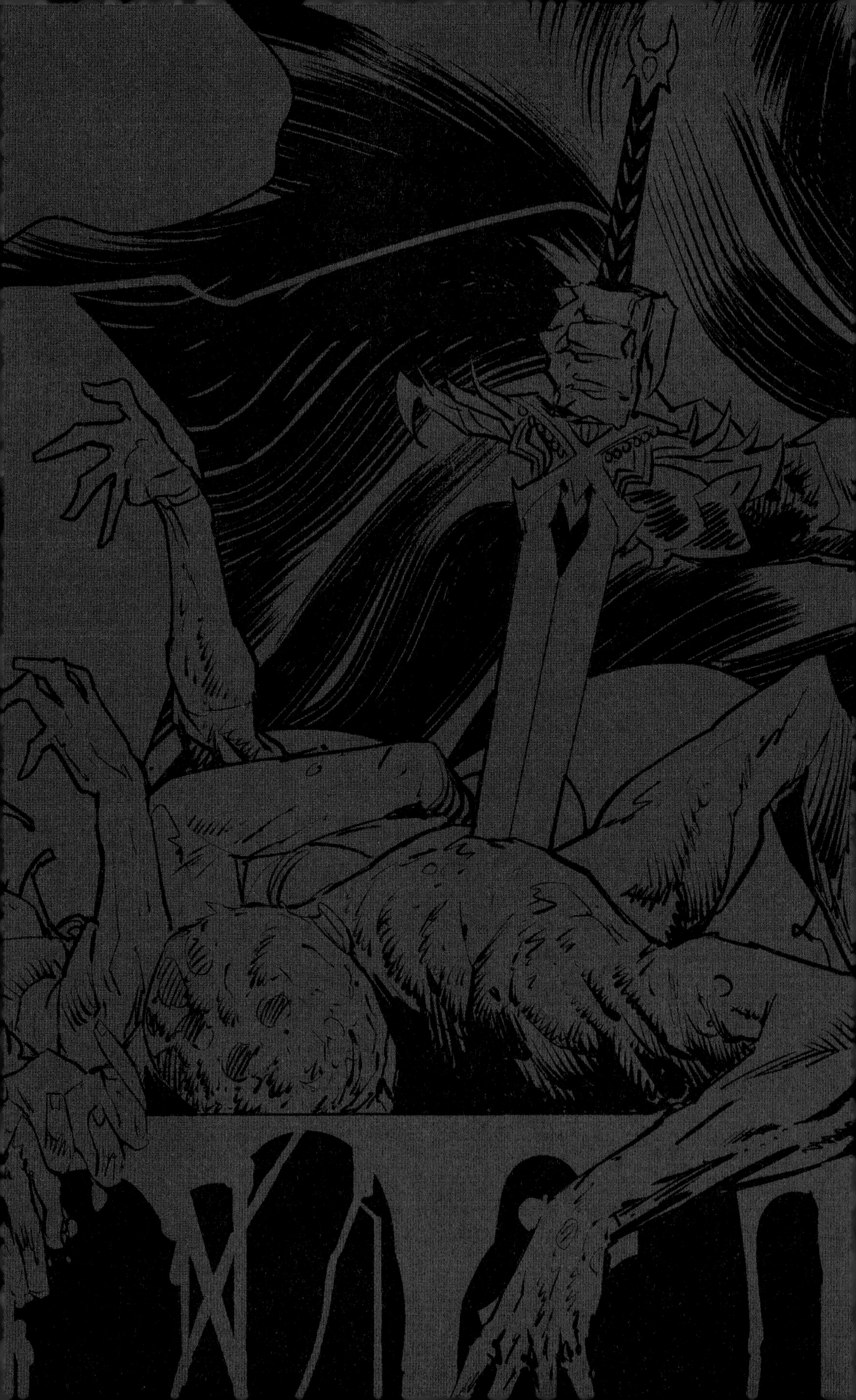

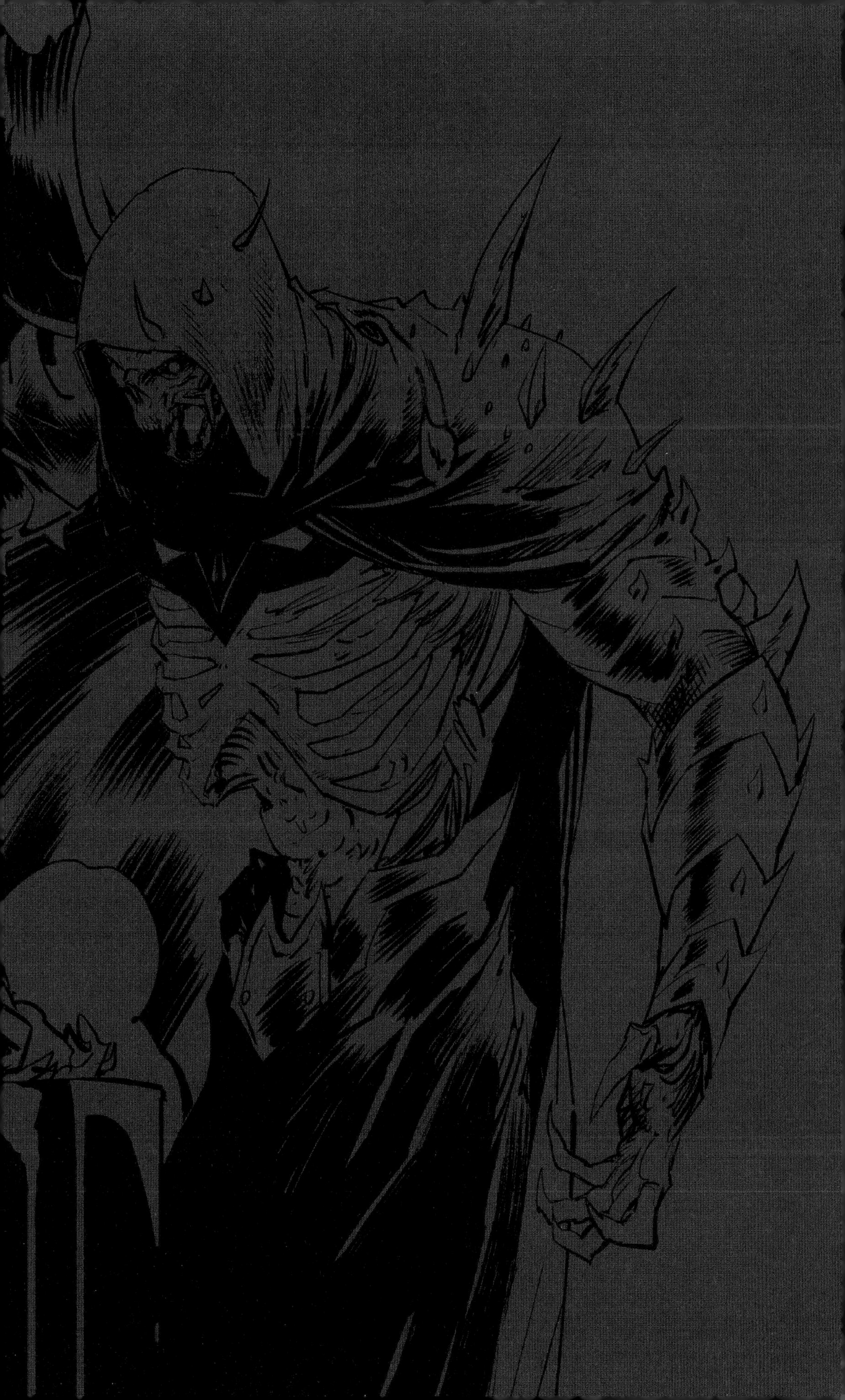

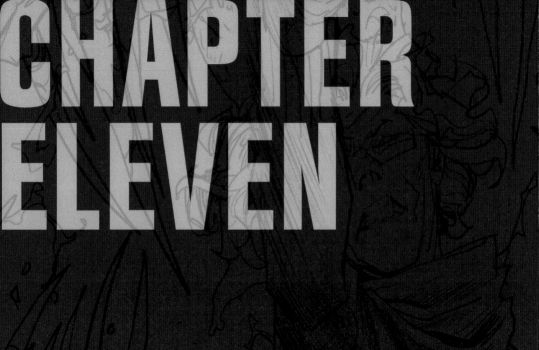

CHAPTER
ELEVEN

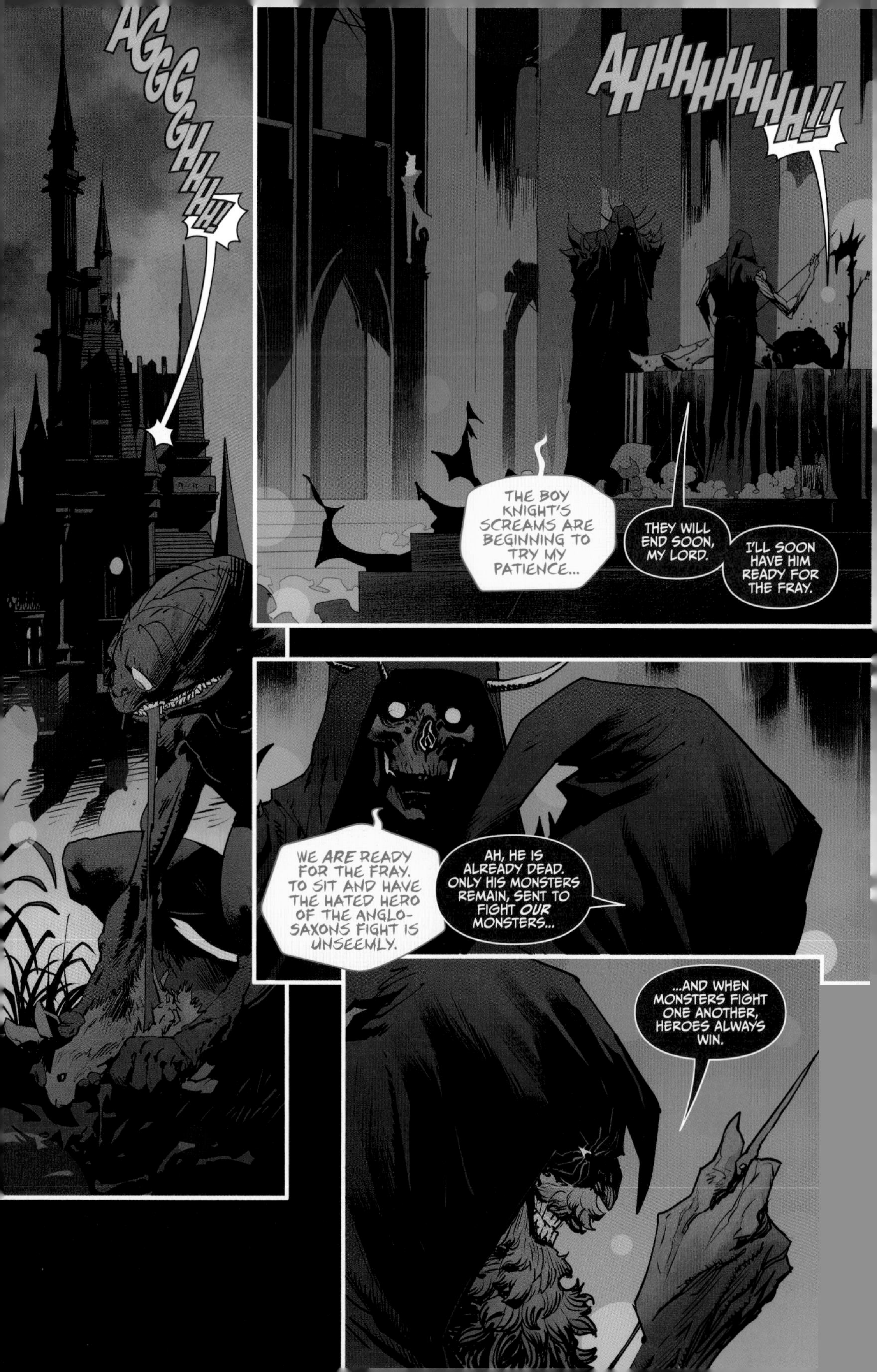
AGGGHHH!
AHHHHHHHH!!!
THE BOY KNIGHT'S SCREAMS ARE BEGINNING TO TRY MY PATIENCE...
THEY WILL END SOON, MY LORD.
I'LL SOON HAVE HIM READY FOR THE FRAY.
WE *ARE* READY FOR THE FRAY. TO SIT AND HAVE THE HATED HERO OF THE ANGLO-SAXONS FIGHT IS UNSEEMLY.
AH, HE IS ALREADY DEAD. ONLY HIS MONSTERS REMAIN, SENT TO FIGHT *OUR* MONSTERS...
...AND WHEN MONSTERS FIGHT ONE ANOTHER, HEROES ALWAYS WIN.

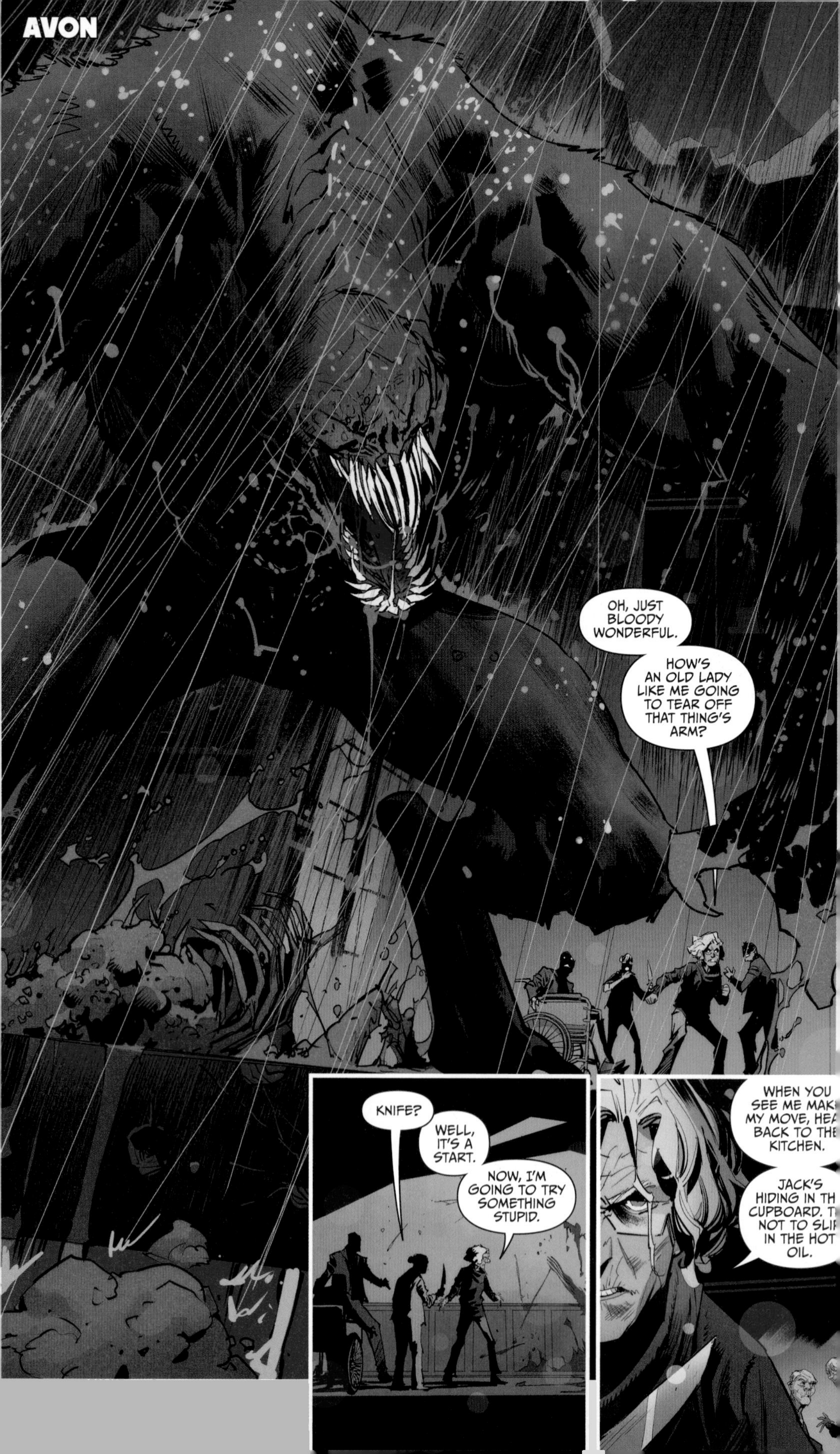
AVON
OH, JUST BLOODY WONDERFUL.
HOW'S AN OLD LADY LIKE ME GOING TO TEAR OFF THAT THING'S ARM?
KNIFE?
WELL, IT'S A START.
NOW, I'M GOING TO TRY SOMETHING STUPID.
WHEN YOU SEE ME MAK MY MOVE, HEA BACK TO THE KITCHEN.
JACK'S HIDING IN TH CUPBOARD. T NOT TO SLI IN THE HOT OIL.

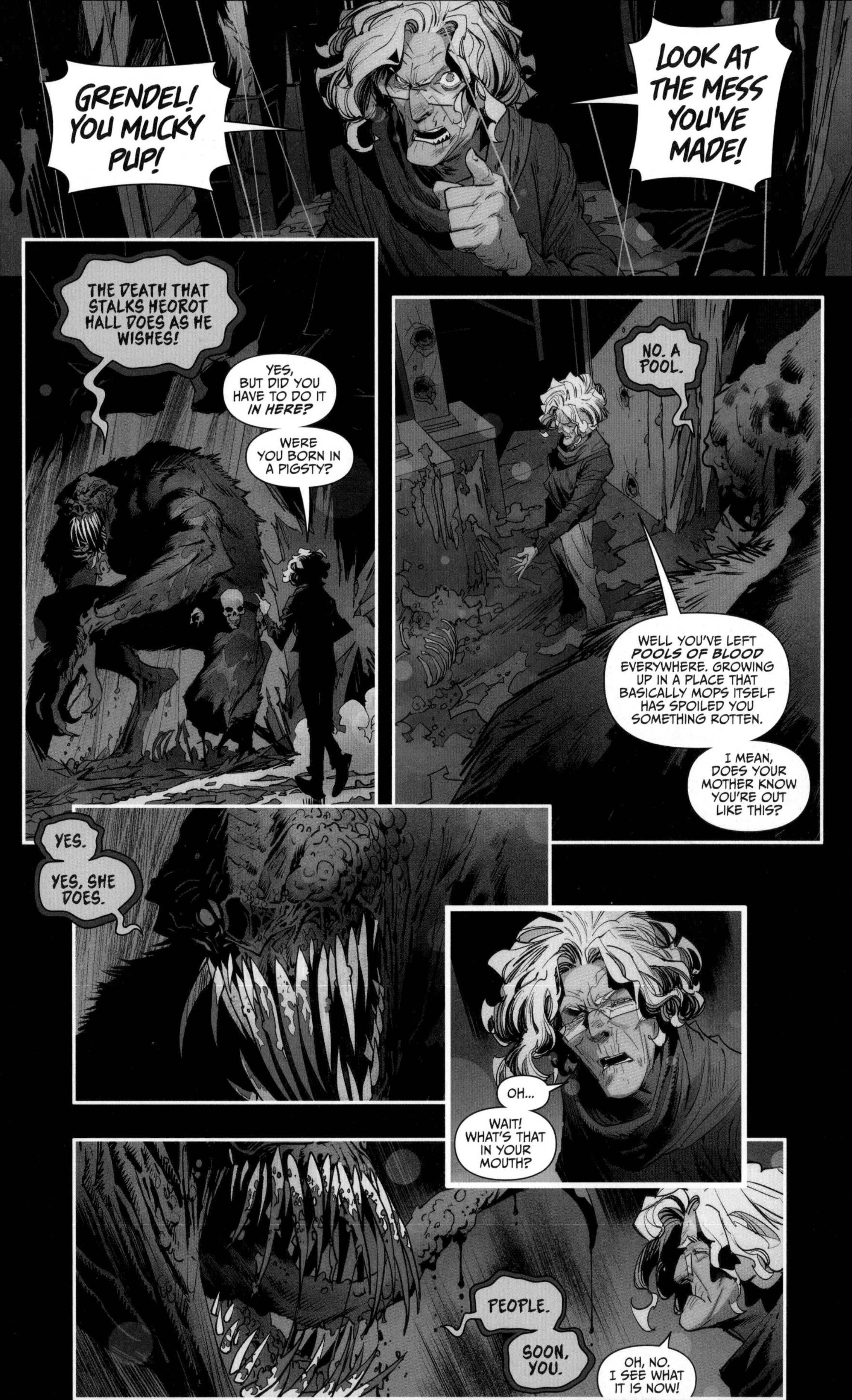
GRENDEL! YOU MUCKY PUP!
LOOK AT THE MESS YOU'VE MADE!
THE DEATH THAT STALKS HEOROT HALL DOES AS HE WISHES!
YES, BUT DID YOU HAVE TO DO IT *IN HERE?*
WERE YOU BORN IN A PIGSTY?
NO. A POOL.
WELL YOU'VE LEFT ***POOLS OF BLOOD*** EVERYWHERE. GROWING UP IN A PLACE THAT BASICALLY MOPS ITSELF HAS SPOILED YOU SOMETHING ROTTEN.
I MEAN, DOES YOUR MOTHER KNOW YOU'RE OUT LIKE THIS?
YES.
YES, SHE DOES.
OH...
WAIT! WHAT'S THAT IN YOUR MOUTH?
PEOPLE.
SOON, YOU.
OH, NO. I SEE WHAT IT IS NOW!

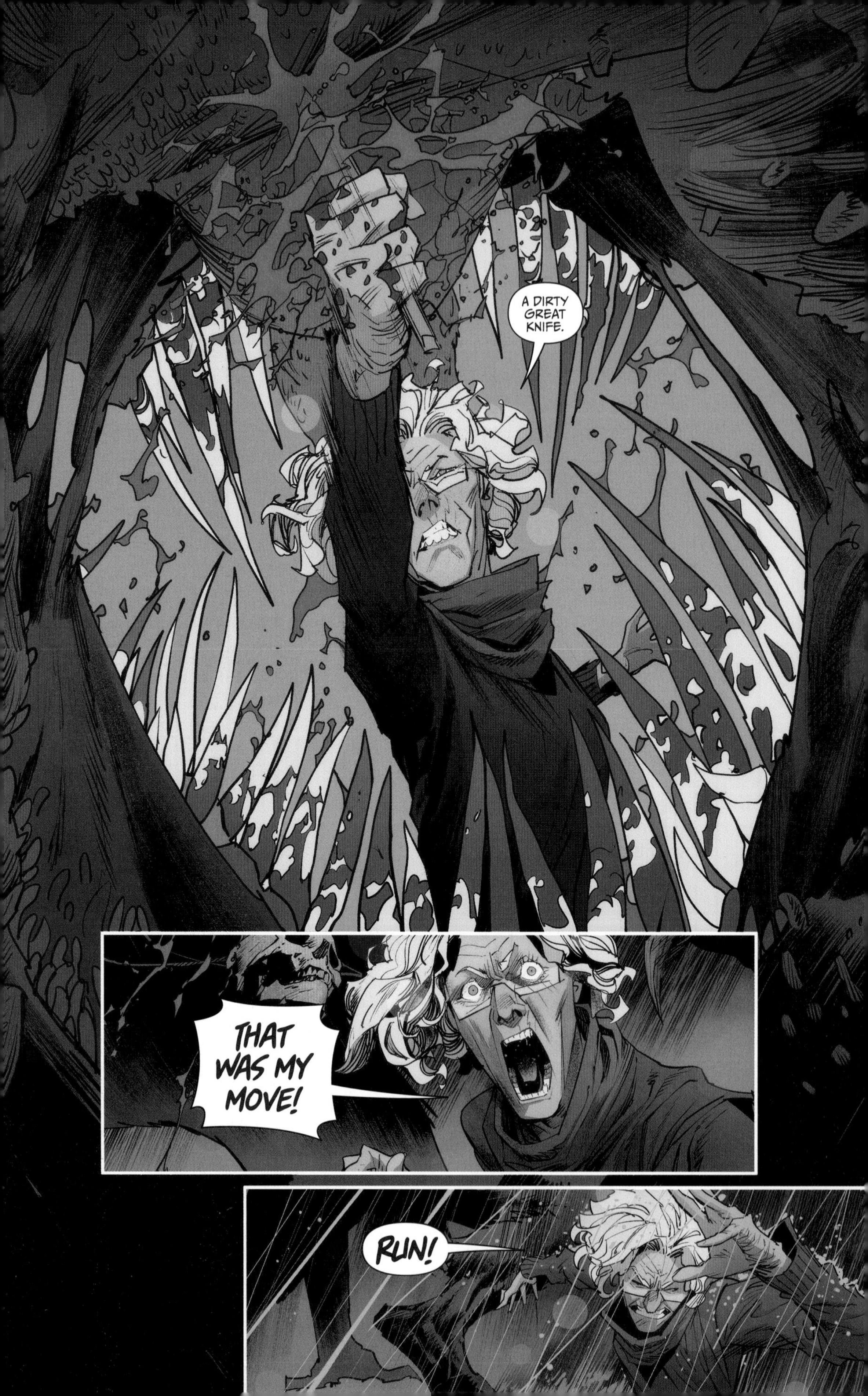
A DIRTY GREAT KNIFE.
THAT WAS MY MOVE!
RUN!

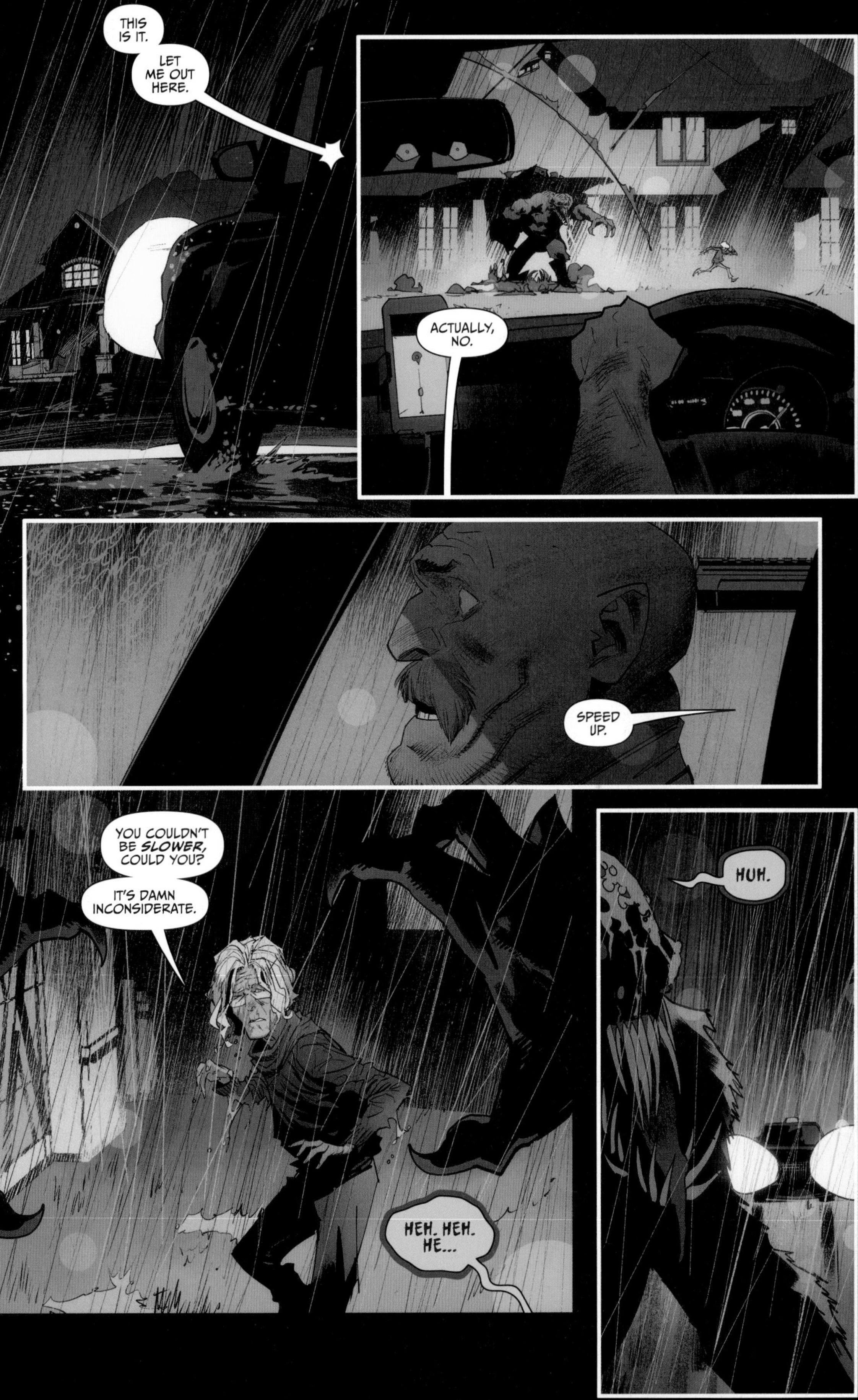
THIS IS IT.
LET ME OUT HERE.
ACTUALLY, NO.
SPEED UP.
YOU COULDN'T BE *SLOWER,* COULD YOU?
IT'S DAMN INCONSIDERATE.
HEH. HEH. HE...
HUH.

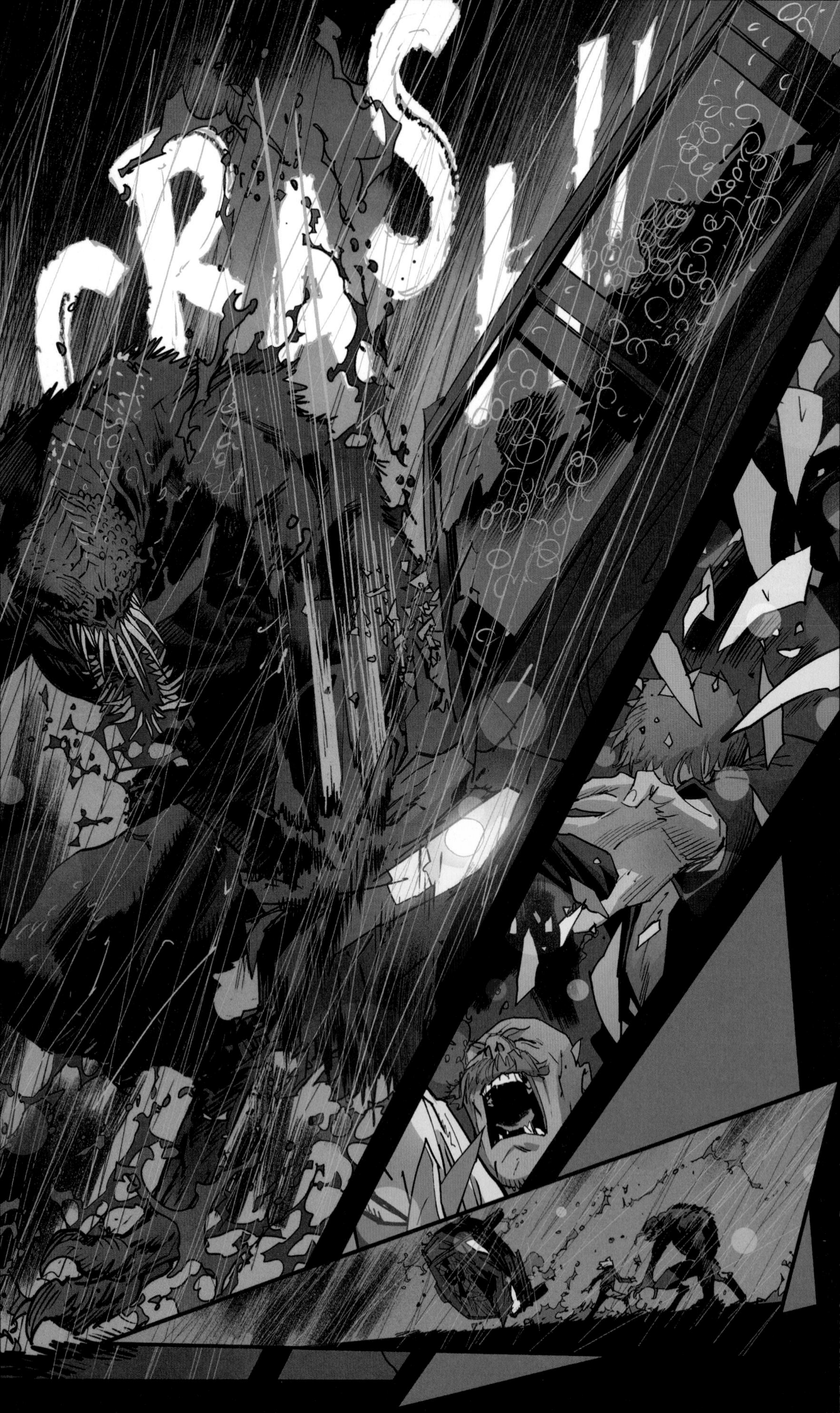
CRASH!!

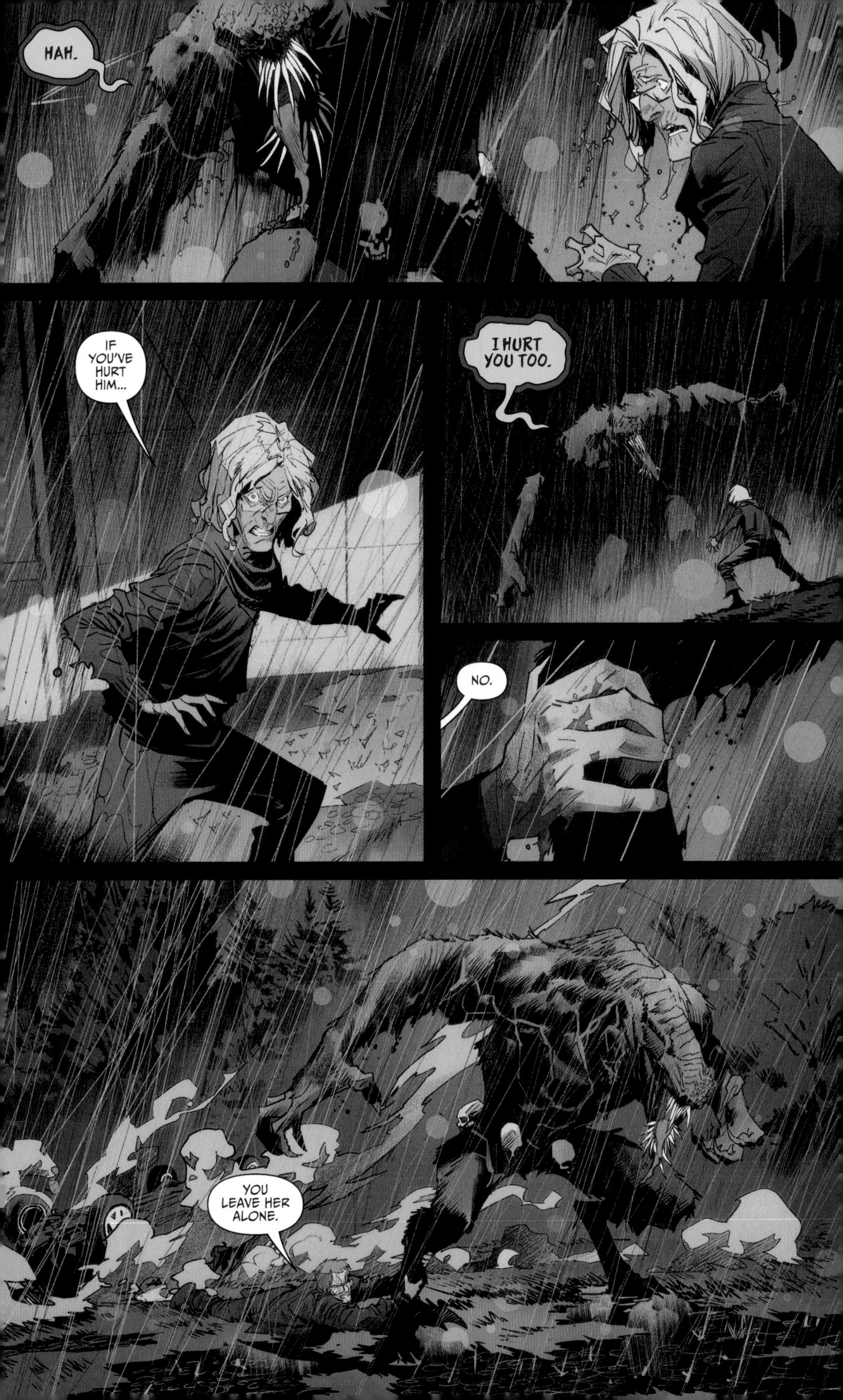
HAH.
IF YOU'VE HURT HIM...
I HURT YOU TOO.
NO.
YOU LEAVE HER ALONE.

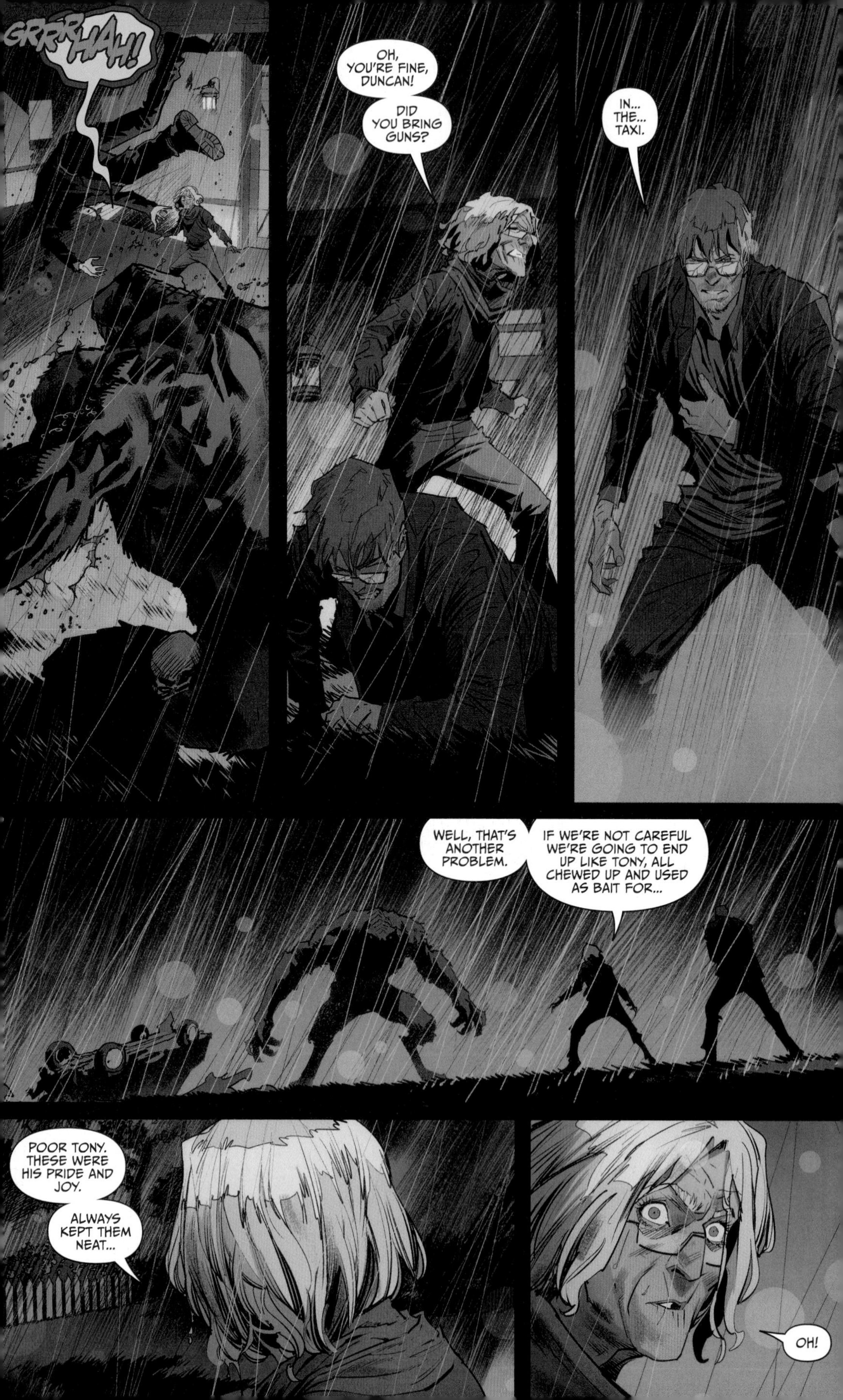
GRRRHAH!!
OH, YOU'RE FINE, DUNCAN!
DID YOU BRING GUNS?
IN... THE... TAXI.
WELL, THAT'S ANOTHER PROBLEM.
IF WE'RE NOT CAREFUL WE'RE GOING TO END UP LIKE TONY, ALL CHEWED UP AND USED AS BAIT FOR...
POOR TONY. THESE WERE HIS PRIDE AND JOY.
ALWAYS KEPT THEM NEAT...
OH!

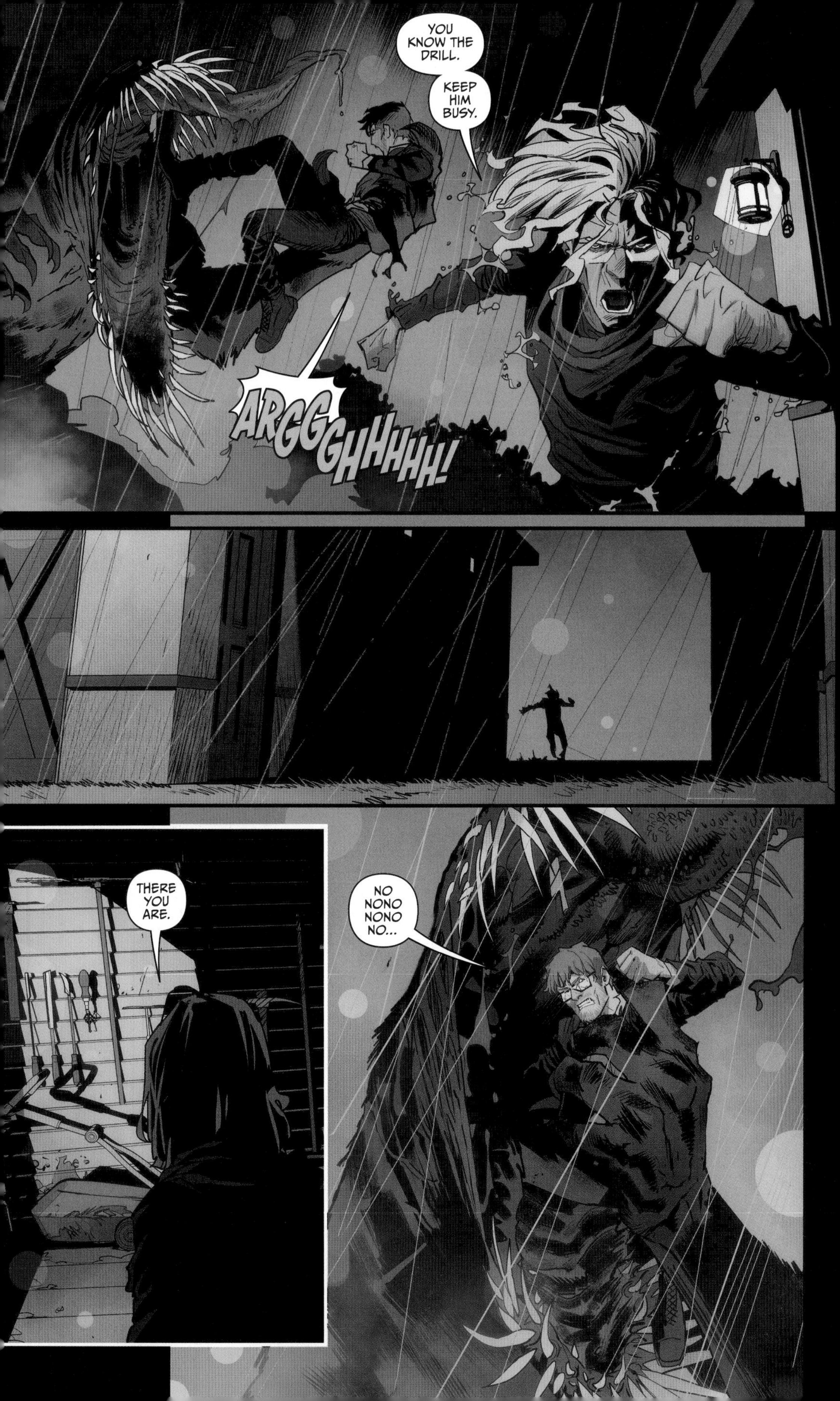
YOU KNOW THE DRILL.
KEEP HIM BUSY.
ARGGGHHHHHH!
THERE YOU ARE.
NO NONO NONO NO...

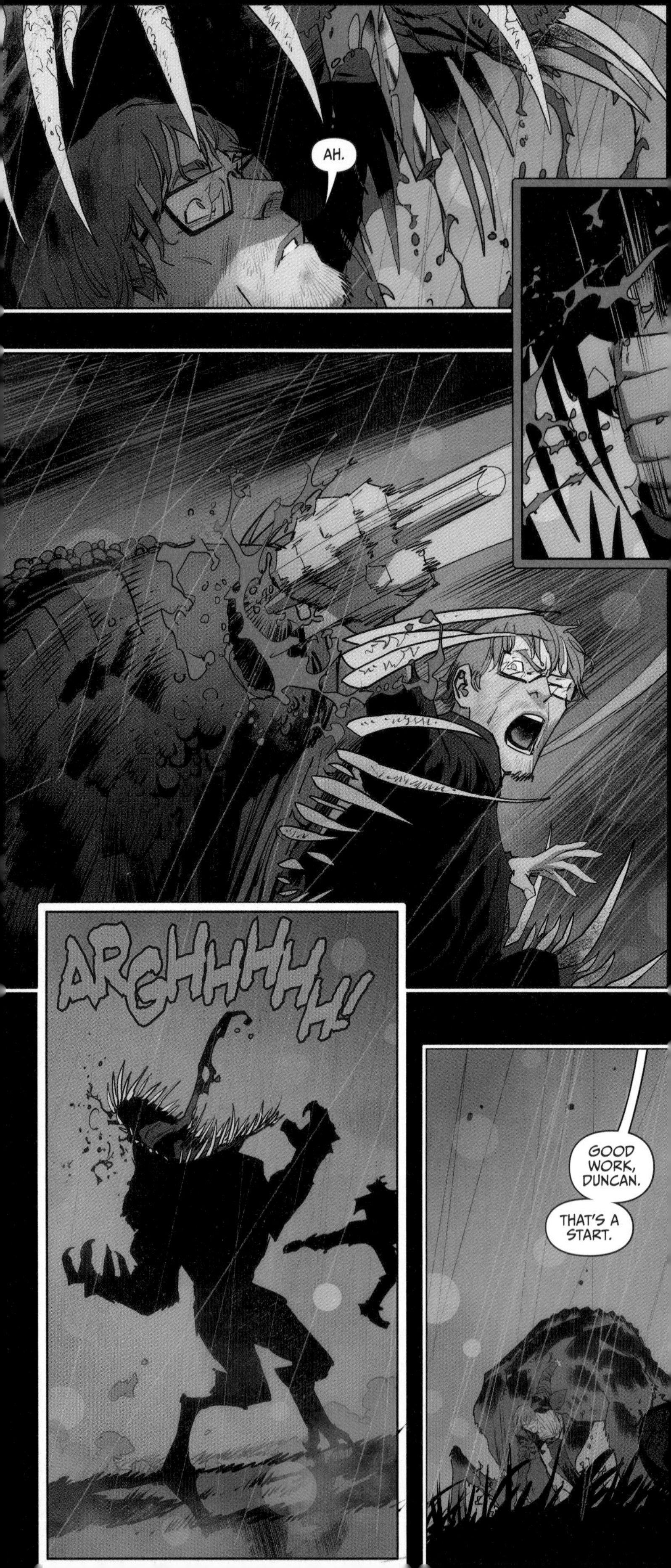
AH.
ARGHHHHH!
GOOD WORK, DUNCAN.
THAT'S A START.

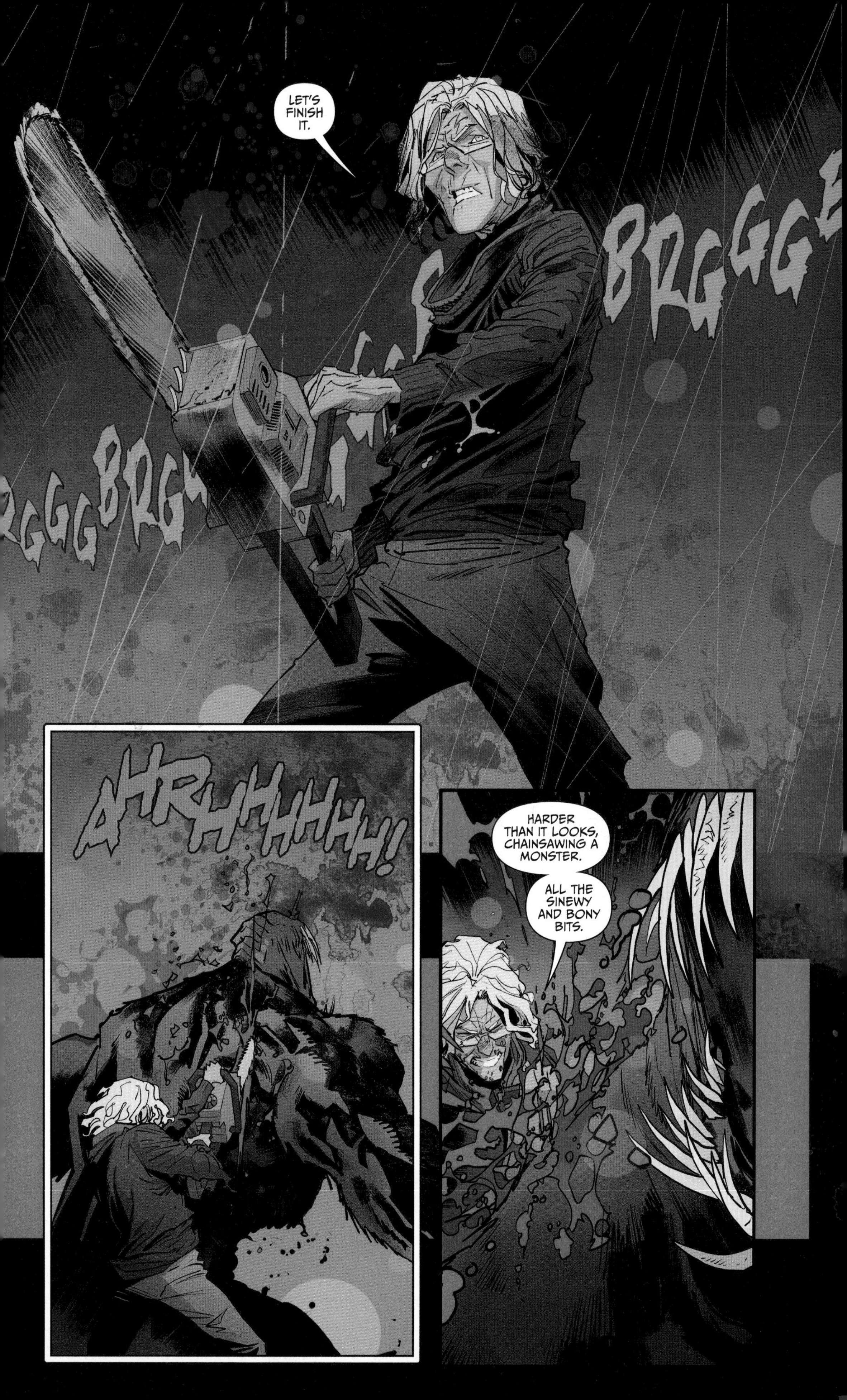
LET'S FINISH IT.
BRGGGE
RGGGBRG
AHRHHHHH!
HARDER THAN IT LOOKS, CHAINSAWING A MONSTER.
ALL THE SINEWY AND BONY BITS.

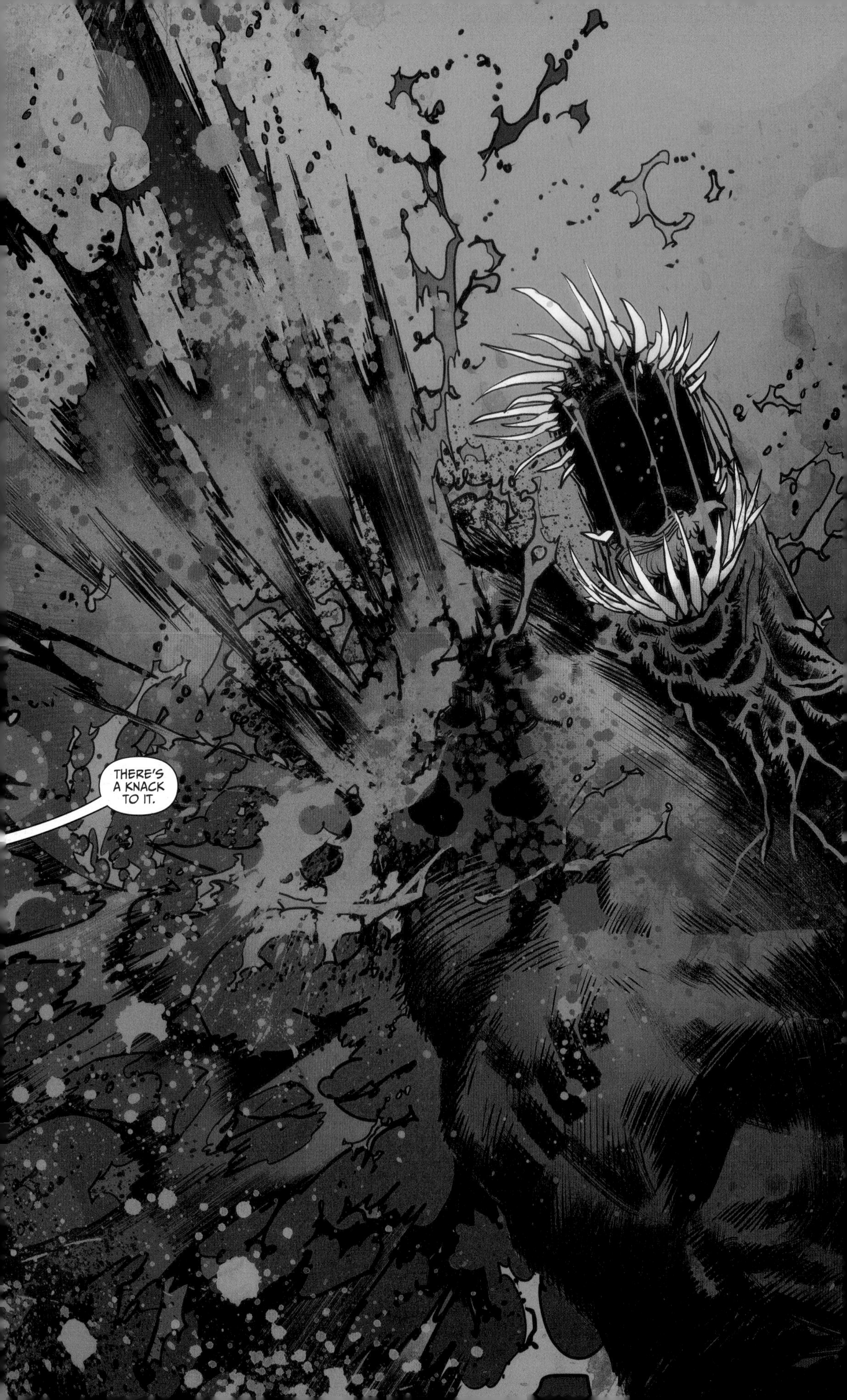
THERE'S A KNACK TO IT.

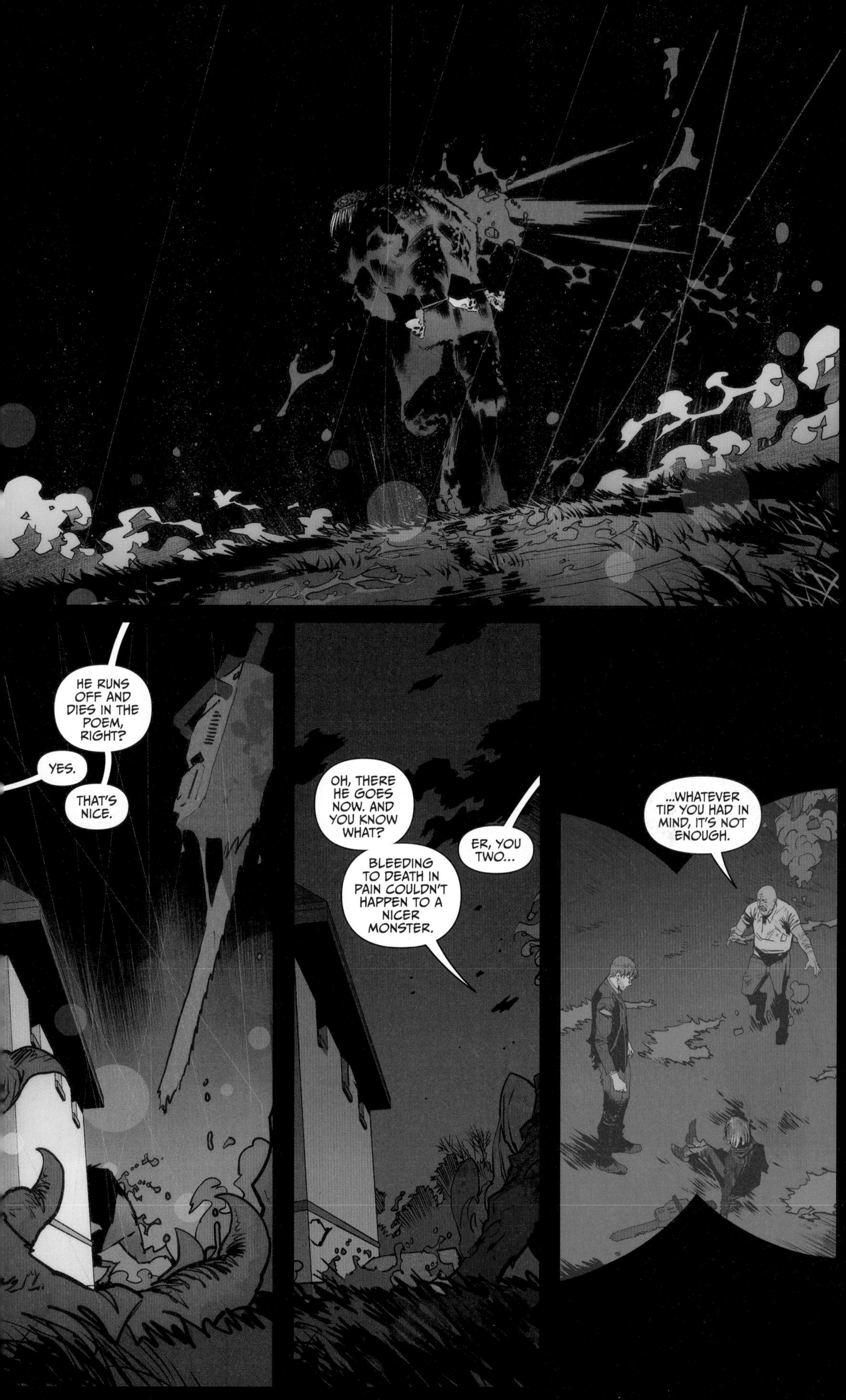
HE RUNS OFF AND DIES IN THE POEM, RIGHT?
YES.
THAT'S NICE.
OH, THERE HE GOES NOW. AND YOU KNOW WHAT?
BLEEDING TO DEATH IN PAIN COULDN'T HAPPEN TO A NICER MONSTER.
ER, YOU TWO...
...WHATEVER TIP YOU HAD IN MIND, IT'S NOT ENOUGH.

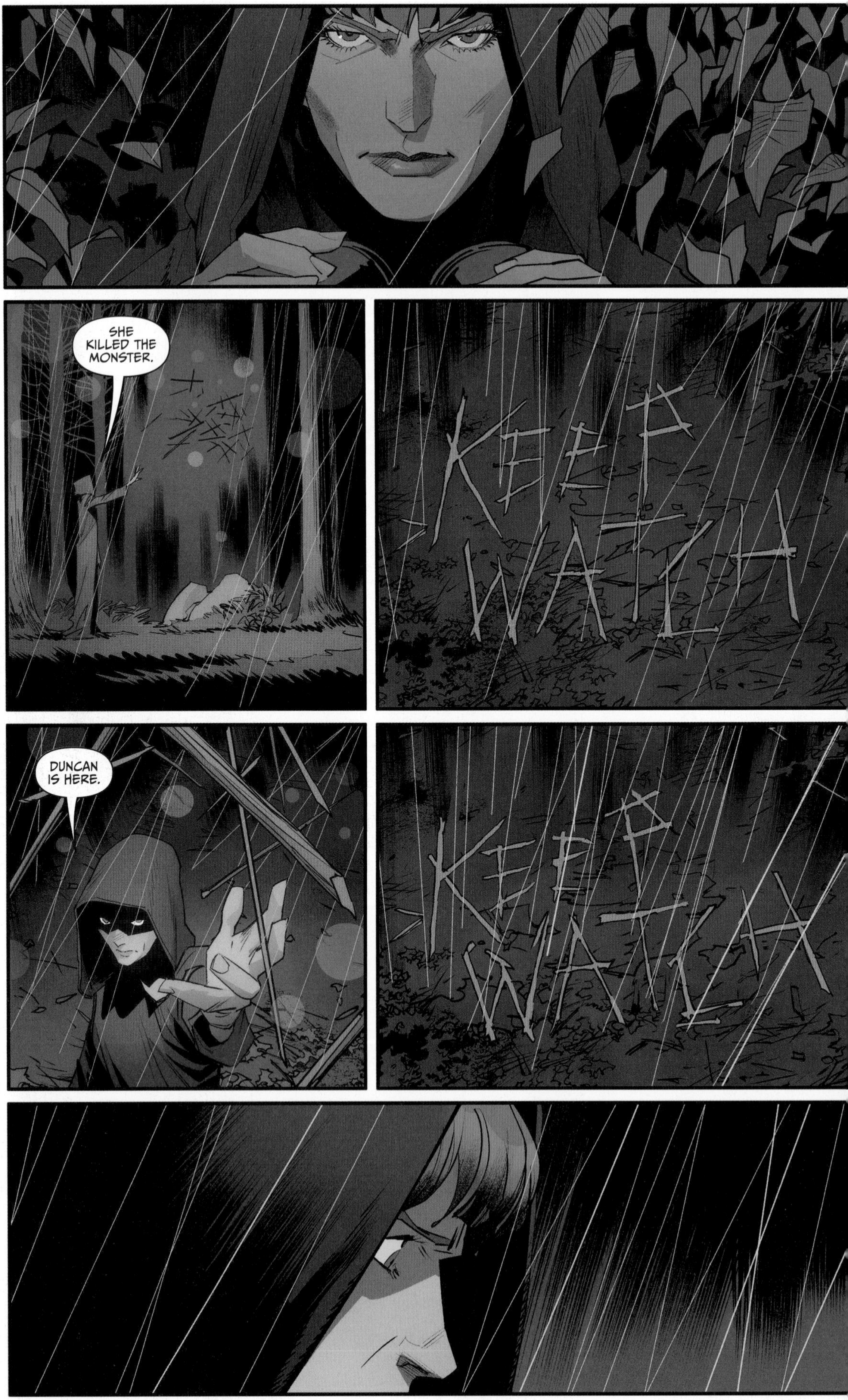
SHE KILLED THE MONSTER.
KEEP WATCH
DUNCAN IS HERE.
KEEP WATCH

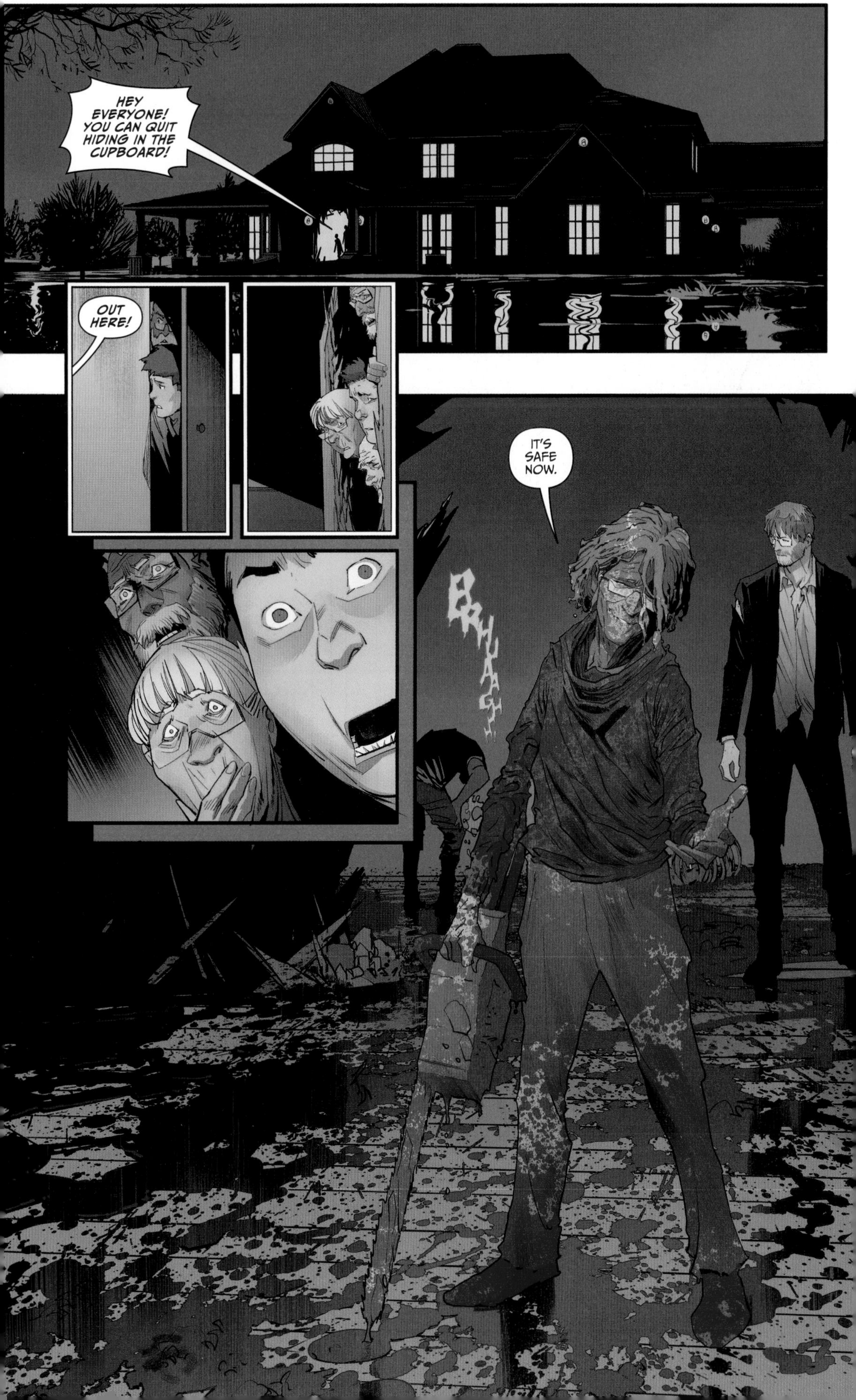
HEY EVERYONE! YOU CAN QUIT HIDING IN THE CUPBOARD!
OUT HERE!
IT'S SAFE NOW.
BRHUAAGH!

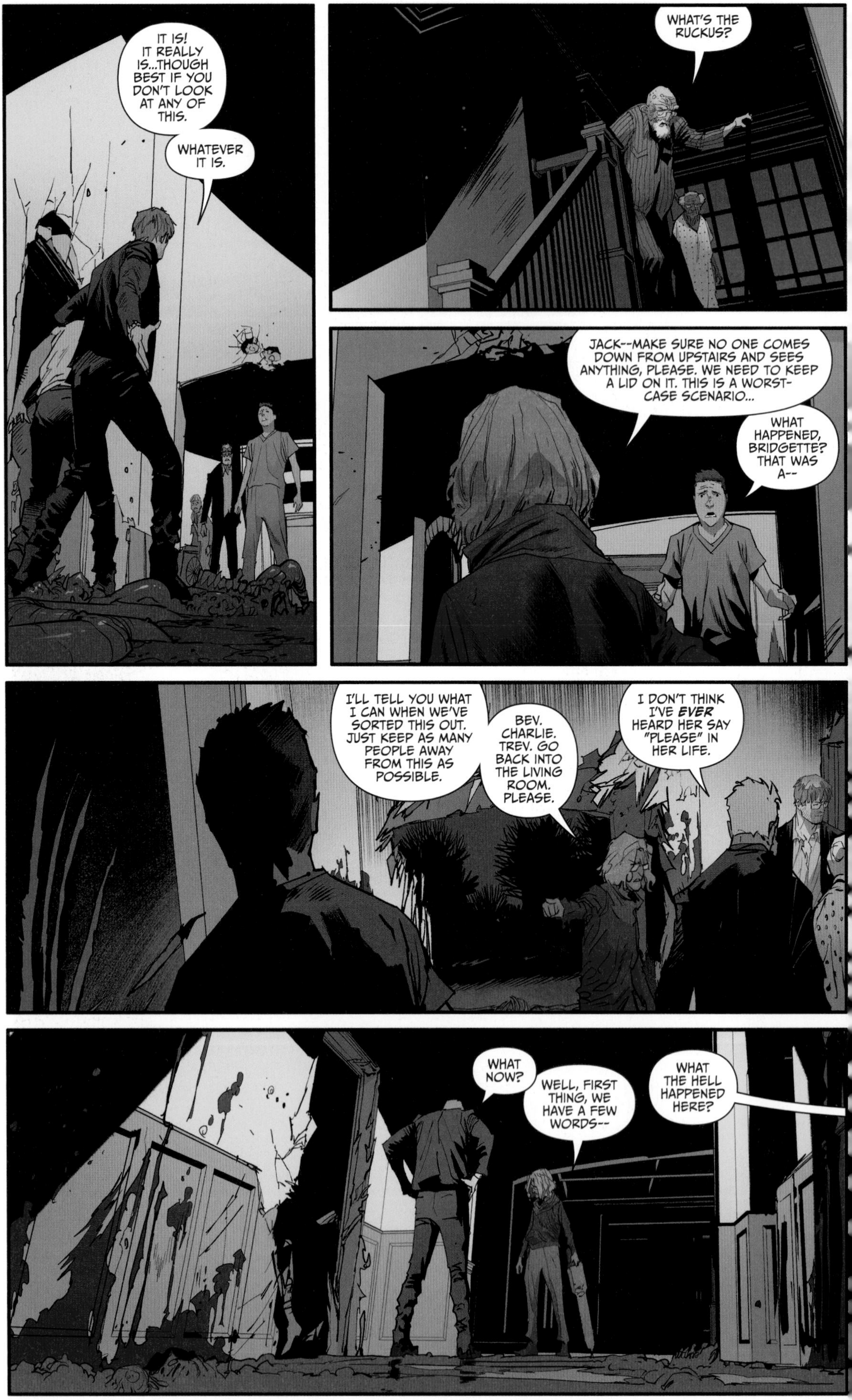

IT IS! IT REALLY IS...THOUGH BEST IF YOU DON'T LOOK AT ANY OF THIS.
WHATEVER IT IS.
WHAT'S THE RUCKUS?
JACK--MAKE SURE NO ONE COMES DOWN FROM UPSTAIRS AND SEES ANYTHING, PLEASE. WE NEED TO KEEP A LID ON IT. THIS IS A WORST-CASE SCENARIO...
WHAT HAPPENED, BRIDGETTE? THAT WAS A--
I'LL TELL YOU WHAT I CAN WHEN WE'VE SORTED THIS OUT. JUST KEEP AS MANY PEOPLE AWAY FROM THIS AS POSSIBLE.
BEV. CHARLIE. TREV. GO BACK INTO THE LIVING ROOM. PLEASE.
I DON'T THINK I'VE *EVER* HEARD HER SAY "PLEASE" IN HER LIFE.
WHAT NOW?
WELL, FIRST THING, WE HAVE A FEW WORDS--
WHAT THE HELL HAPPENED HERE?

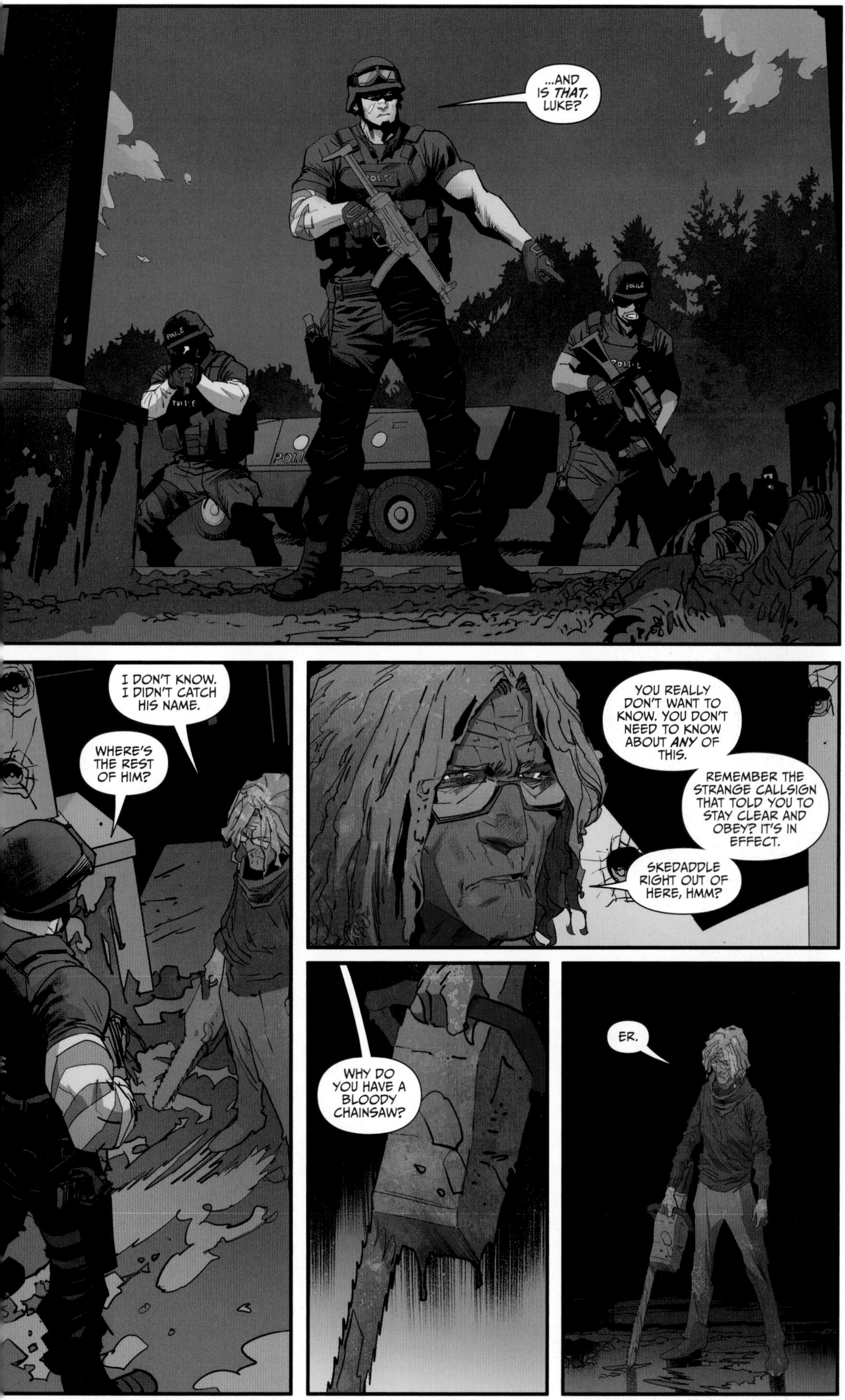
...AND IS THAT, LUKE?
I DON'T KNOW. I DIDN'T CATCH HIS NAME.
WHERE'S THE REST OF HIM?
YOU REALLY DON'T WANT TO KNOW. YOU DON'T NEED TO KNOW ABOUT ANY OF THIS.
REMEMBER THE STRANGE CALLSIGN THAT TOLD YOU TO STAY CLEAR AND OBEY? IT'S IN EFFECT.
SKEDADDLE RIGHT OUT OF HERE, HMM?
WHY DO YOU HAVE A BLOODY CHAINSAW?
ER.

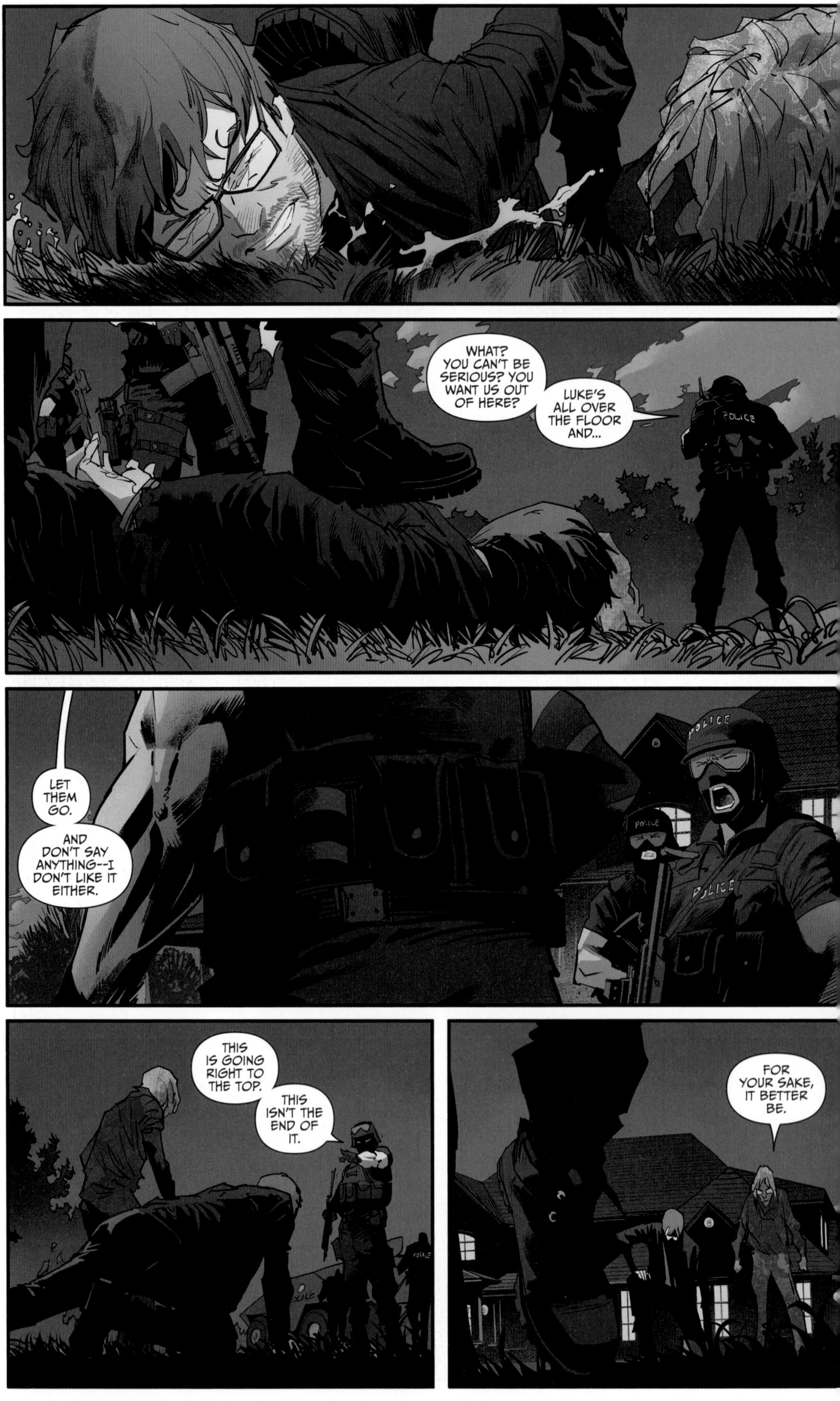

WHAT? YOU CAN'T BE SERIOUS? YOU WANT US OUT OF HERE?
LUKE'S ALL OVER THE FLOOR AND...
LET THEM GO.
AND DON'T SAY ANYTHING--I DON'T LIKE IT EITHER.
THIS IS GOING RIGHT TO THE TOP.
THIS ISN'T THE END OF IT.
FOR YOUR SAKE, IT BETTER BE.

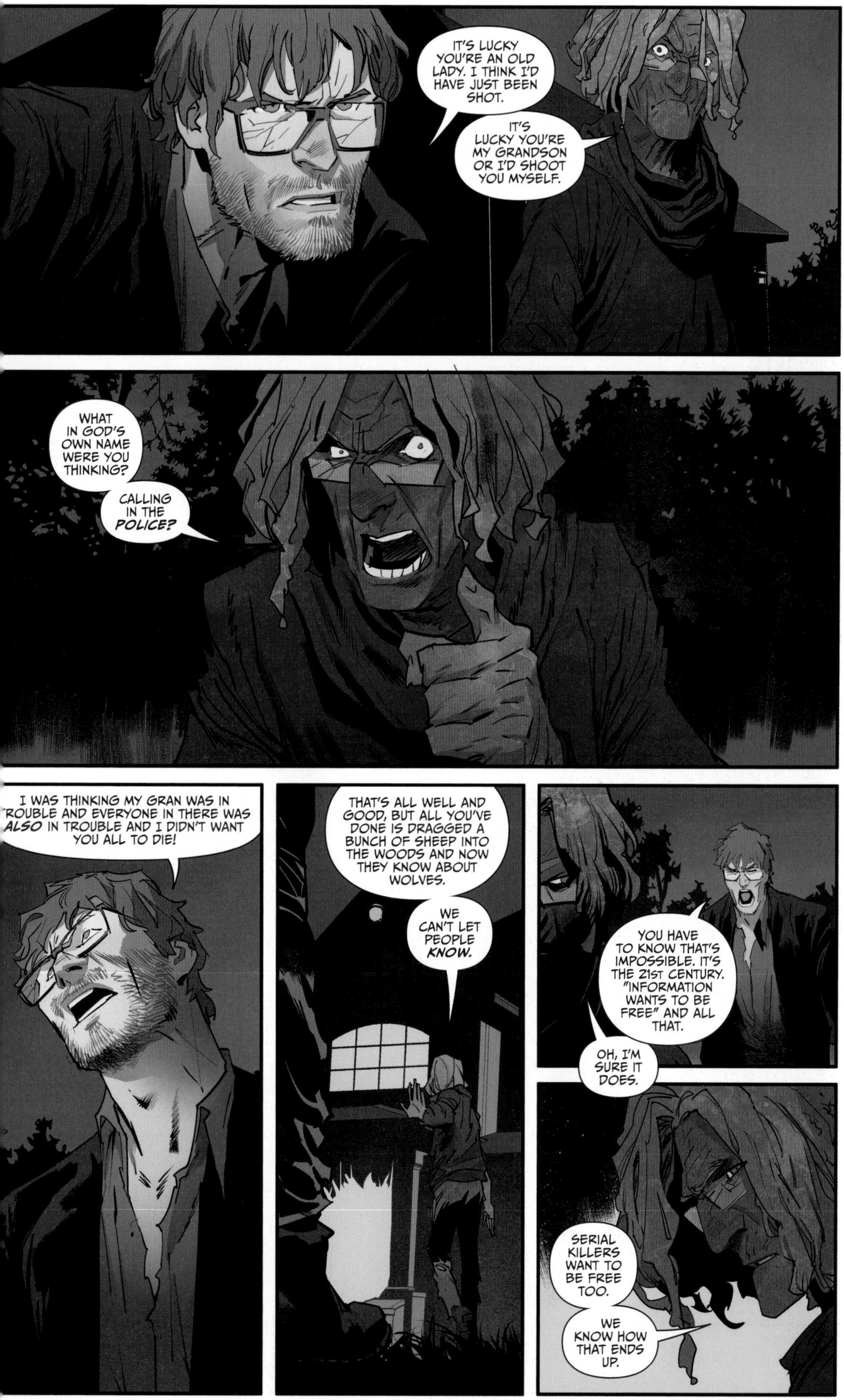
IT'S LUCKY YOU'RE AN OLD LADY. I THINK I'D HAVE JUST BEEN SHOT.
IT'S LUCKY YOU'RE MY GRANDSON OR I'D SHOOT YOU MYSELF.
WHAT IN GOD'S OWN NAME WERE YOU THINKING?
CALLING IN THE *POLICE?*
I WAS THINKING MY GRAN WAS IN TROUBLE AND EVERYONE IN THERE WAS *ALSO* IN TROUBLE AND I DIDN'T WANT YOU ALL TO DIE!
THAT'S ALL WELL AND GOOD, BUT ALL YOU'VE DONE IS DRAGGED A BUNCH OF SHEEP INTO THE WOODS AND NOW THEY KNOW ABOUT WOLVES.
WE CAN'T LET PEOPLE *KNOW.*
YOU HAVE TO KNOW THAT'S IMPOSSIBLE. IT'S THE 21ST CENTURY. "INFORMATION WANTS TO BE FREE" AND ALL THAT.
OH, I'M SURE IT DOES.
SERIAL KILLERS WANT TO BE FREE TOO.
WE KNOW HOW THAT ENDS UP.

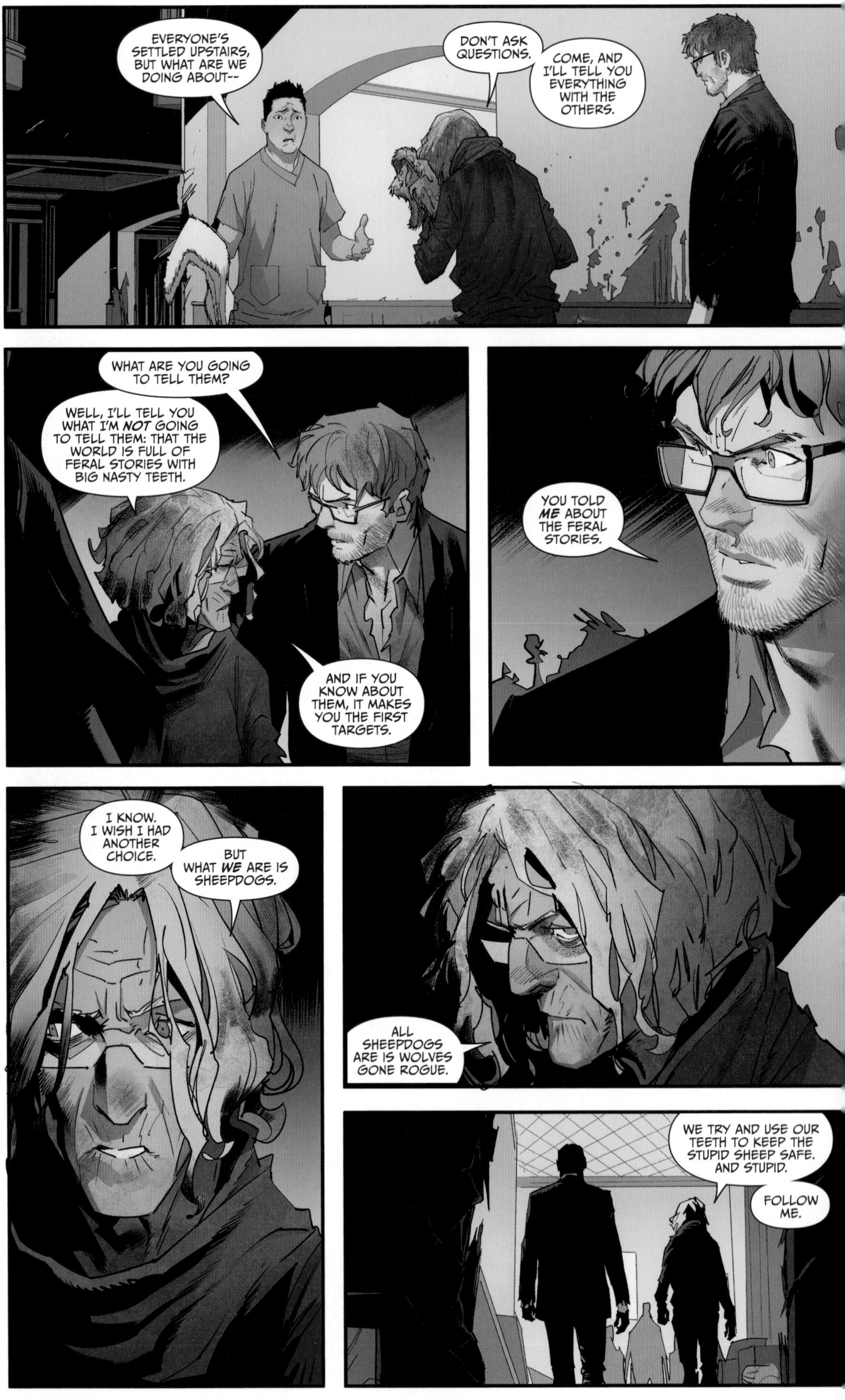
EVERYONE'S SETTLED UPSTAIRS, BUT WHAT ARE WE DOING ABOUT--
DON'T ASK QUESTIONS.
COME, AND I'LL TELL YOU EVERYTHING WITH THE OTHERS.
WHAT ARE YOU GOING TO TELL THEM?
WELL, I'LL TELL YOU WHAT I'M NOT GOING TO TELL THEM: THAT THE WORLD IS FULL OF FERAL STORIES WITH BIG NASTY TEETH.
AND IF YOU KNOW ABOUT THEM, IT MAKES YOU THE FIRST TARGETS.
YOU TOLD ME ABOUT THE FERAL STORIES.
I KNOW. I WISH I HAD ANOTHER CHOICE.
BUT WHAT WE ARE IS SHEEPDOGS.
ALL SHEEPDOGS ARE IS WOLVES GONE ROGUE.
WE TRY AND USE OUR TEETH TO KEEP THE STUPID SHEEP SAFE. AND STUPID.
FOLLOW ME.

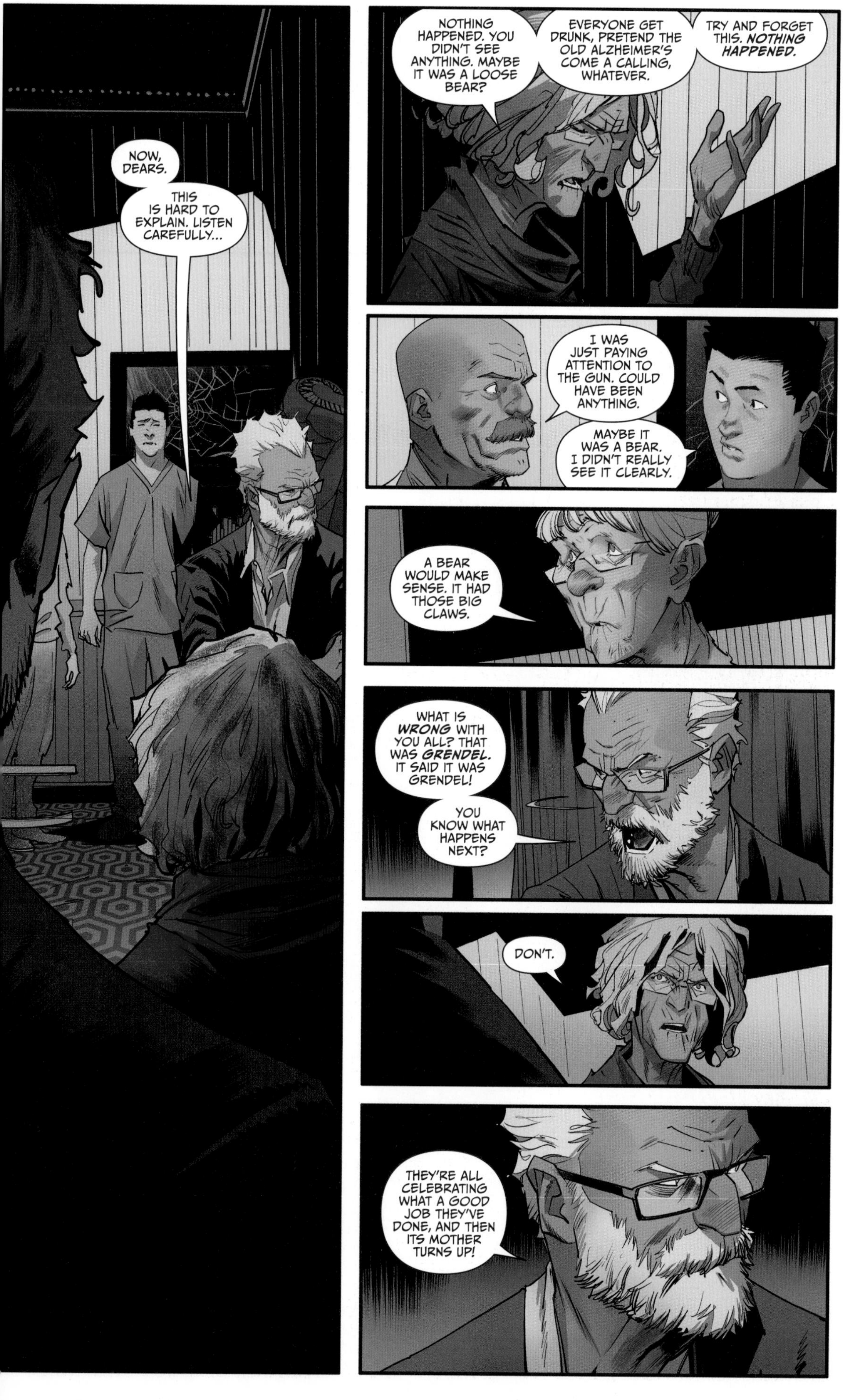
NOW, DEARS.
THIS IS HARD TO EXPLAIN. LISTEN CAREFULLY...
NOTHING HAPPENED. YOU DIDN'T SEE ANYTHING. MAYBE IT WAS A LOOSE BEAR?
EVERYONE GET DRUNK, PRETEND THE OLD ALZHEIMER'S COME A CALLING, WHATEVER.
TRY AND FORGET THIS. NOTHING HAPPENED.
I WAS JUST PAYING ATTENTION TO THE GUN. COULD HAVE BEEN ANYTHING.
MAYBE IT WAS A BEAR. I DIDN'T REALLY SEE IT CLEARLY.
A BEAR WOULD MAKE SENSE. IT HAD THOSE BIG CLAWS.
WHAT IS WRONG WITH YOU ALL? THAT WAS GRENDEL. IT SAID IT WAS GRENDEL!
YOU KNOW WHAT HAPPENS NEXT?
DON'T.
THEY'RE ALL CELEBRATING WHAT A GOOD JOB THEY'VE DONE, AND THEN ITS MOTHER TURNS UP!

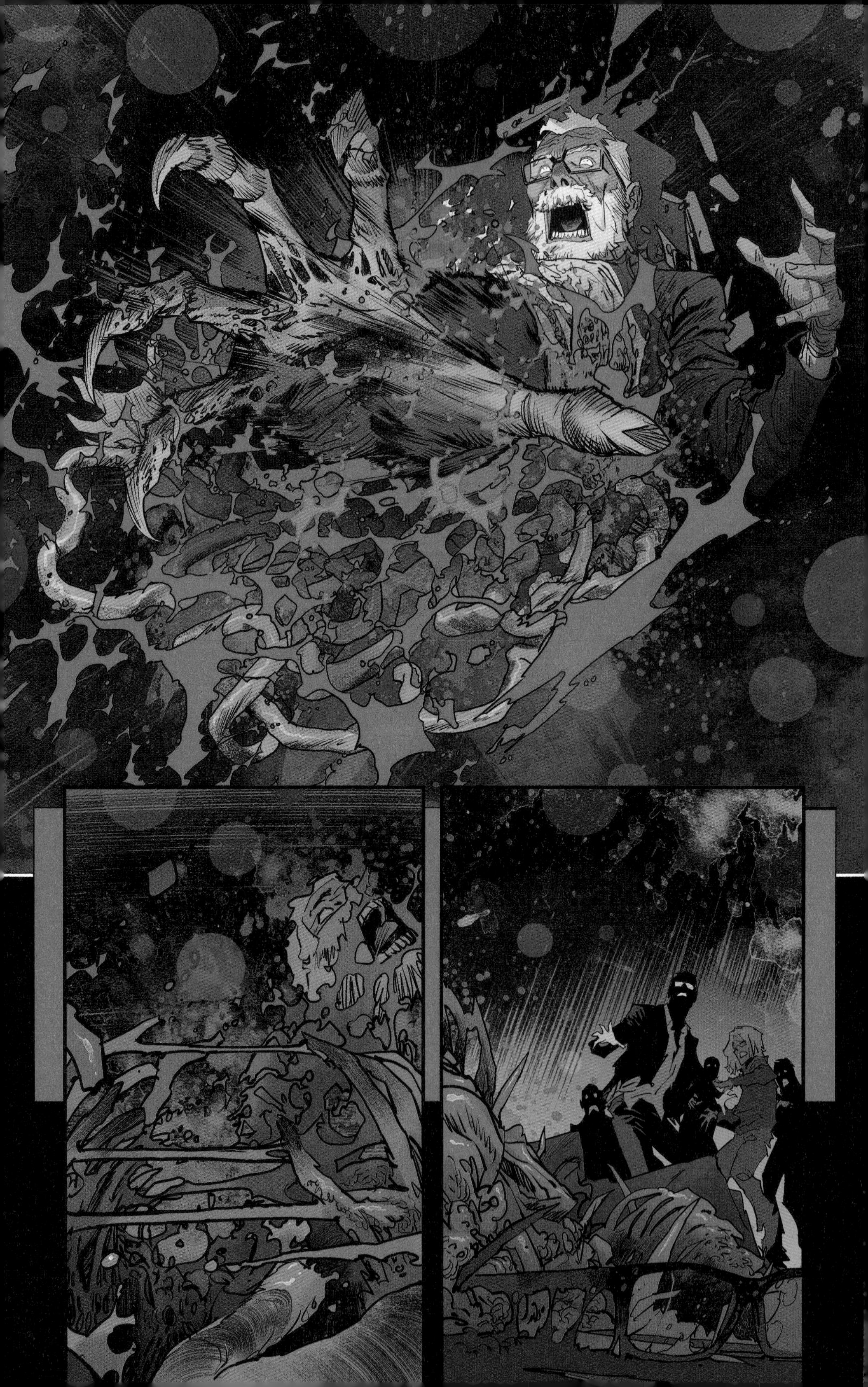

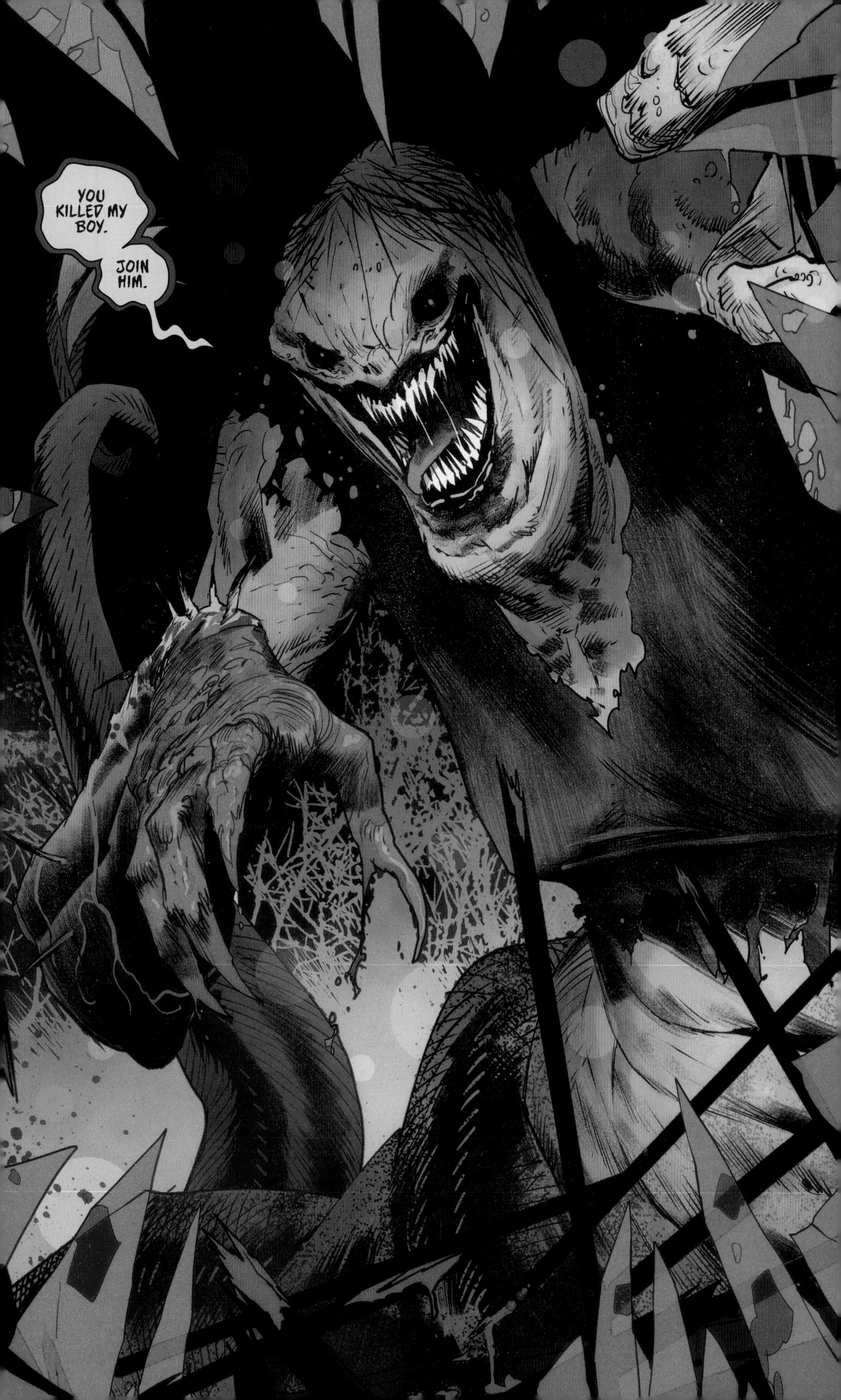
YOU KILLED MY BOY.
JOIN HIM.

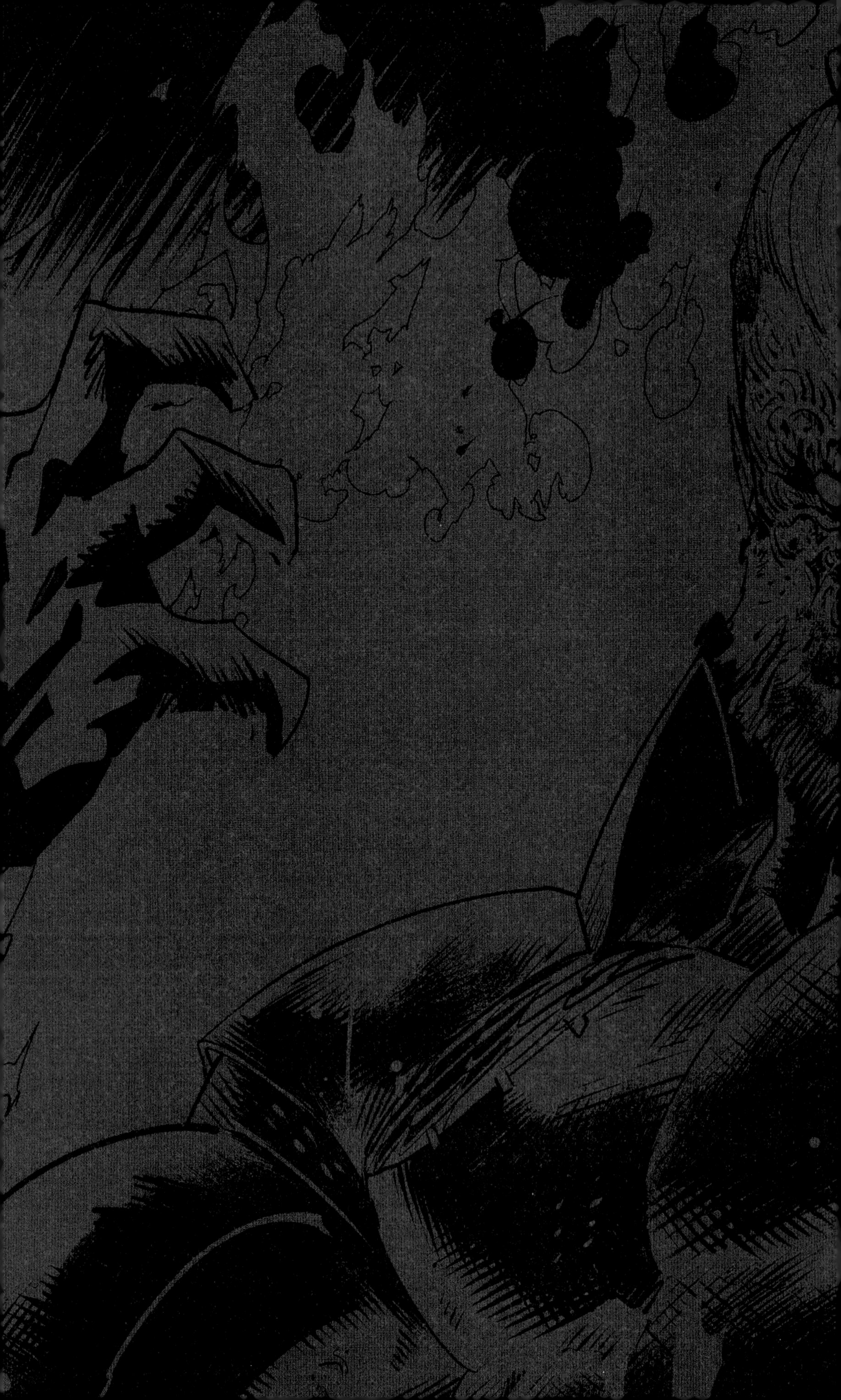

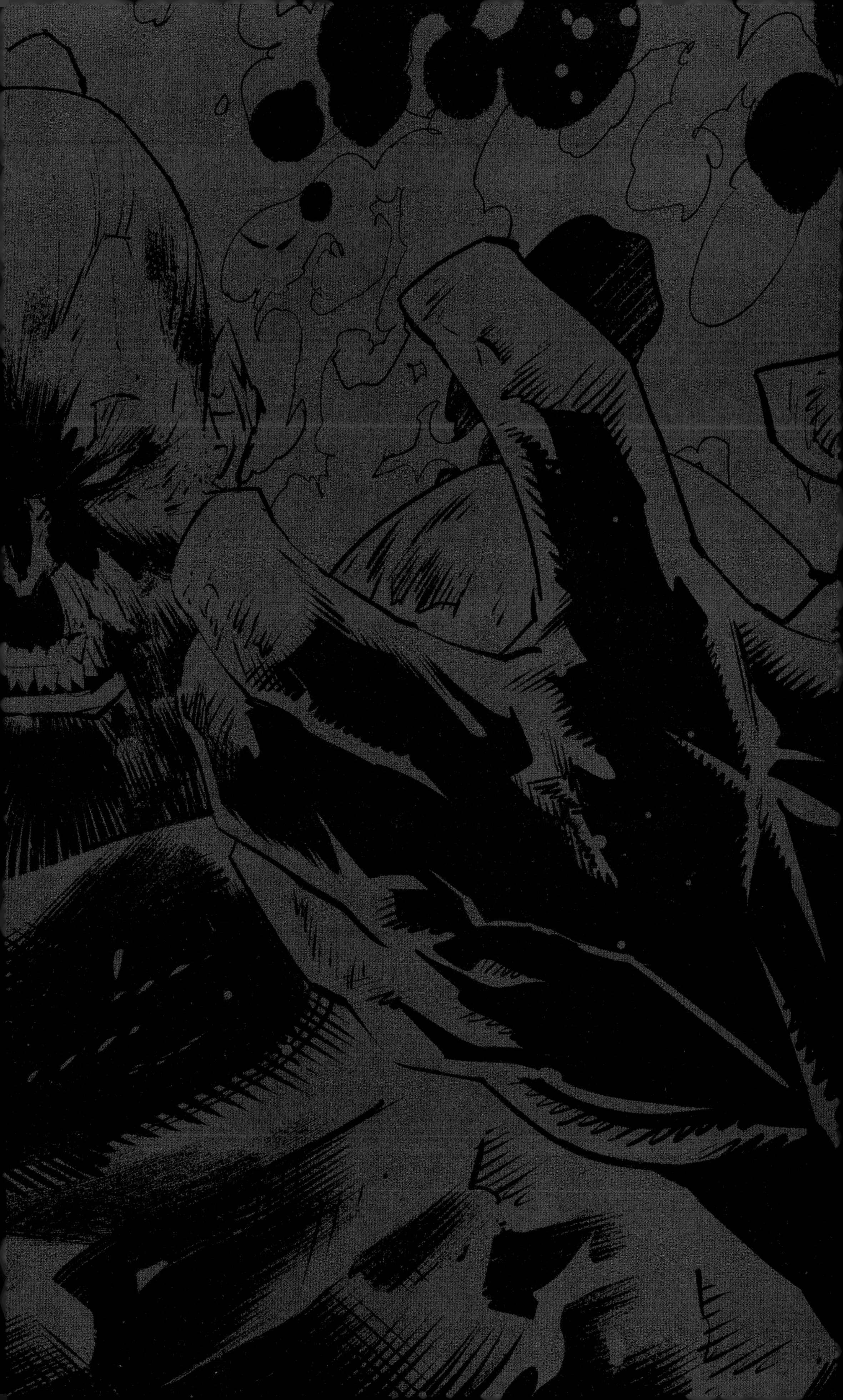

CHAPTER TWELVE

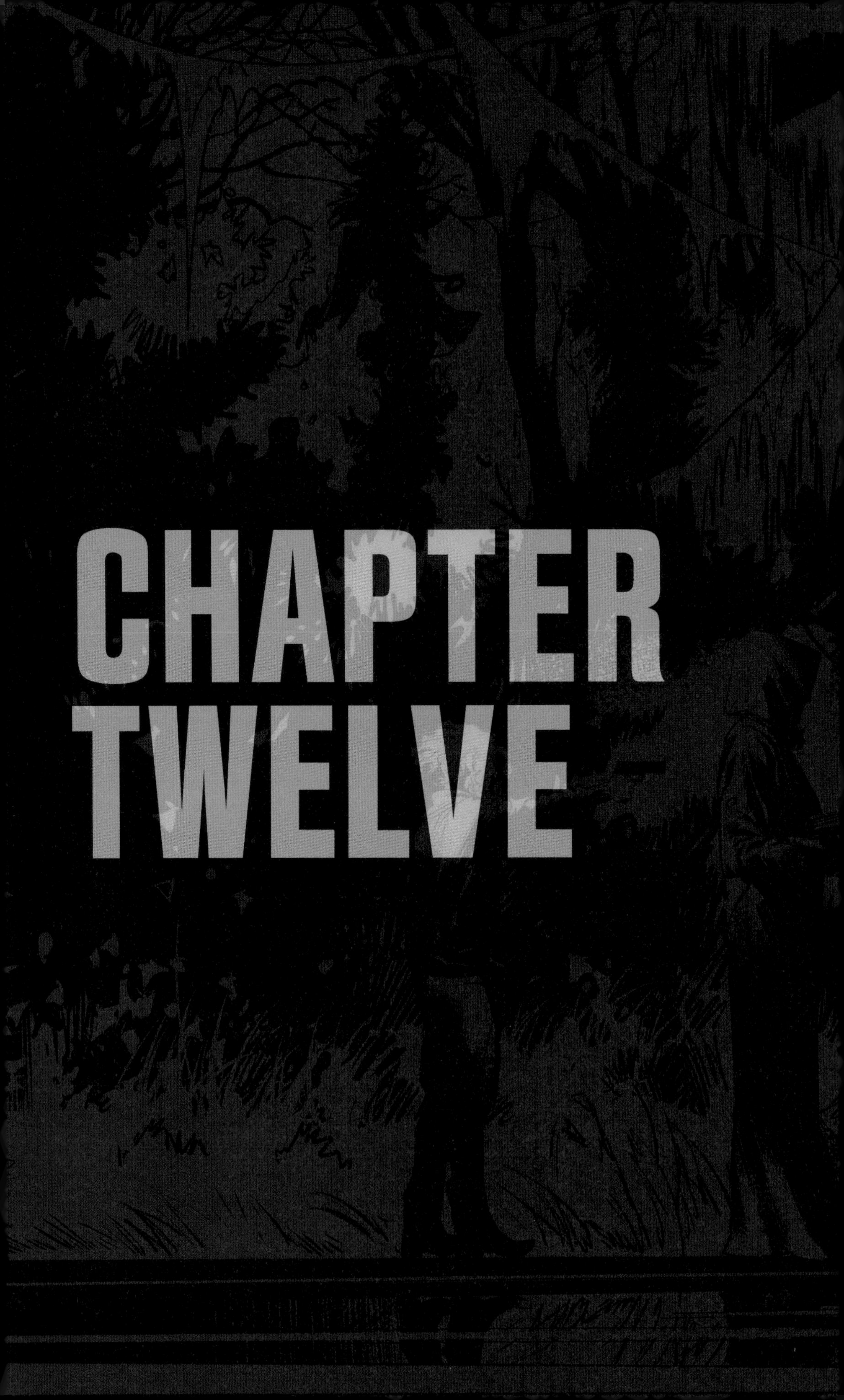

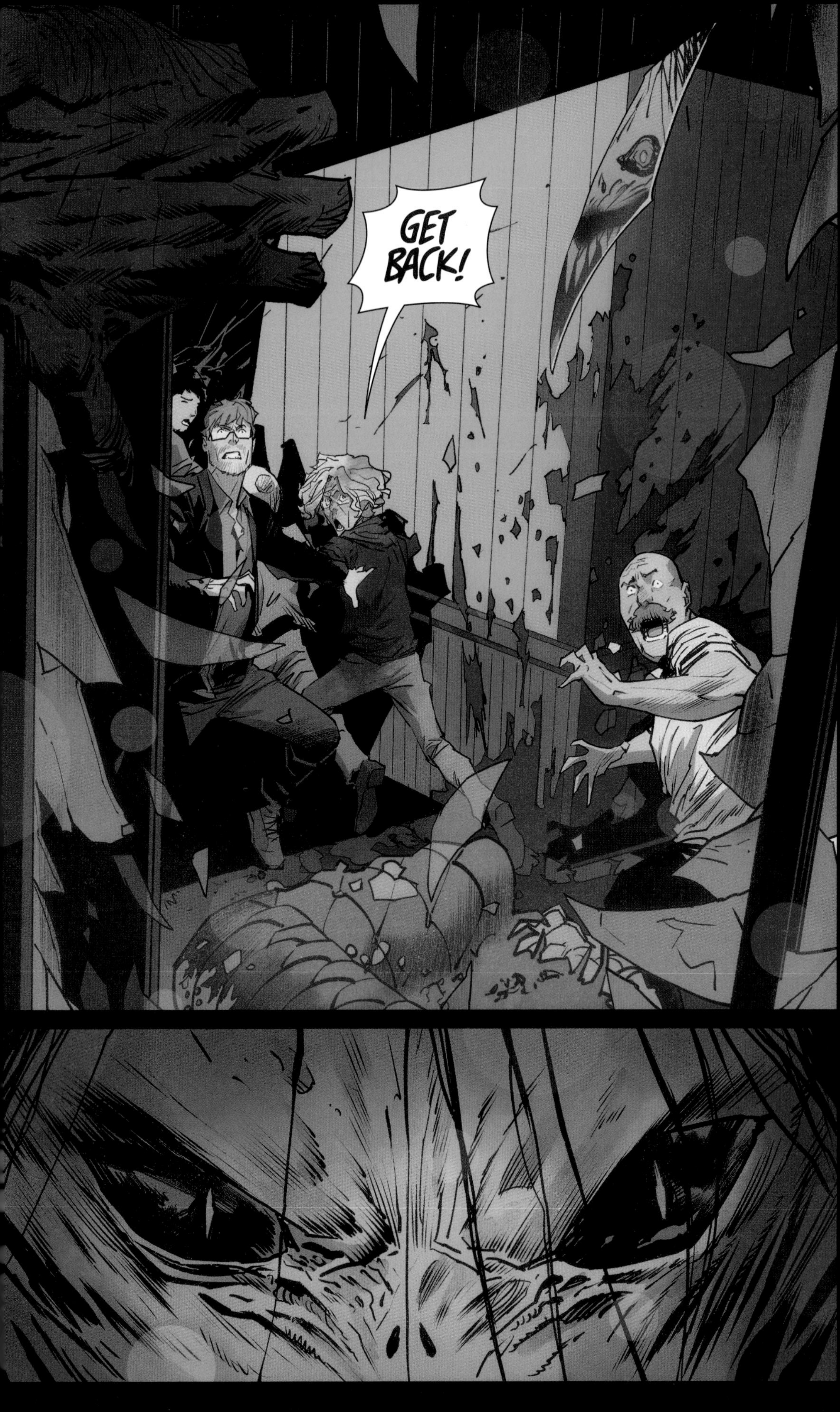
GET BACK!

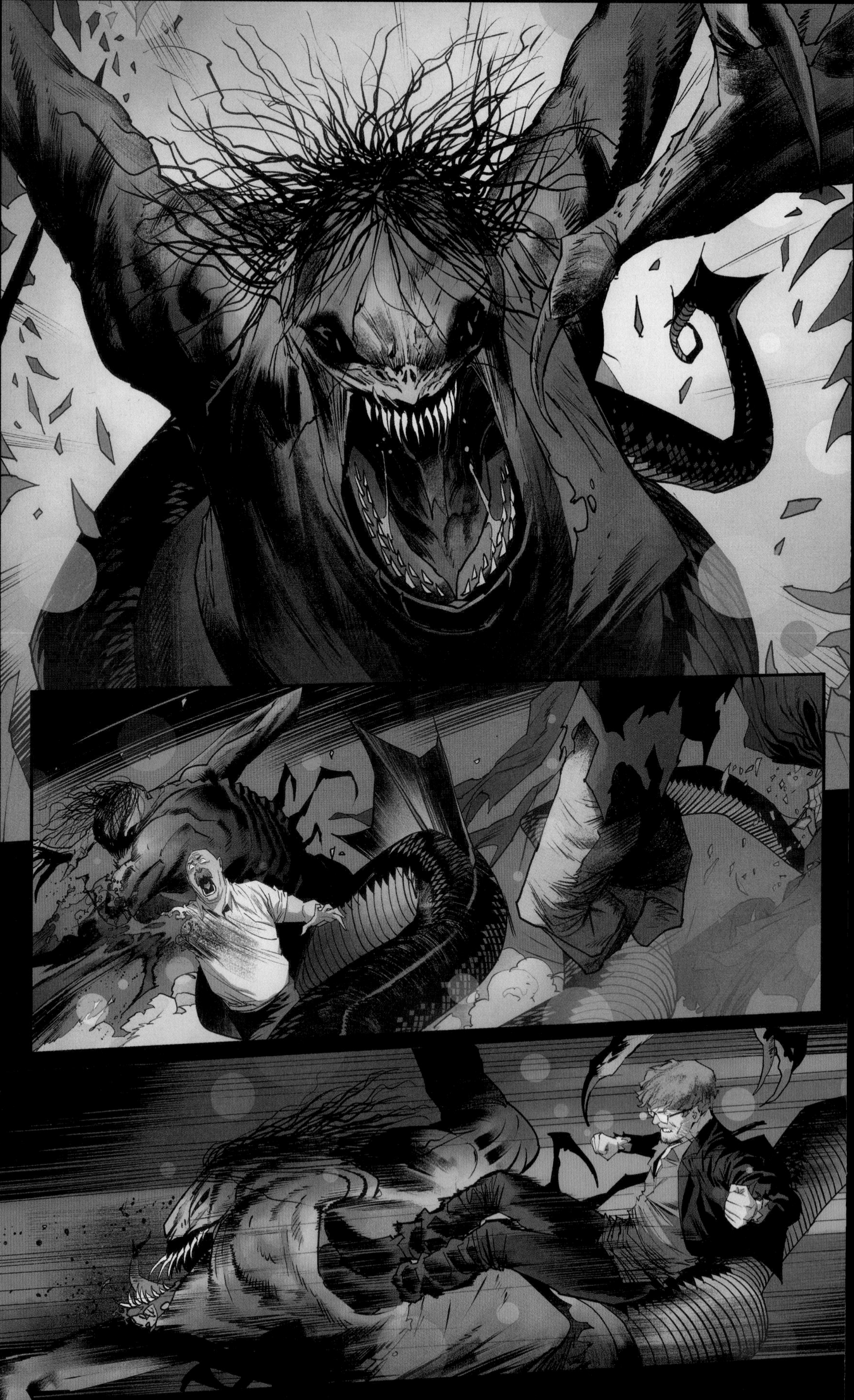

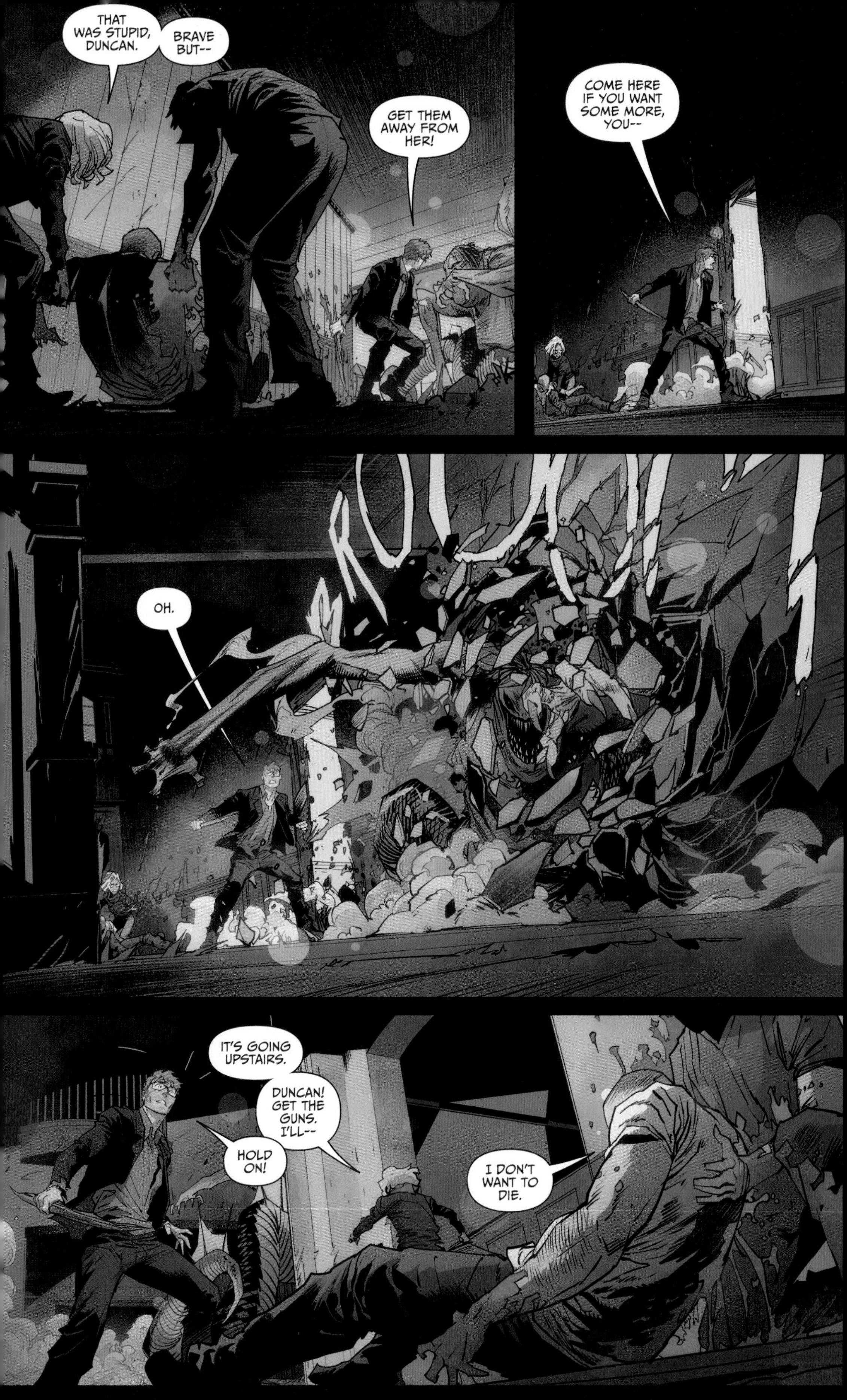
THAT WAS STUPID, DUNCAN.
BRAVE BUT--
GET THEM AWAY FROM HER!
COME HERE IF YOU WANT SOME MORE, YOU--
OH.
IT'S GOING UPSTAIRS.
DUNCAN! GET THE GUNS. I'LL--
HOLD ON!
I DON'T WANT TO DIE.

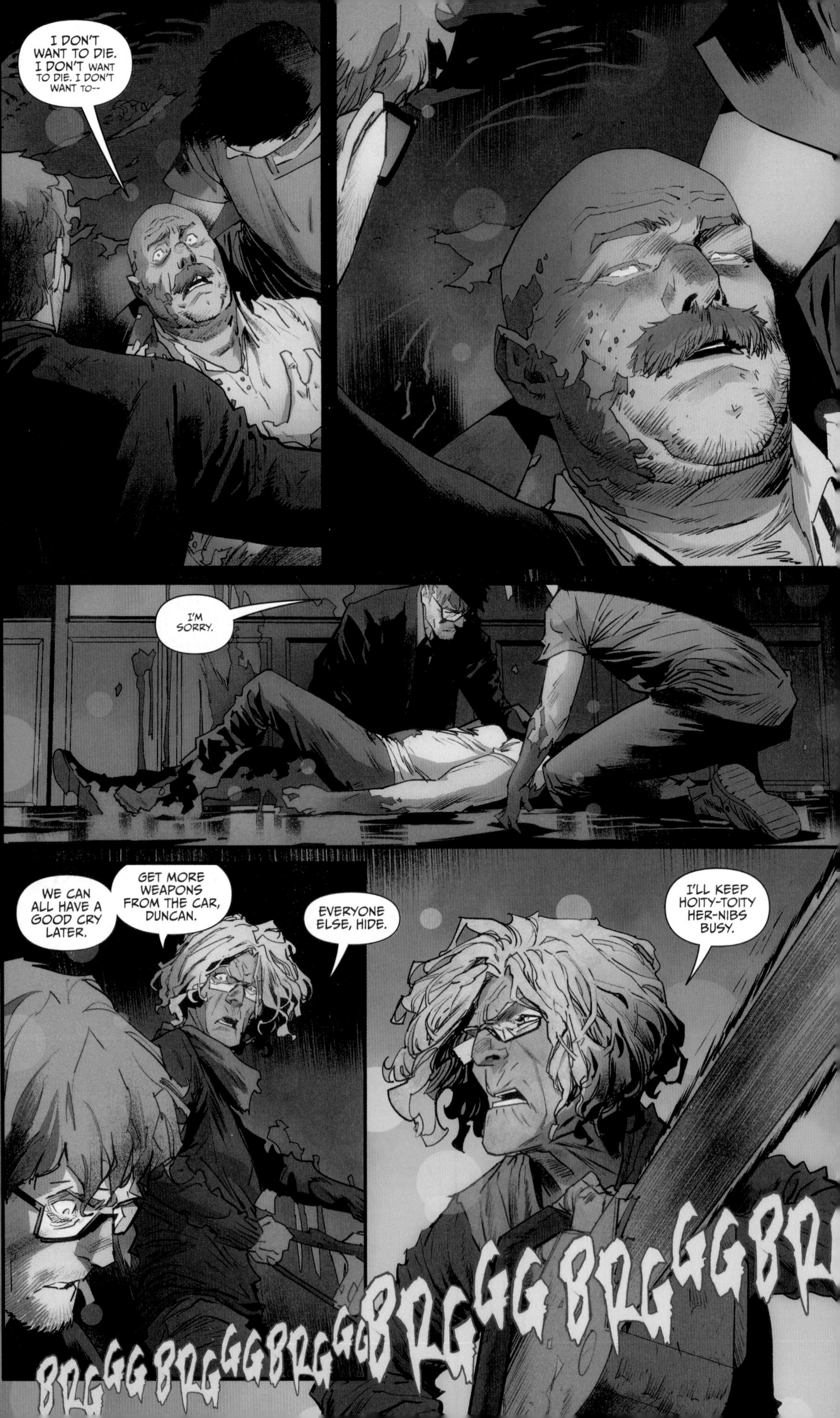
I DON'T WANT TO DIE. I DON'T WANT TO DIE. I DON'T WANT TO--
I'M SORRY.
WE CAN ALL HAVE A GOOD CRY LATER.
GET MORE WEAPONS FROM THE CAR, DUNCAN.
EVERYONE ELSE, HIDE.
I'LL KEEP HOITY-TOITY HER-NIBS BUSY.
BRGGG BRGGG BRGGG BRGGG BRGGG BRGGBR

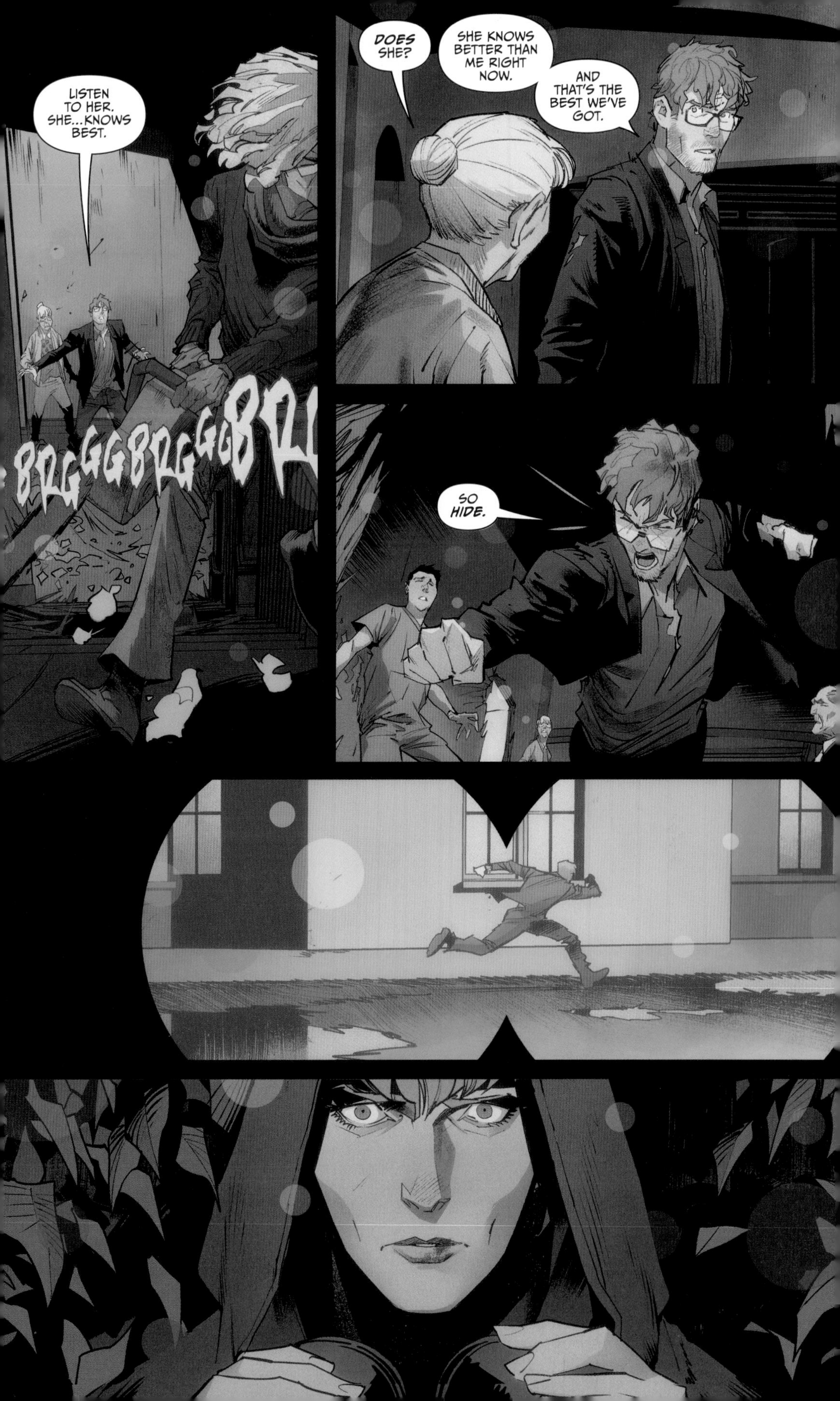

LISTEN TO HER. SHE...KNOWS BEST.
BRGGGBRGGGBR
DOES SHE?
SHE KNOWS BETTER THAN ME RIGHT NOW.
AND THAT'S THE BEST WE'VE GOT.
SO HIDE.

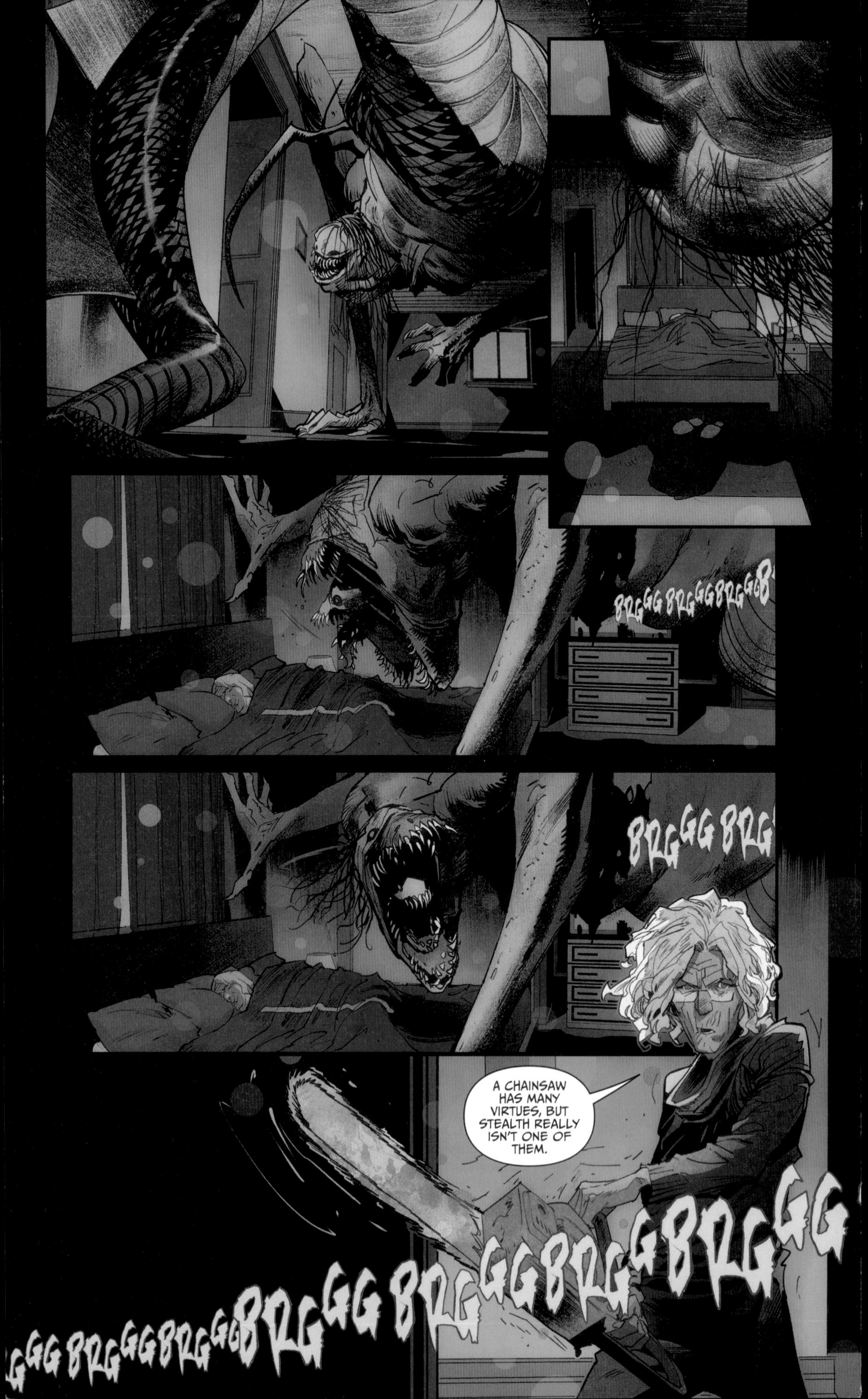
BRGG BRGGGBRGGBR
BRGG BRG
A CHAINSAW HAS MANY VIRTUES, BUT STEALTH REALLY ISN'T ONE OF THEM.
GGG BRGGGBRGGGBRGGG BRGGGBRGGBRGGG

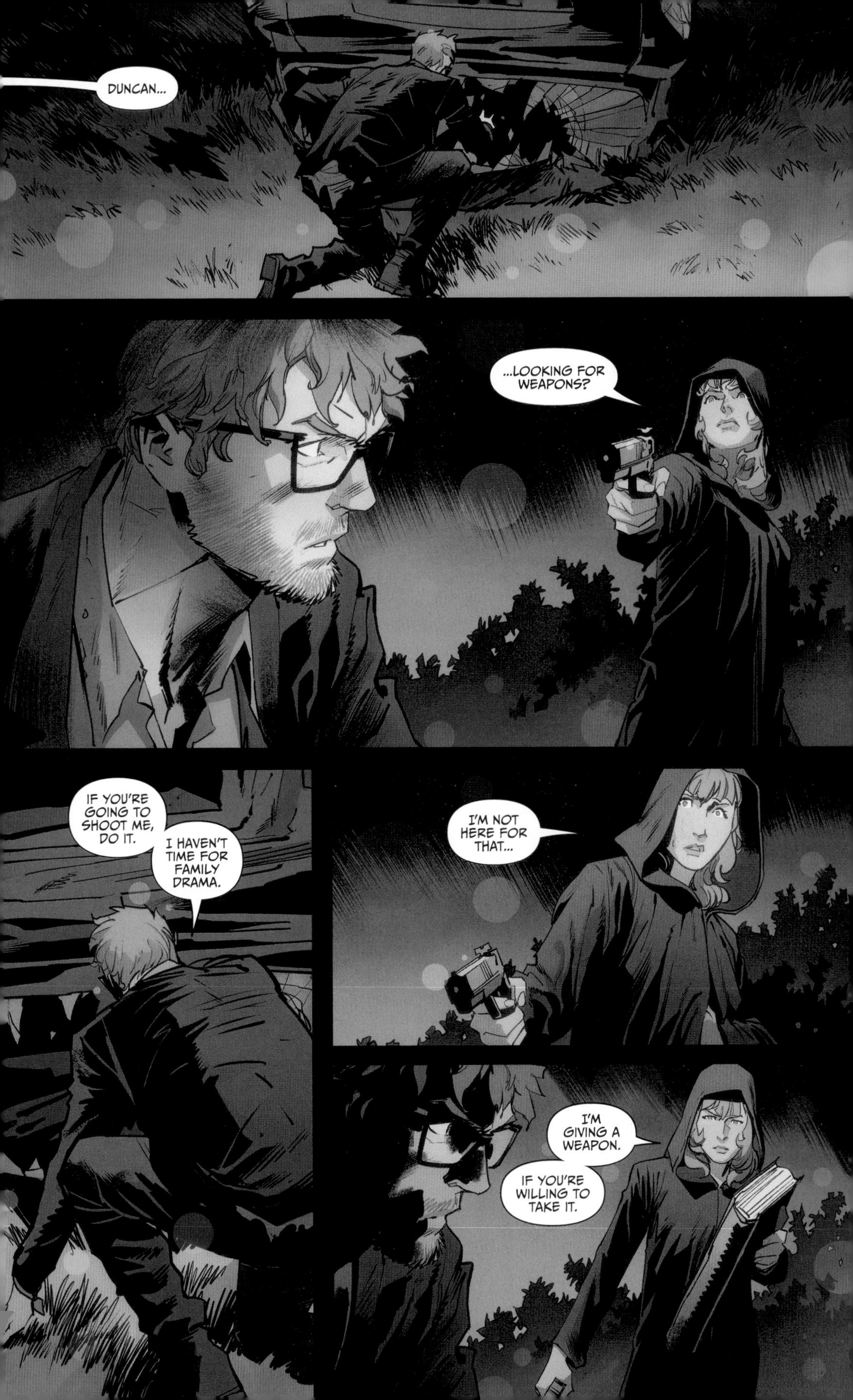
DUNCAN...
...LOOKING FOR WEAPONS?
IF YOU'RE GOING TO SHOOT ME, DO IT.
I HAVEN'T TIME FOR FAMILY DRAMA.
I'M NOT HERE FOR THAT...
I'M GIVING A WEAPON.
IF YOU'RE WILLING TO TAKE IT.

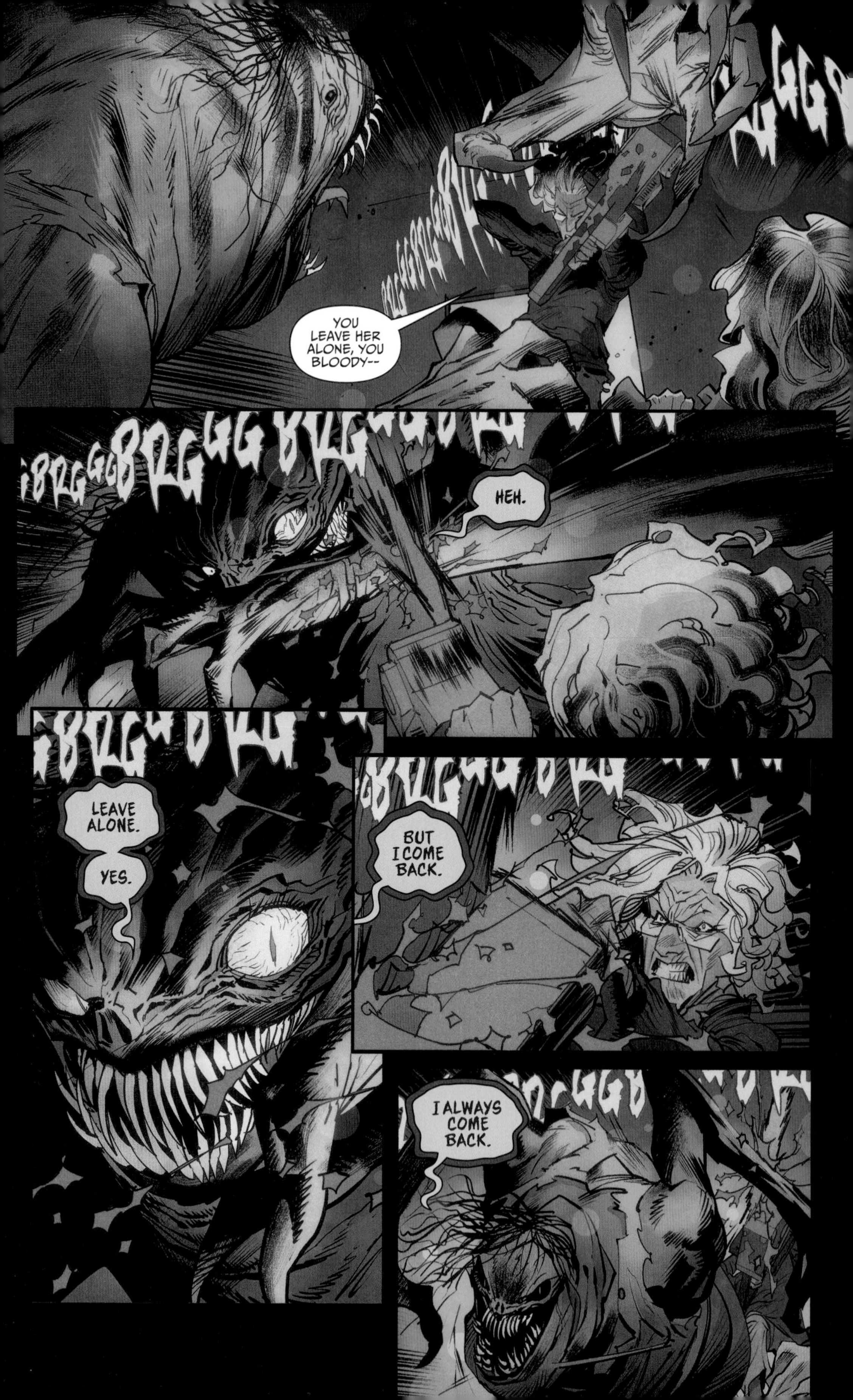
YOU LEAVE HER ALONE, YOU BLOODY--
HEH.
LEAVE ALONE.
YES.
BUT I COME BACK.
I ALWAYS COME BACK.

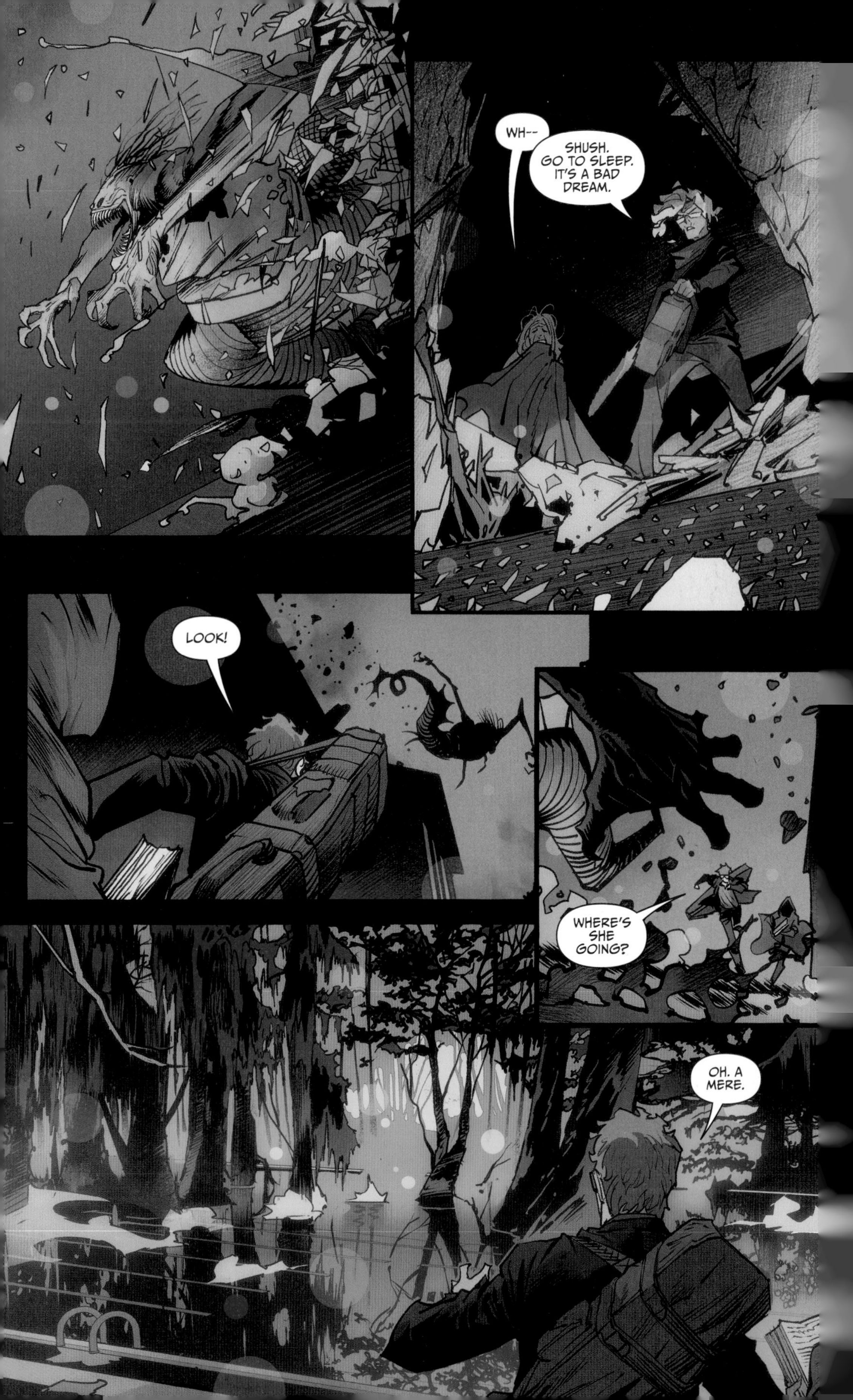
WH--
SHUSH. GO TO SLEEP. IT'S A BAD DREAM.
LOOK!
WHERE'S SHE GOING?
OH. A MERE.

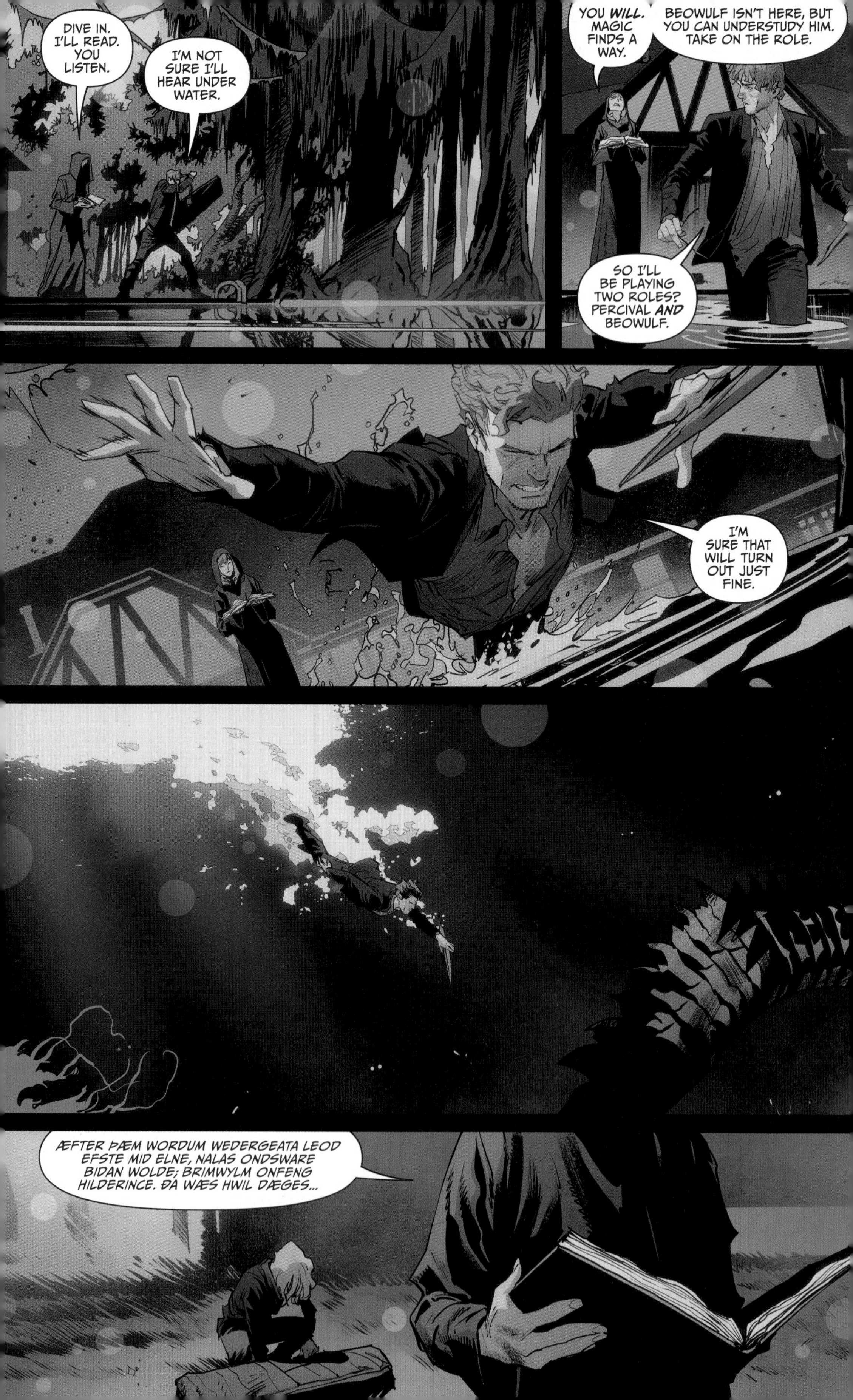
DIVE IN. I'LL READ. YOU LISTEN.
I'M NOT SURE I'LL HEAR UNDER WATER.
YOU *WILL.* MAGIC FINDS A WAY.
BEOWULF ISN'T HERE, BUT YOU CAN UNDERSTUDY HIM. TAKE ON THE ROLE.
SO I'LL BE PLAYING TWO ROLES? PERCIVAL *AND* BEOWULF.
I'M SURE THAT WILL TURN OUT JUST FINE.
ÆFTER ÞÆM WORDUM WEDERGEATA LEOD EFSTE MID ELNE, NALAS ONDSWARE BIDAN WOLDE; BRIMWYLM ONFENG HILDERINCE. ÐA WÆS HWIL DÆGES...

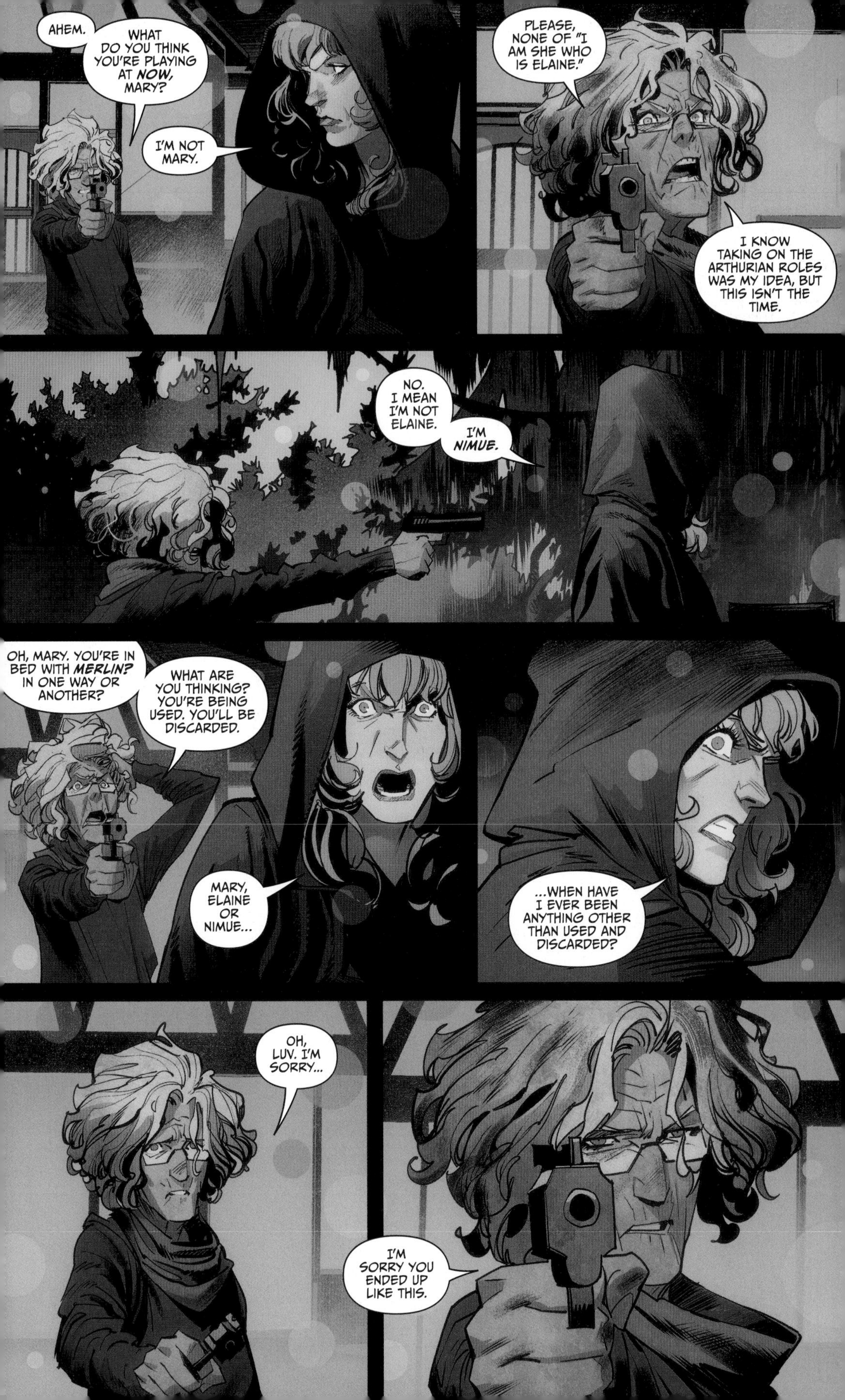
AHEM.
WHAT DO YOU THINK YOU'RE PLAYING AT *NOW,* MARY?
I'M NOT MARY.
PLEASE, NONE OF "I AM SHE WHO IS ELAINE."
I KNOW TAKING ON THE ARTHURIAN ROLES WAS MY IDEA, BUT THIS ISN'T THE TIME.
NO. I MEAN I'M NOT ELAINE.
I'M *NIMUE.*
OH, MARY. YOU'RE IN BED WITH *MERLIN?* IN ONE WAY OR ANOTHER?
WHAT ARE YOU THINKING? YOU'RE BEING USED. YOU'LL BE DISCARDED.
MARY, ELAINE OR NIMUE...
...WHEN HAVE I EVER BEEN ANYTHING OTHER THAN USED AND DISCARDED?
OH, LUV. I'M SORRY...
I'M SORRY YOU ENDED UP LIKE THIS.

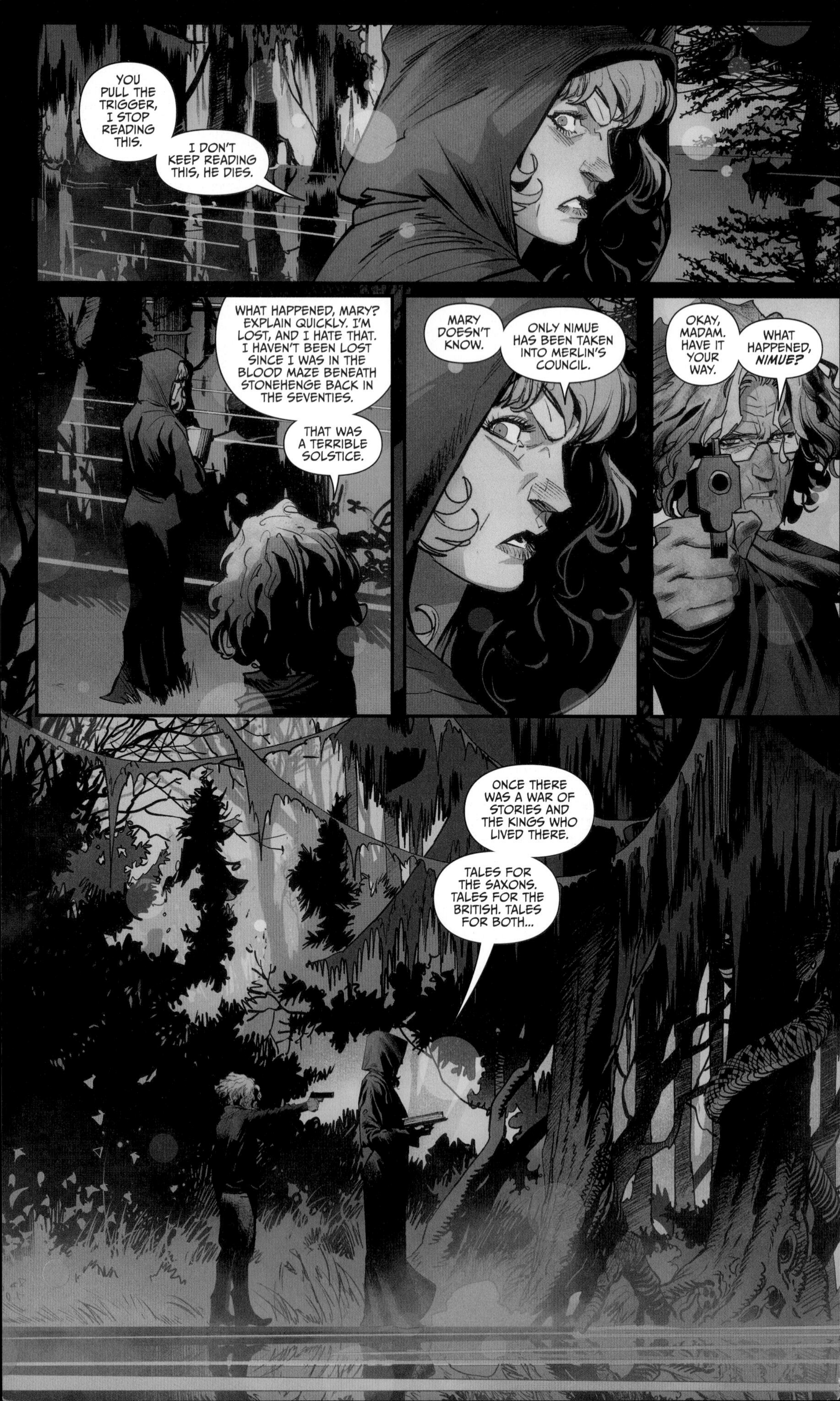
YOU PULL THE TRIGGER, I STOP READING THIS.
I DON'T KEEP READING THIS, HE DIES.
WHAT HAPPENED, MARY? EXPLAIN QUICKLY. I'M LOST, AND I HATE THAT. I HAVEN'T BEEN LOST SINCE I WAS IN THE BLOOD MAZE BENEATH STONEHENGE BACK IN THE SEVENTIES.
THAT WAS A TERRIBLE SOLSTICE.
MARY DOESN'T KNOW.
ONLY NIMUE HAS BEEN TAKEN INTO MERLIN'S COUNCIL.
OKAY, MADAM. HAVE IT YOUR WAY.
WHAT HAPPENED, *NIMUE?*
ONCE THERE WAS A WAR OF STORIES AND THE KINGS WHO LIVED THERE.
TALES FOR THE SAXONS. TALES FOR THE BRITISH. TALES FOR BOTH...

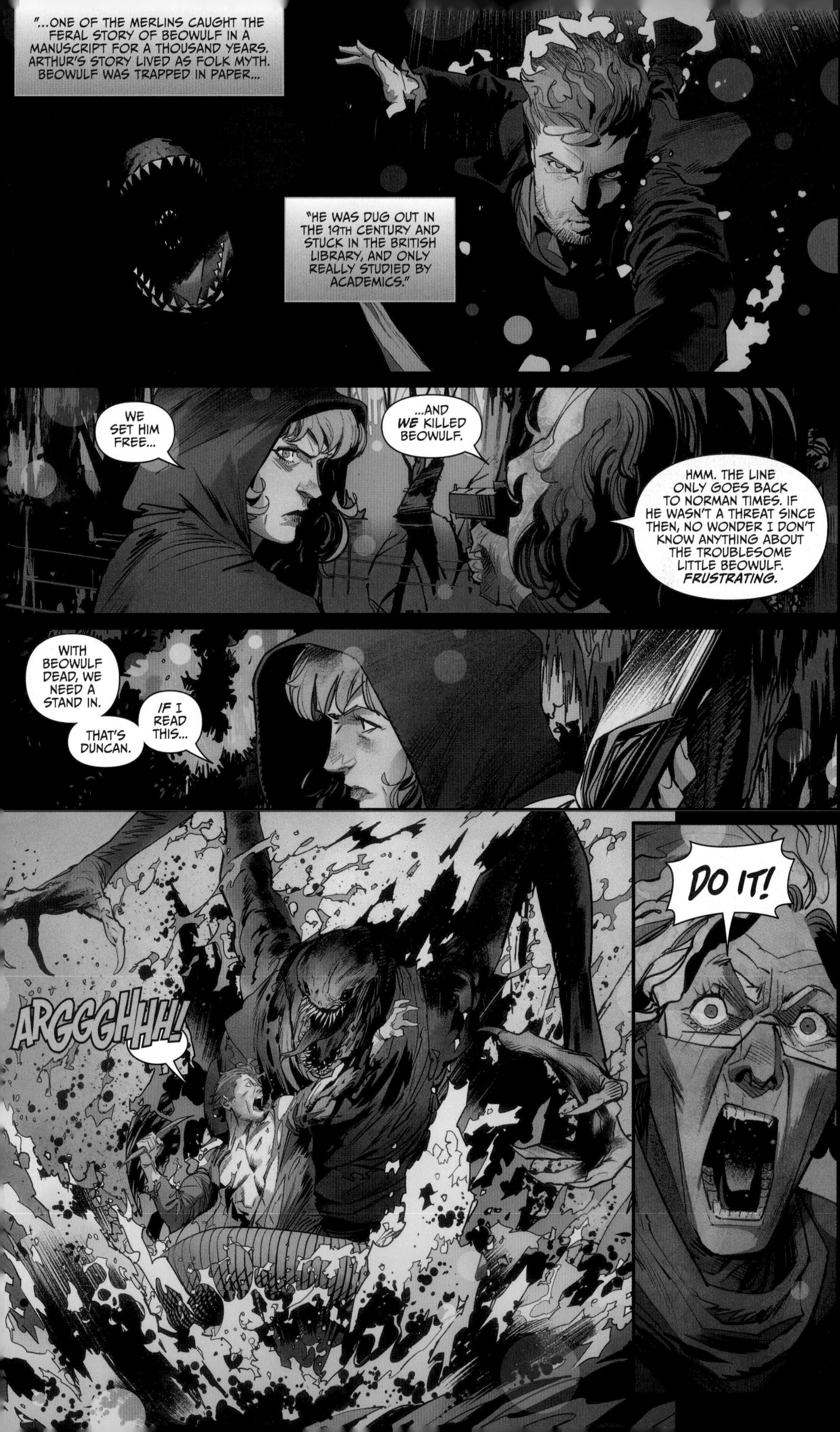
"...ONE OF THE MERLINS CAUGHT THE FERAL STORY OF BEOWULF IN A MANUSCRIPT FOR A THOUSAND YEARS. ARTHUR'S STORY LIVED AS FOLK MYTH. BEOWULF WAS TRAPPED IN PAPER...
"HE WAS DUG OUT IN THE 19TH CENTURY AND STUCK IN THE BRITISH LIBRARY, AND ONLY REALLY STUDIED BY ACADEMICS."
WE SET HIM FREE...
...AND WE KILLED BEOWULF.
HMM. THE LINE ONLY GOES BACK TO NORMAN TIMES. IF HE WASN'T A THREAT SINCE THEN, NO WONDER I DON'T KNOW ANYTHING ABOUT THE TROUBLESOME LITTLE BEOWULF. FRUSTRATING.
WITH BEOWULF DEAD, WE NEED A STAND IN.
THAT'S DUNCAN.
IF I READ THIS...
ARGGGHHH!
DO IT!

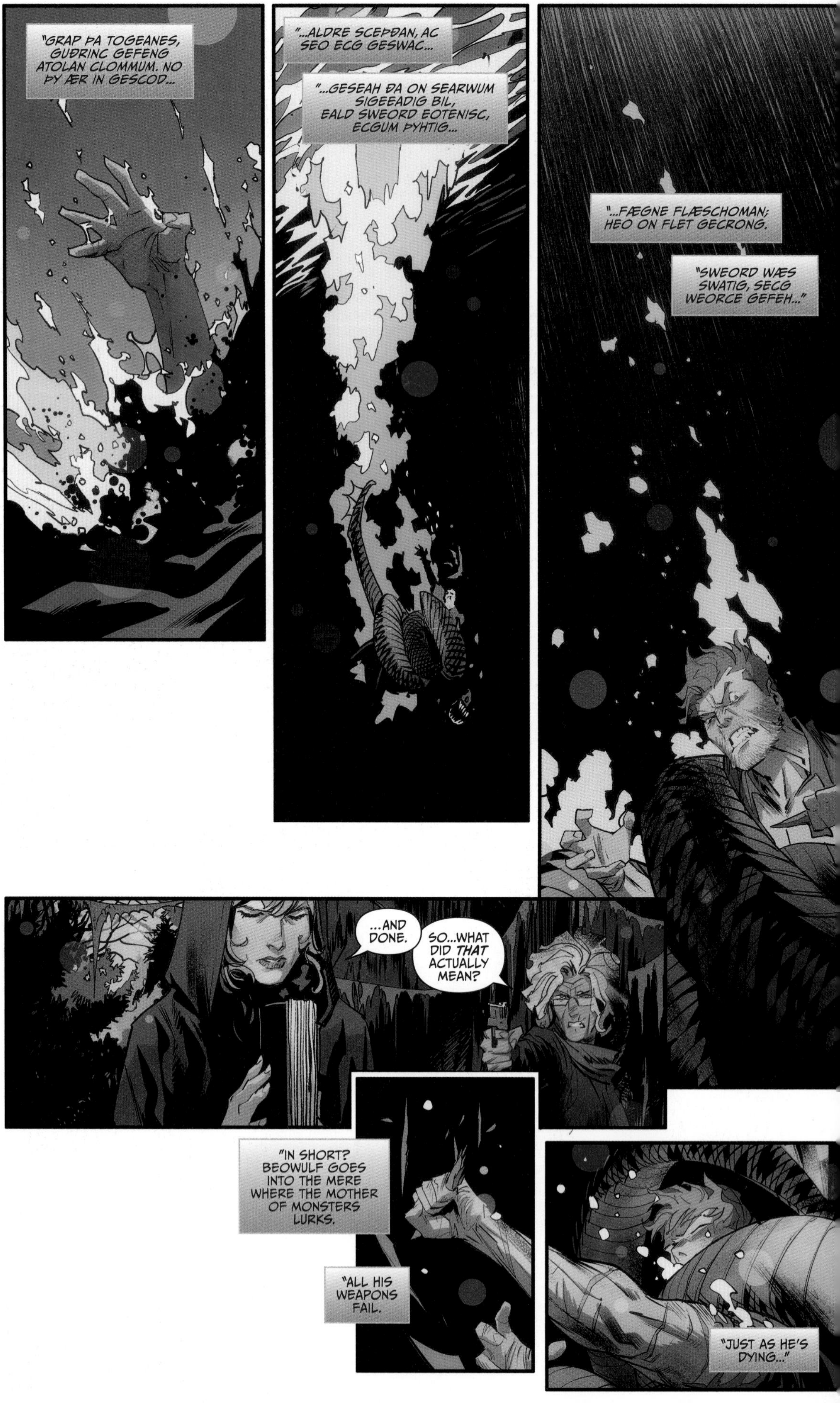
"GRAP ÞA TOGEANES, GUÐRINC GEFENG ATOLAN CLOMMUM. NO ÞY ÆR IN GESCOD...
"...ALDRE SCEÞÐAN, AC SEO ECG GESWAC...
"...GESEAH ÐA ON SEARWUM SIGEEADIG BIL, EALD SWEORD EOTENISC, ECGUM ÞYHTIG...
"...FÆGNE FLÆSCHOMAN; HEO ON FLET GECRONG.
"SWEORD WÆS SWATIG, SECG WEORCE GEFEH..."
...AND DONE.
SO...WHAT DID THAT ACTUALLY MEAN?
"IN SHORT? BEOWULF GOES INTO THE MERE WHERE THE MOTHER OF MONSTERS LURKS.
"ALL HIS WEAPONS FAIL.
"JUST AS HE'S DYING..."

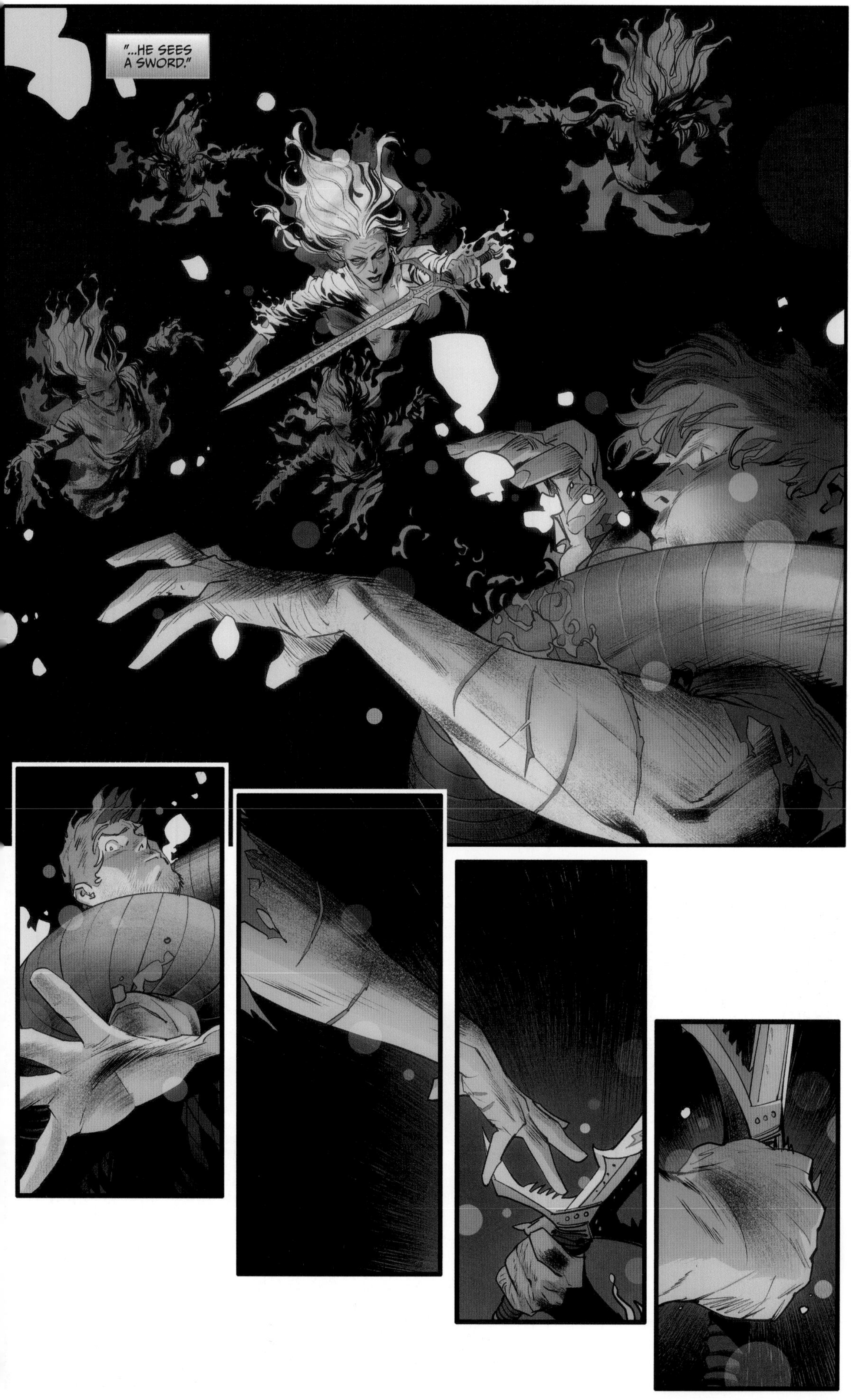
"...HE SEES A SWORD."

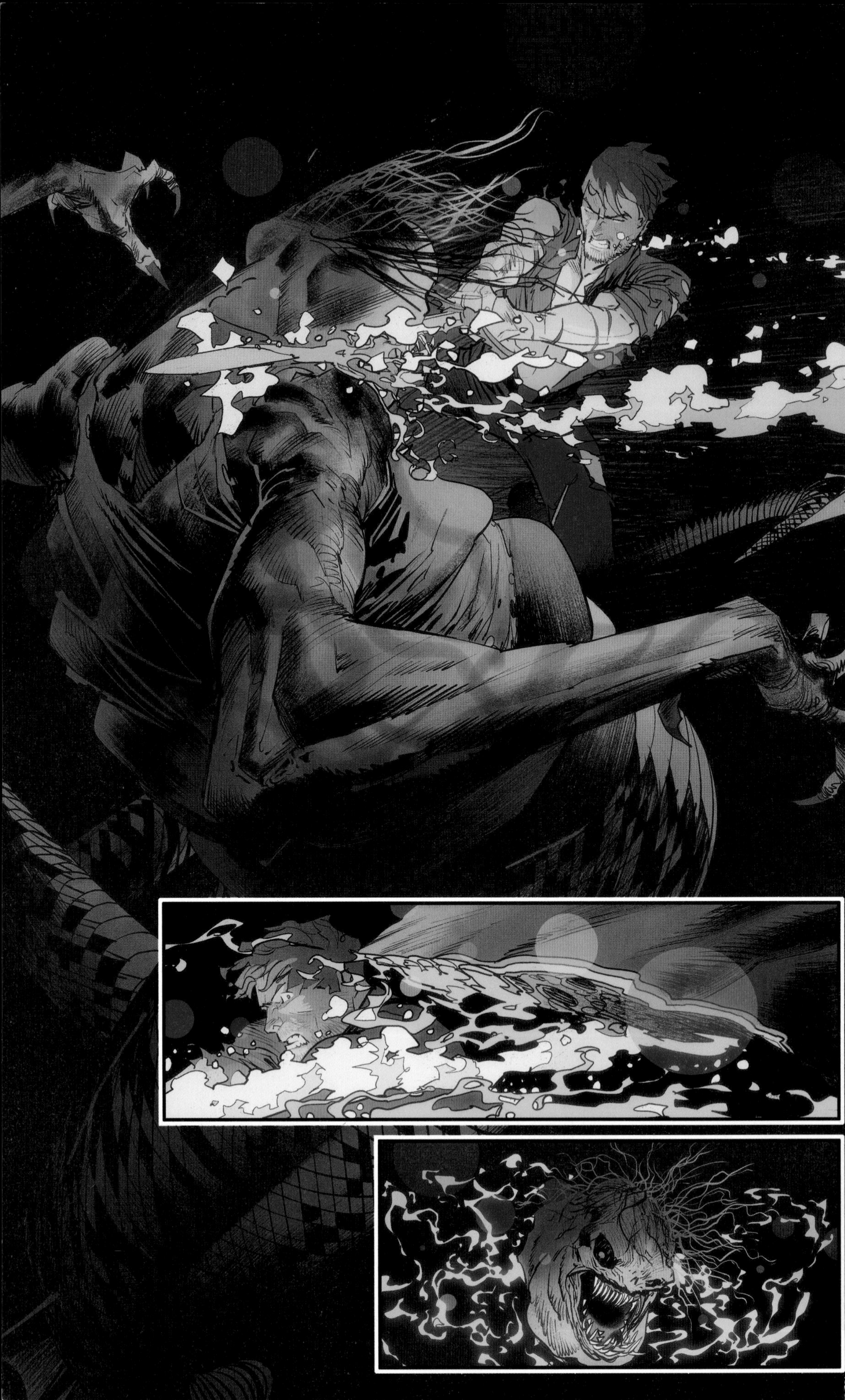

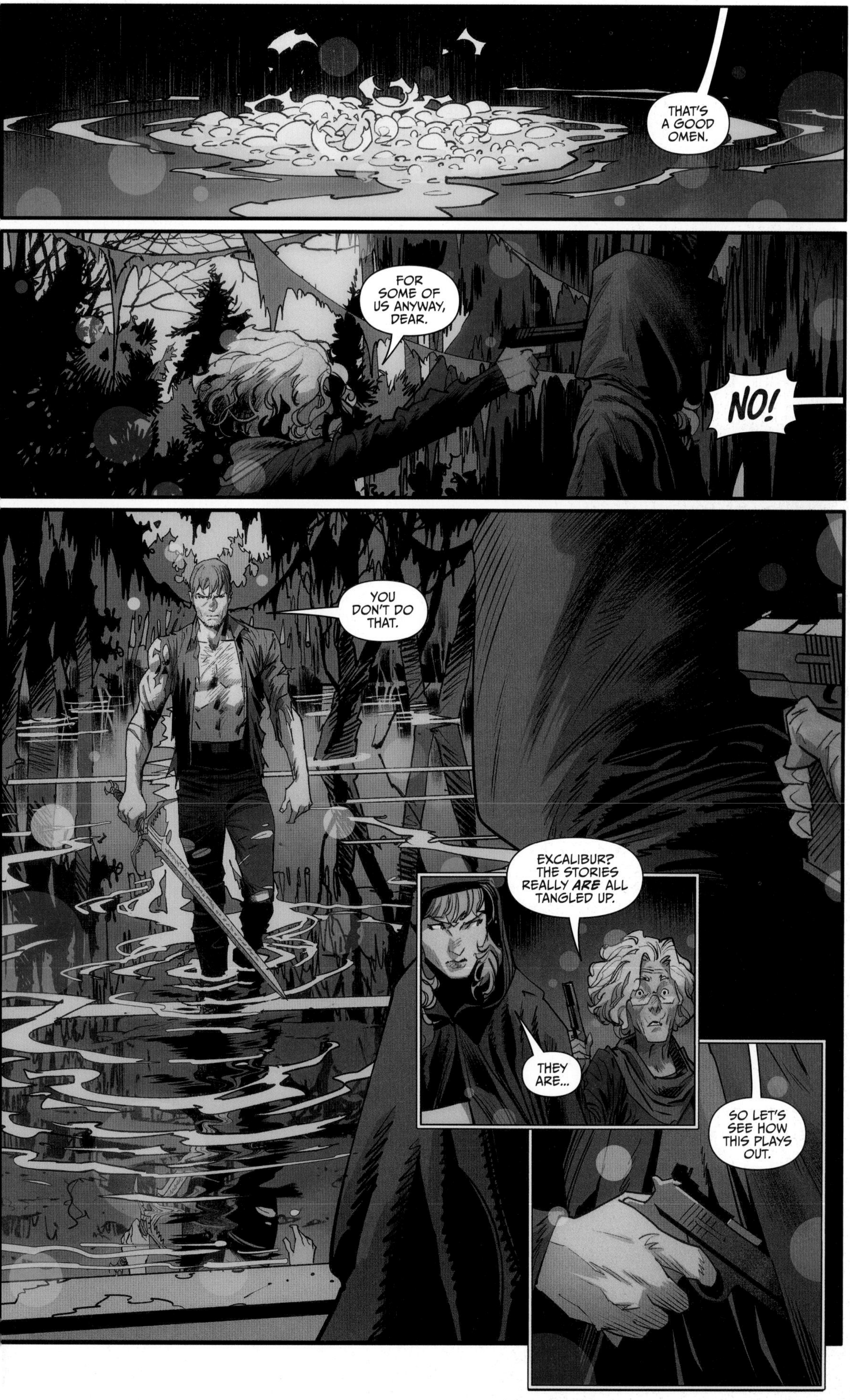
THAT'S A GOOD OMEN.
FOR SOME OF US ANYWAY, DEAR.
NO!
YOU DON'T DO THAT.
EXCALIBUR? THE STORIES REALLY ARE ALL TANGLED UP.
THEY ARE...
SO LET'S SEE HOW THIS PLAYS OUT.

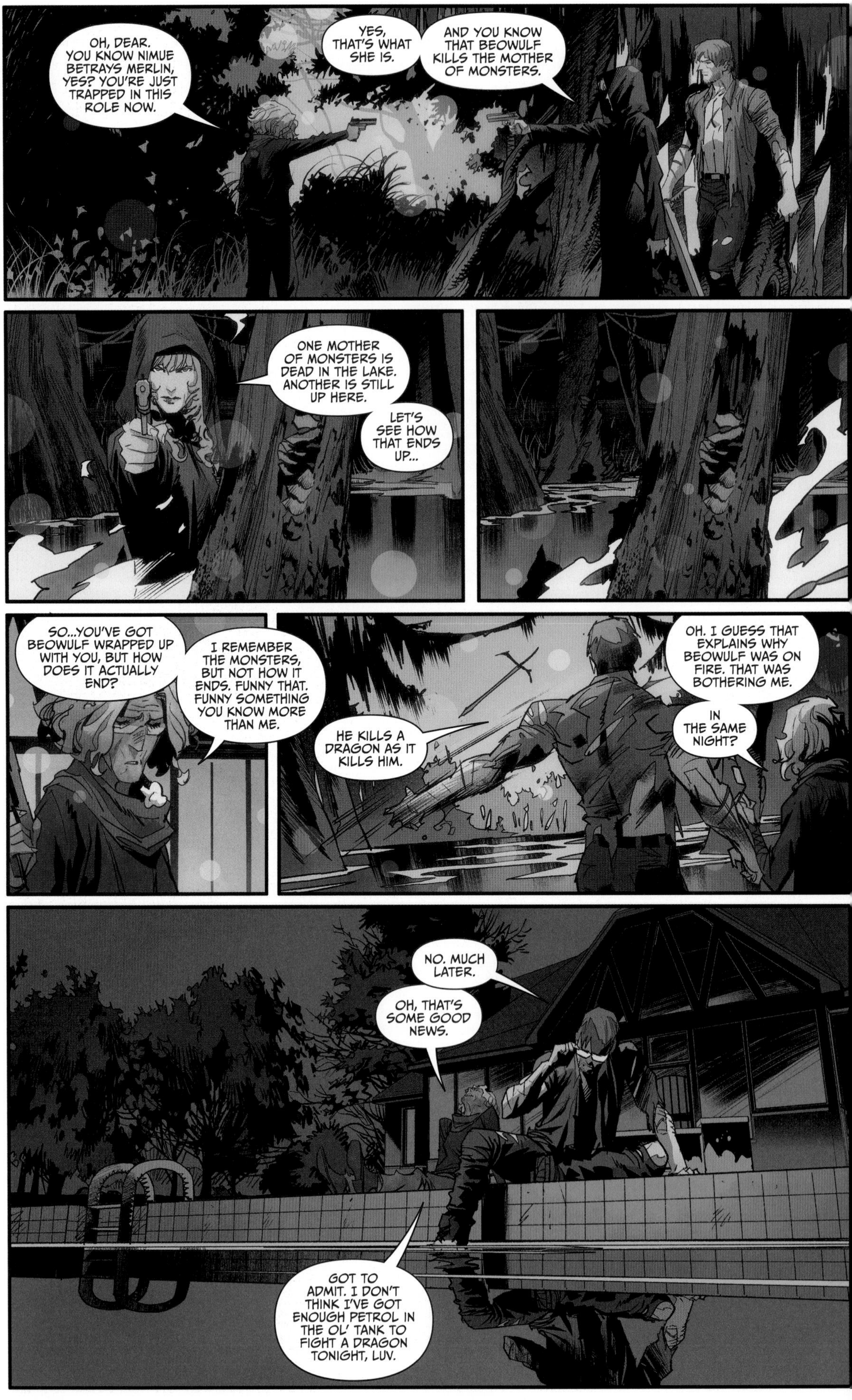
OH, DEAR. YOU KNOW NIMUE BETRAYS MERLIN, YES? YOU'RE JUST TRAPPED IN THIS ROLE NOW.
YES, THAT'S WHAT SHE IS.
AND YOU KNOW THAT BEOWULF KILLS THE MOTHER OF MONSTERS.
ONE MOTHER OF MONSTERS IS DEAD IN THE LAKE. ANOTHER IS STILL UP HERE.
LET'S SEE HOW THAT ENDS UP...
SO...YOU'VE GOT BEOWULF WRAPPED UP WITH YOU, BUT HOW DOES IT ACTUALLY END?
I REMEMBER THE MONSTERS, BUT NOT HOW IT ENDS. FUNNY THAT. FUNNY SOMETHING YOU KNOW MORE THAN ME.
HE KILLS A DRAGON AS IT KILLS HIM.
OH. I GUESS THAT EXPLAINS WHY BEOWULF WAS ON FIRE. THAT WAS BOTHERING ME.
IN THE SAME NIGHT?
NO. MUCH LATER.
OH, THAT'S SOME GOOD NEWS.
GOT TO ADMIT. I DON'T THINK I'VE GOT ENOUGH PETROL IN THE OL' TANK TO FIGHT A DRAGON TONIGHT, LUV.

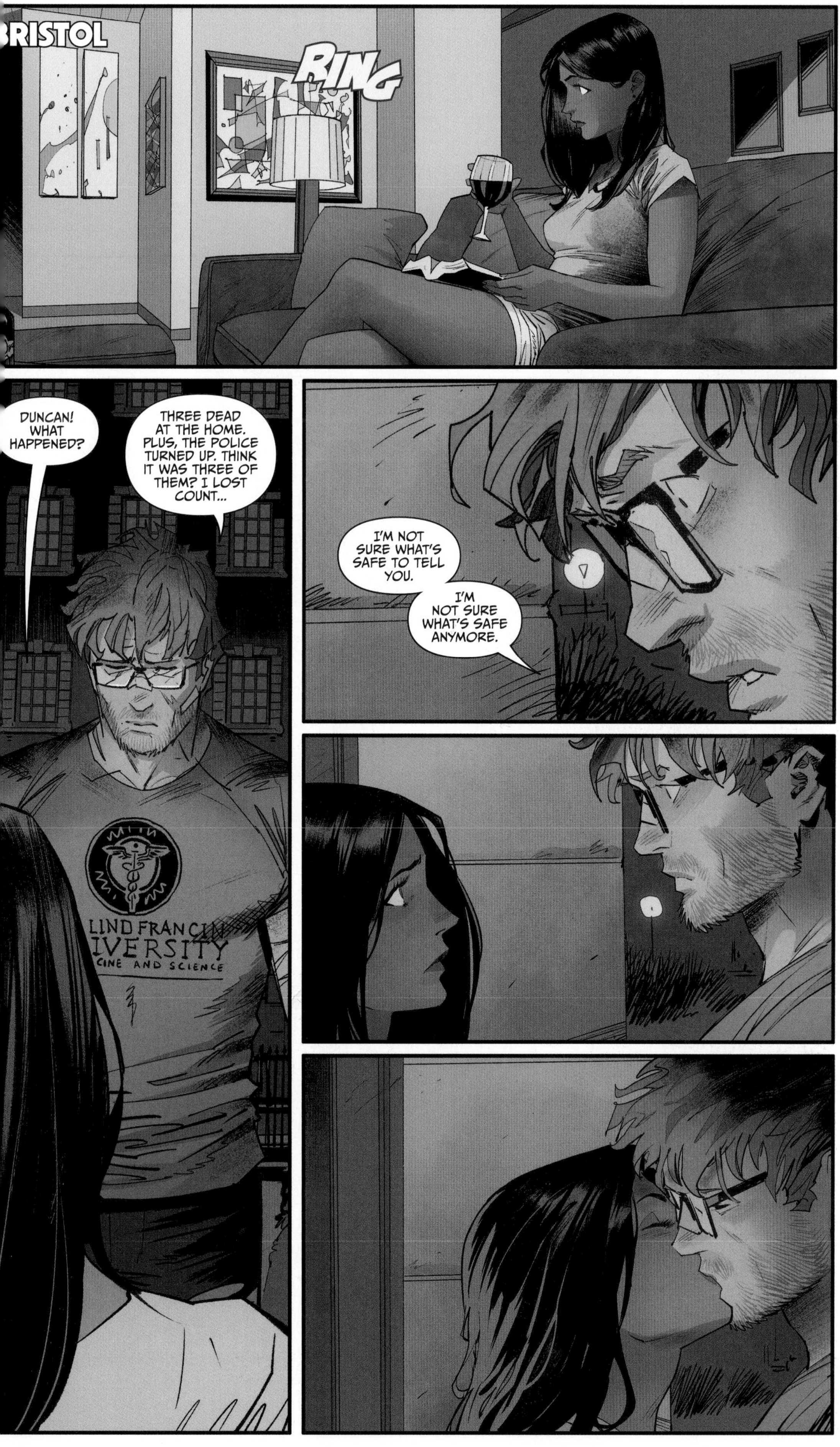
BRISTOL
RING
DUNCAN! WHAT HAPPENED?
THREE DEAD AT THE HOME. PLUS, THE POLICE TURNED UP. THINK IT WAS THREE OF THEM? I LOST COUNT...
I'M NOT SURE WHAT'S SAFE TO TELL YOU.
I'M NOT SURE WHAT'S SAFE ANYMORE.

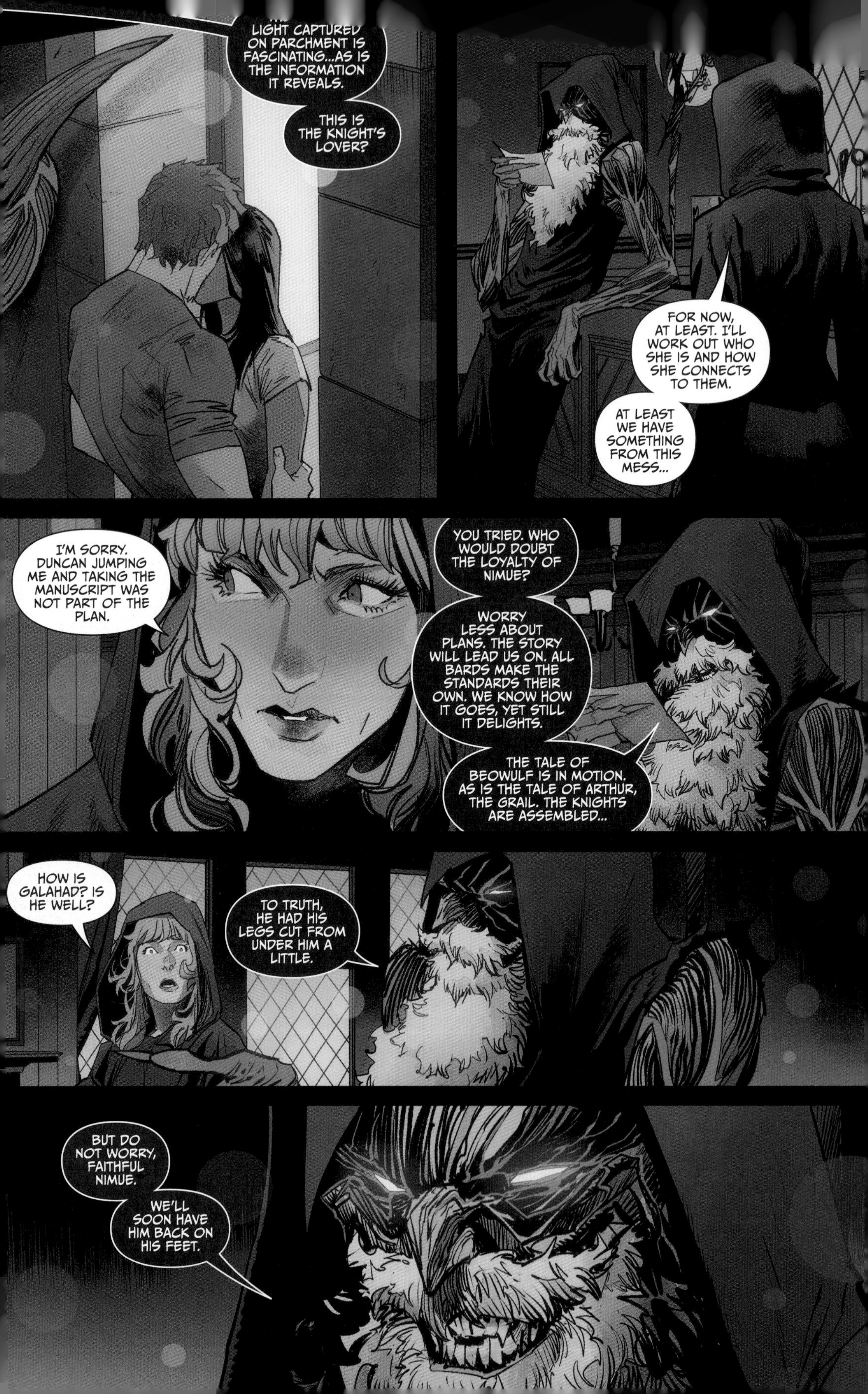
LIGHT CAPTURED ON PARCHMENT IS FASCINATING...AS IS THE INFORMATION IT REVEALS.
THIS IS THE KNIGHT'S LOVER?
FOR NOW, AT LEAST. I'LL WORK OUT WHO SHE IS AND HOW SHE CONNECTS TO THEM.
AT LEAST WE HAVE SOMETHING FROM THIS MESS...
I'M SORRY. DUNCAN JUMPING ME AND TAKING THE MANUSCRIPT WAS NOT PART OF THE PLAN.
YOU TRIED. WHO WOULD DOUBT THE LOYALTY OF NIMUE?
WORRY LESS ABOUT PLANS. THE STORY WILL LEAD US ON. ALL BARDS MAKE THE STANDARDS THEIR OWN. WE KNOW HOW IT GOES, YET STILL IT DELIGHTS.
THE TALE OF BEOWULF IS IN MOTION. AS IS THE TALE OF ARTHUR, THE GRAIL. THE KNIGHTS ARE ASSEMBLED...
HOW IS GALAHAD? IS HE WELL?
TO TRUTH, HE HAD HIS LEGS CUT FROM UNDER HIM A LITTLE.
BUT DO NOT WORRY, FAITHFUL NIMUE.
WE'LL SOON HAVE HIM BACK ON HIS FEET.

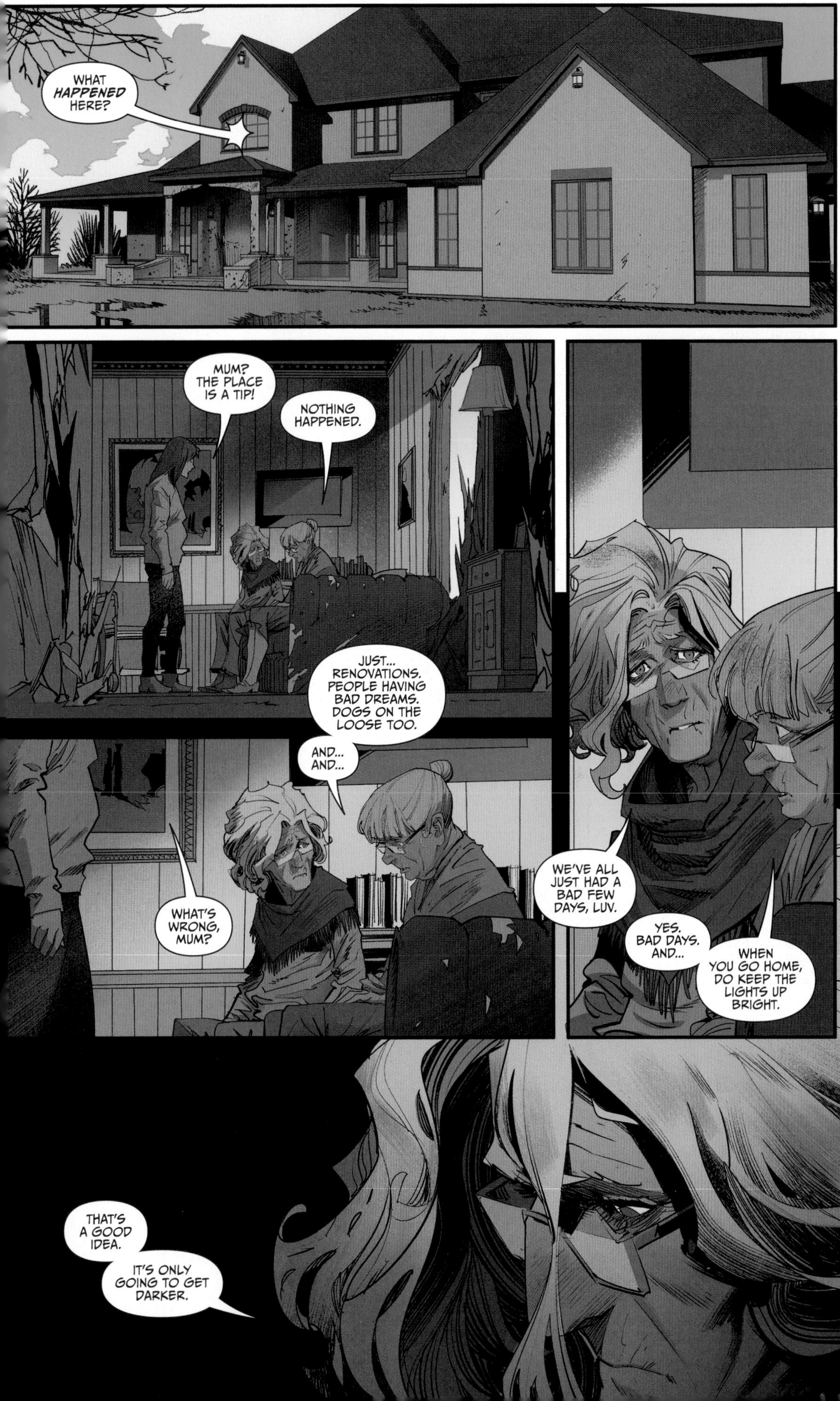
WHAT *HAPPENED* HERE?
MUM? THE PLACE IS A TIP!
NOTHING HAPPENED.
JUST... RENOVATIONS. PEOPLE HAVING BAD DREAMS. DOGS ON THE LOOSE TOO.
AND... AND...
WHAT'S WRONG, MUM?
WE'VE ALL JUST HAD A BAD FEW DAYS, LUV.
YES. BAD DAYS. AND...
WHEN YOU GO HOME, DO KEEP THE LIGHTS UP BRIGHT.
THAT'S A GOOD IDEA.
IT'S ONLY GOING TO GET DARKER.

ONCE & FUTURE ™

OLD ENGLISH

GILLEN

MORA

BONVILLAIN

DUKESHIRE

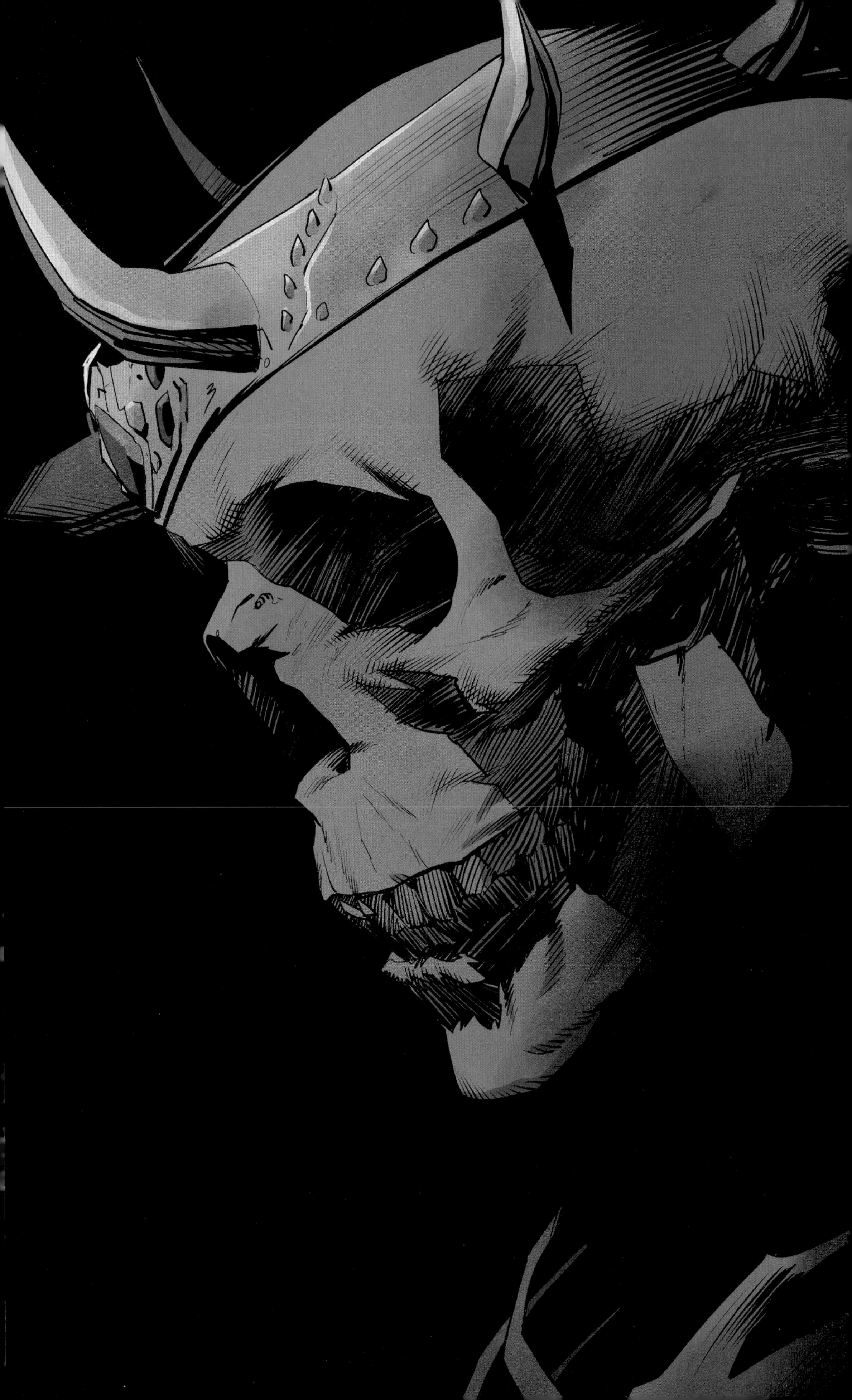

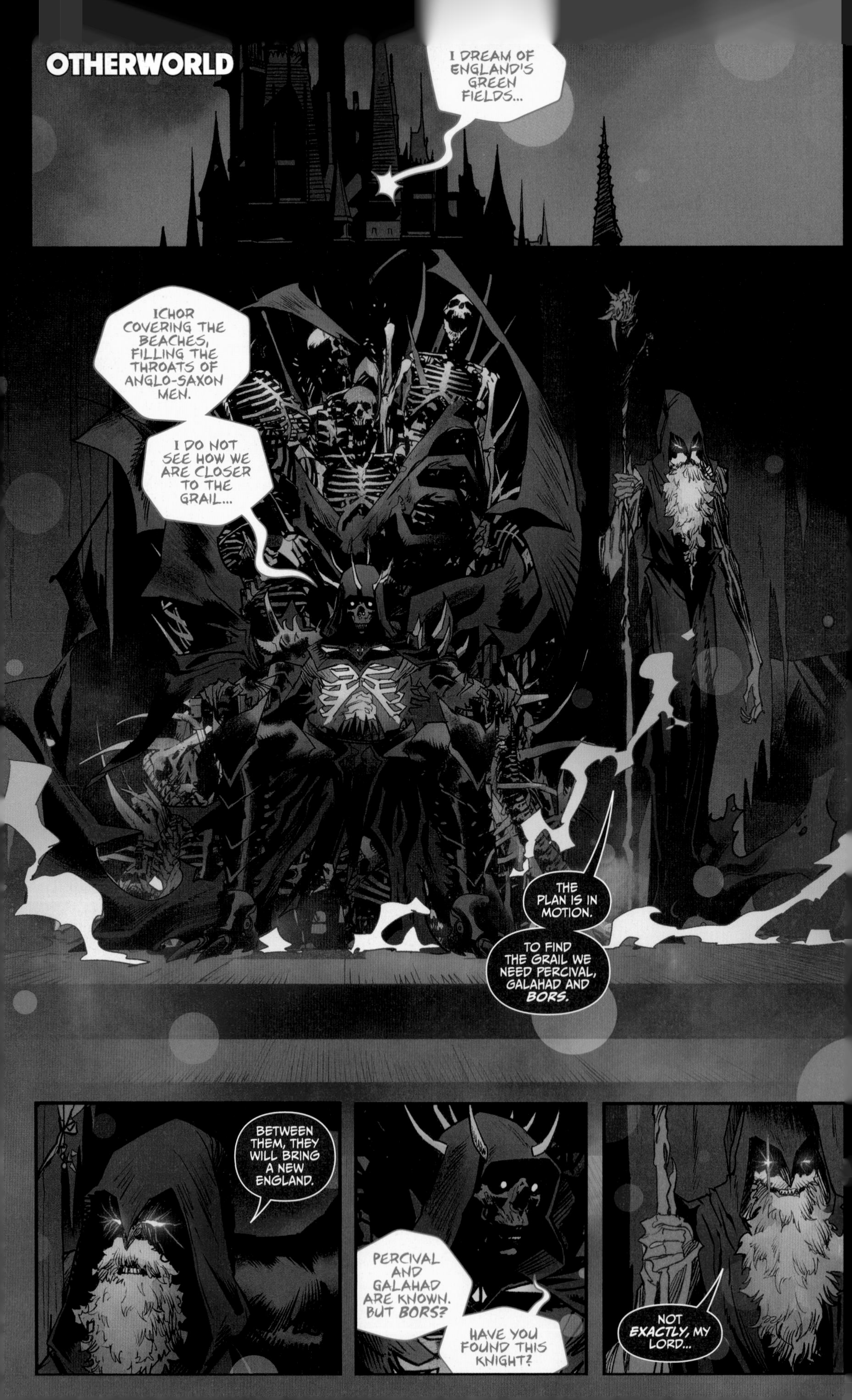
OTHERWORLD
I DREAM OF ENGLAND'S GREEN FIELDS...
ICHOR COVERING THE BEACHES, FILLING THE THROATS OF ANGLO-SAXON MEN.
I DO NOT SEE HOW WE ARE CLOSER TO THE GRAIL...
THE PLAN IS IN MOTION.
TO FIND THE GRAIL WE NEED PERCIVAL, GALAHAD AND BORS.
BETWEEN THEM, THEY WILL BRING A NEW ENGLAND.
PERCIVAL AND GALAHAD ARE KNOWN. BUT BORS?
HAVE YOU FOUND THIS KNIGHT?
NOT EXACTLY, MY LORD...

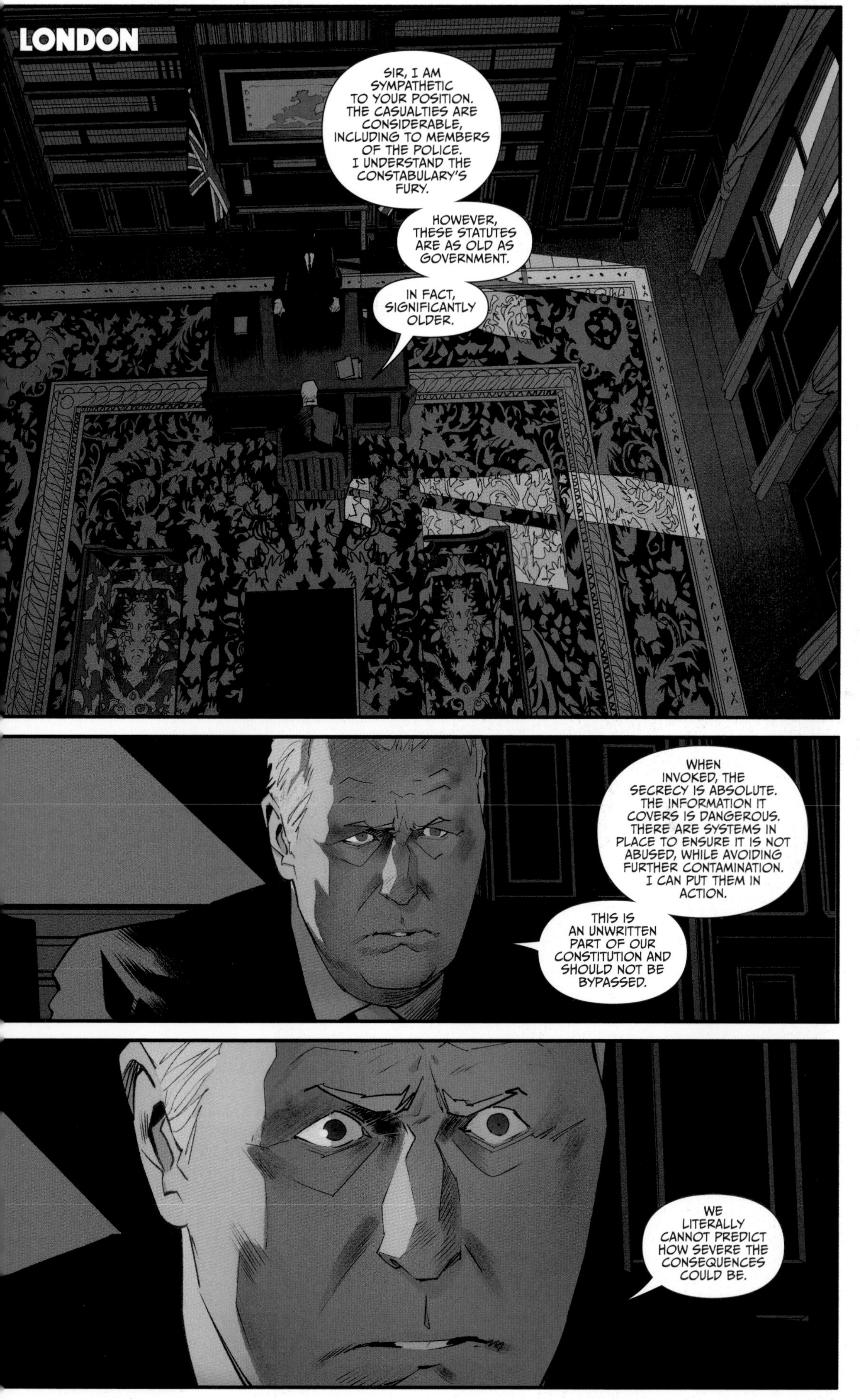
LONDON
SIR, I AM SYMPATHETIC TO YOUR POSITION. THE CASUALTIES ARE CONSIDERABLE, INCLUDING TO MEMBERS OF THE POLICE. I UNDERSTAND THE CONSTABULARY'S FURY.
HOWEVER, THESE STATUTES ARE AS OLD AS GOVERNMENT.
IN FACT, SIGNIFICANTLY OLDER.
WHEN INVOKED, THE SECRECY IS ABSOLUTE. THE INFORMATION IT COVERS IS DANGEROUS. THERE ARE SYSTEMS IN PLACE TO ENSURE IT IS NOT ABUSED, WHILE AVOIDING FURTHER CONTAMINATION. I CAN PUT THEM IN ACTION.
THIS IS AN UNWRITTEN PART OF OUR CONSTITUTION AND SHOULD NOT BE BYPASSED.
WE LITERALLY CANNOT PREDICT HOW SEVERE THE CONSEQUENCES COULD BE.

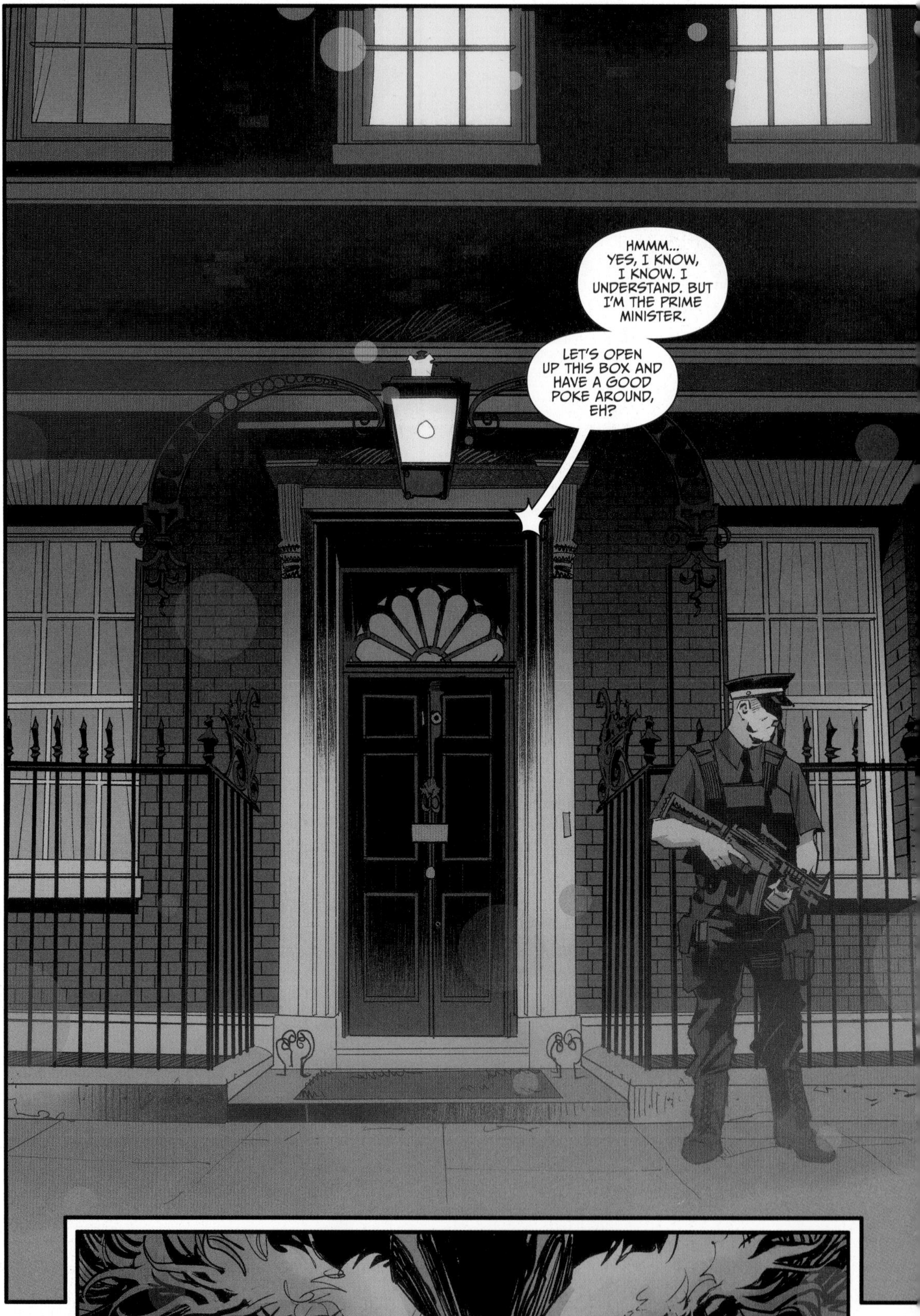
HMMM... YES, I KNOW, I KNOW. I UNDERSTAND. BUT I'M THE PRIME MINISTER.
LET'S OPEN UP THIS BOX AND HAVE A GOOD POKE AROUND, EH?

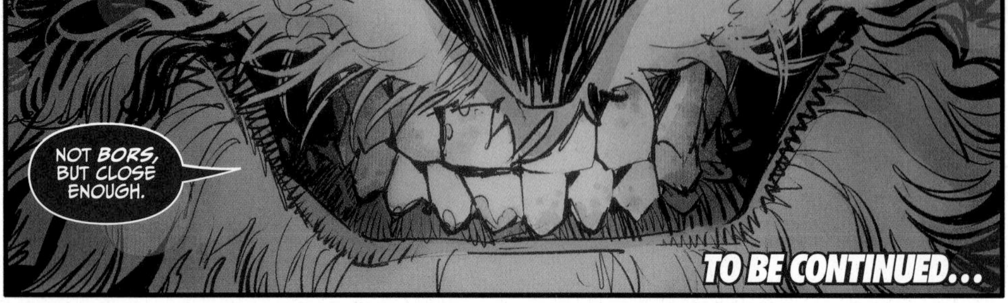
NOT *BORS*, BUT CLOSE ENOUGH.
TO BE CONTINUED...

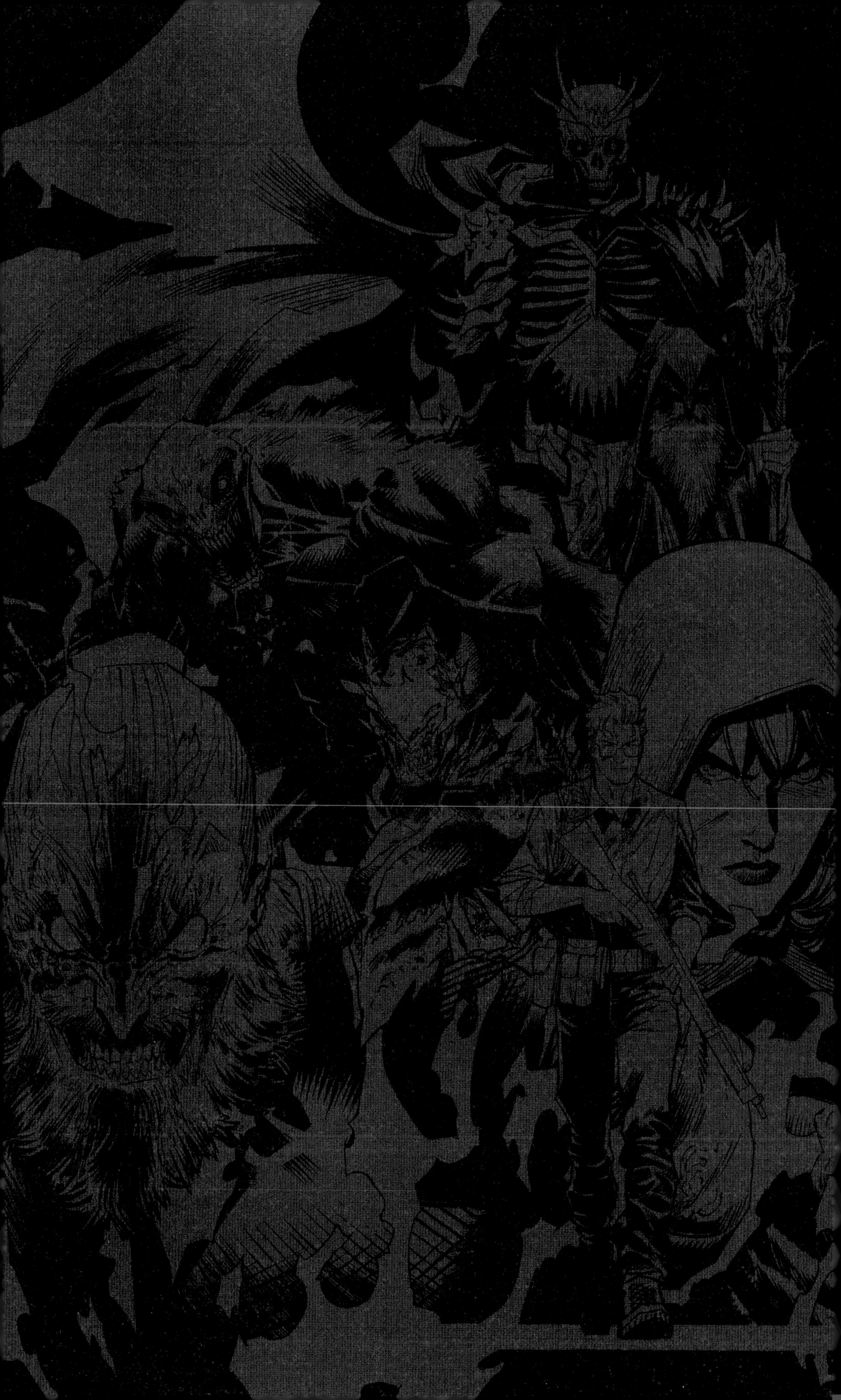

COVER GALLERY

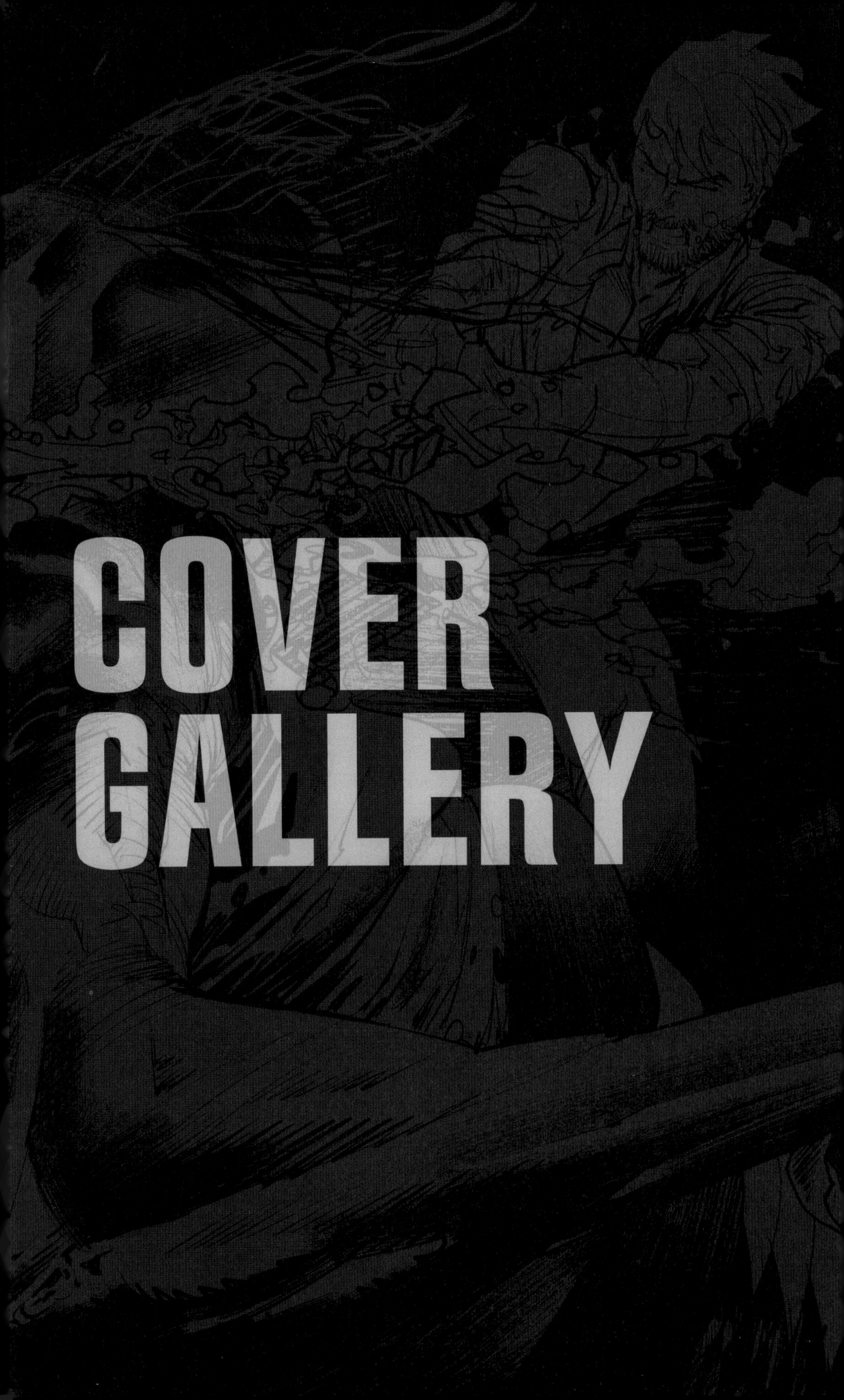

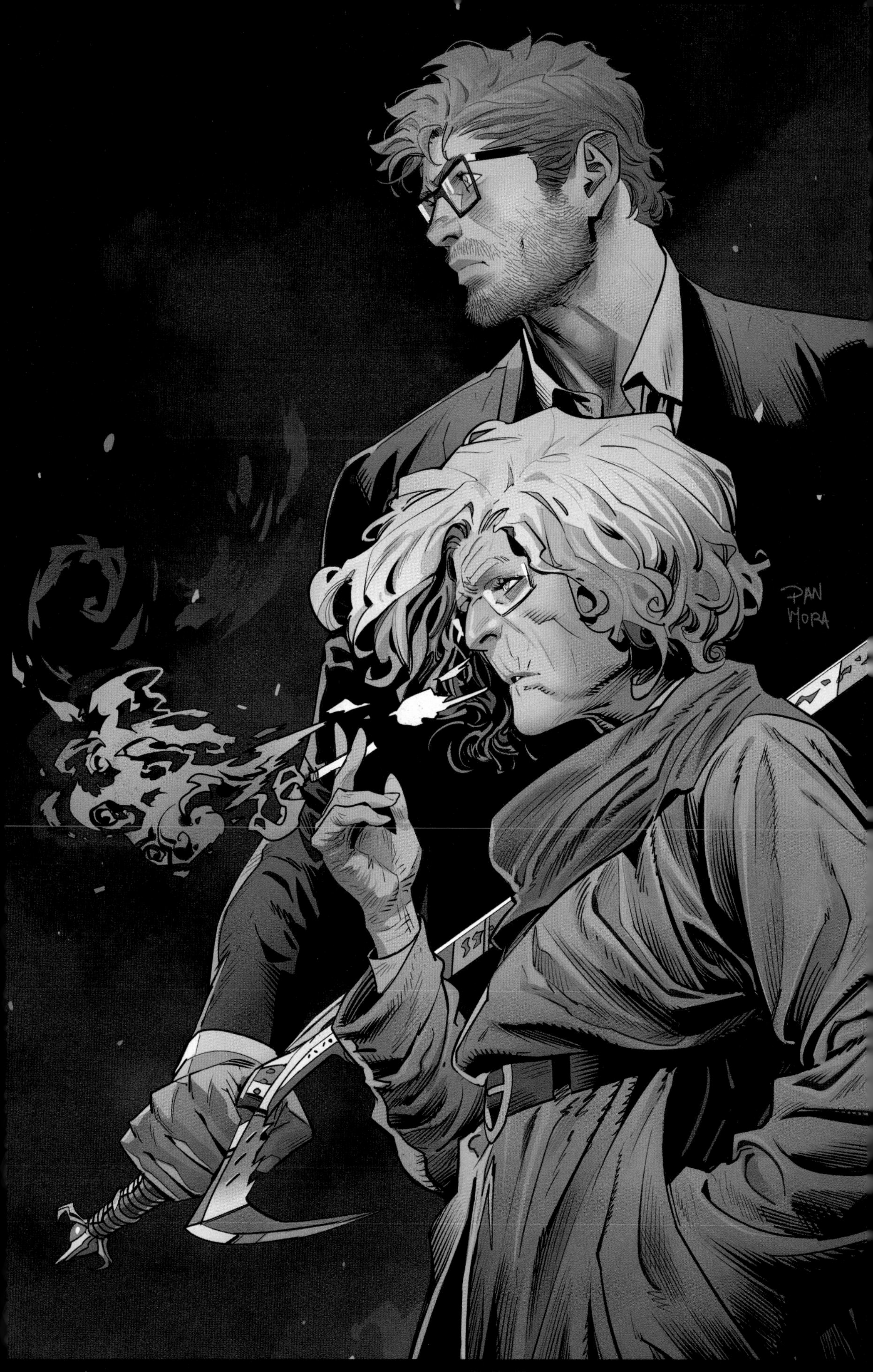
DAN
MORA

ISSUE SEVEN COVER BY **DAN MORA**

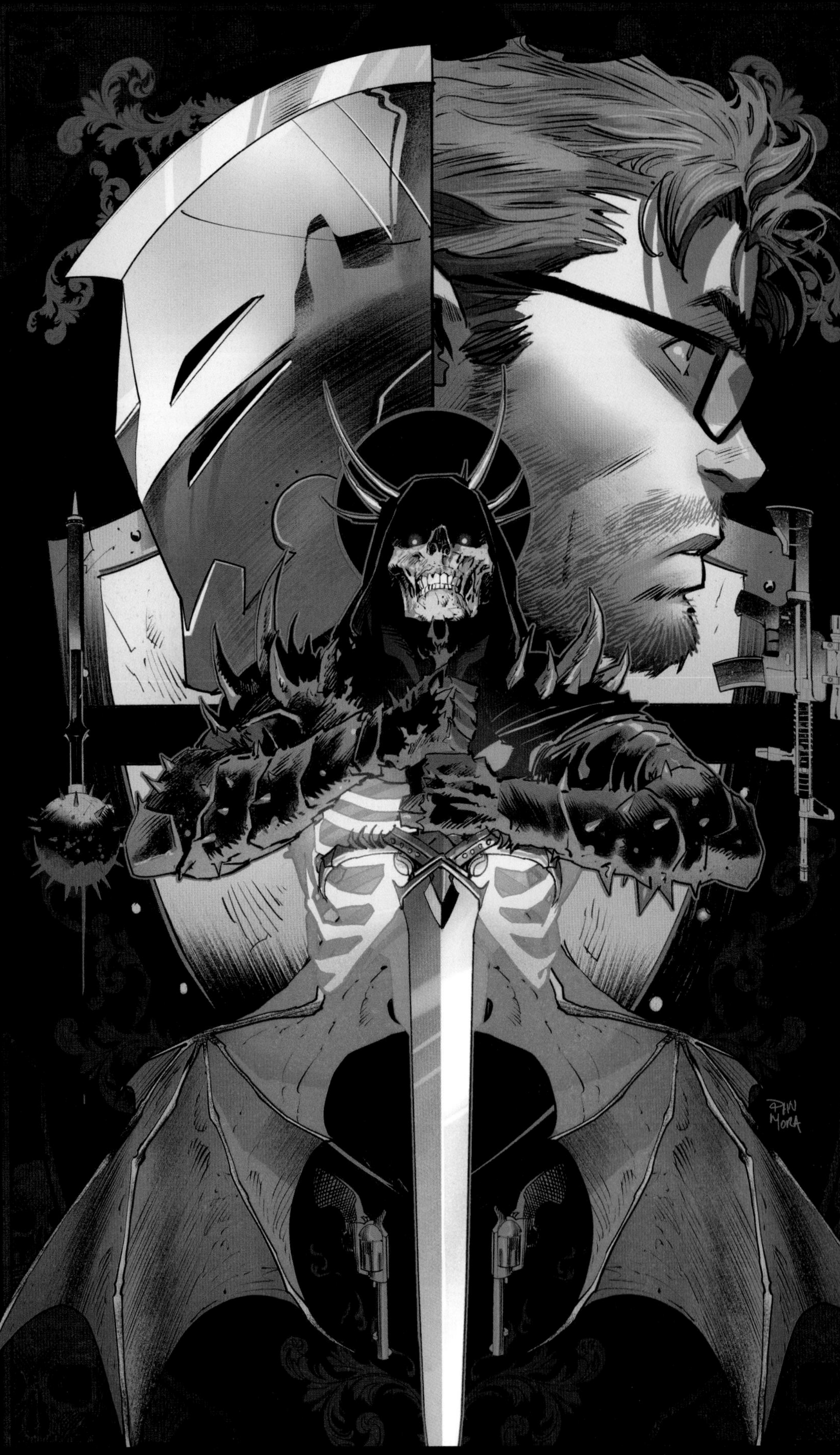

ISSUE SEVEN ONE-PER-STORE "THANK YOU" VARIANT COVER BY **DAN MORA**

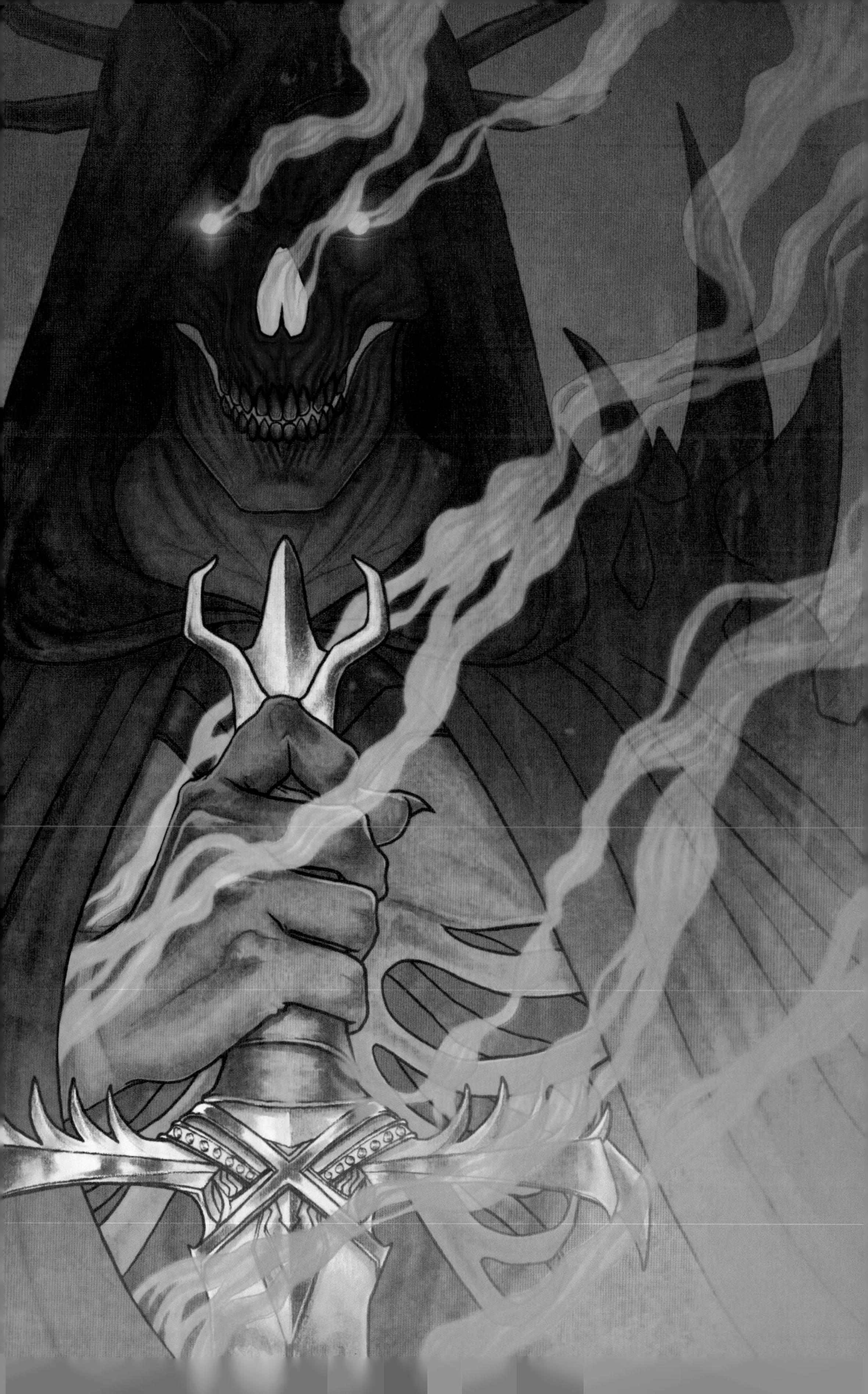

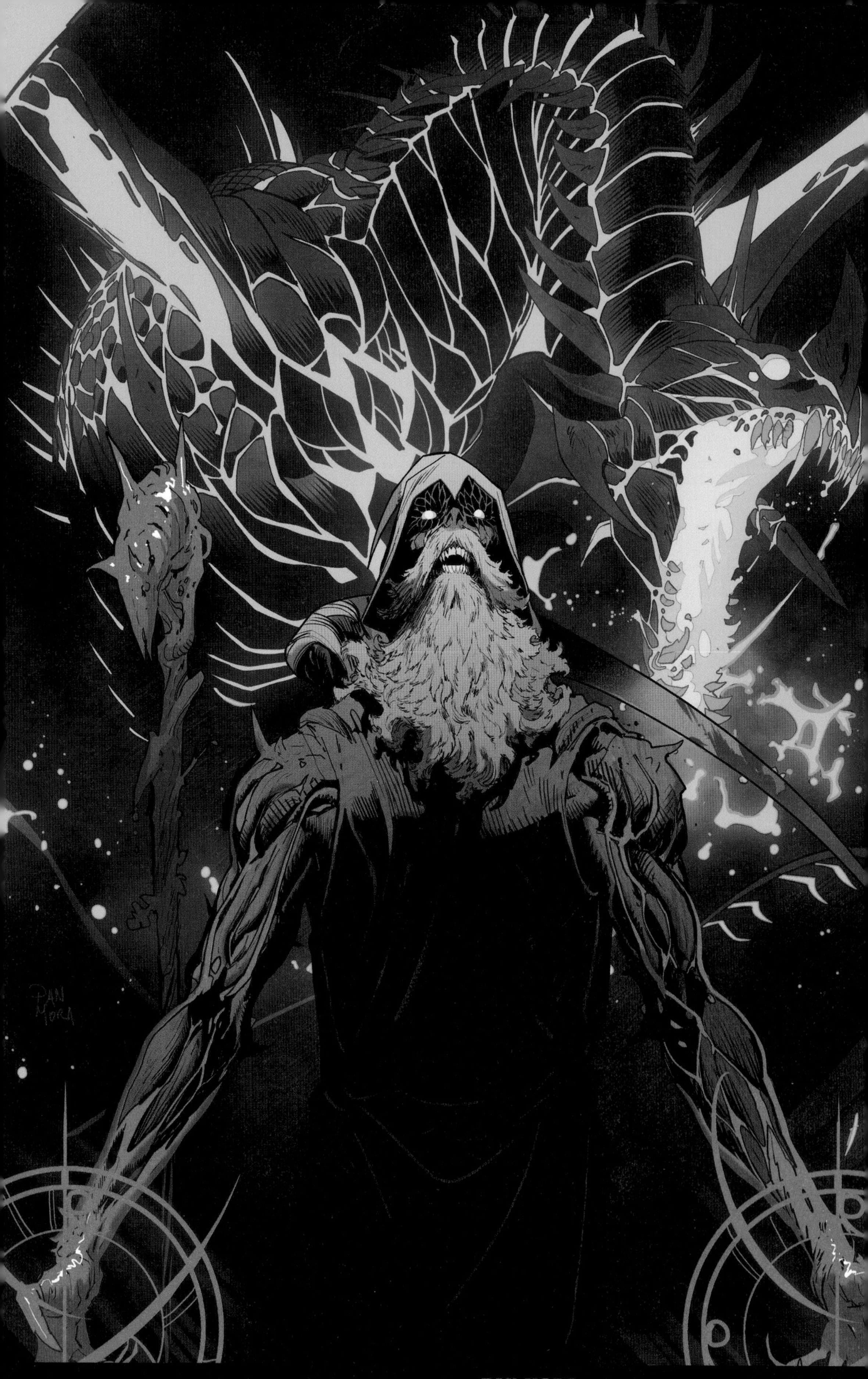
DAN MORA

ISSUE EIGHT COVER BY **DAN MORA**

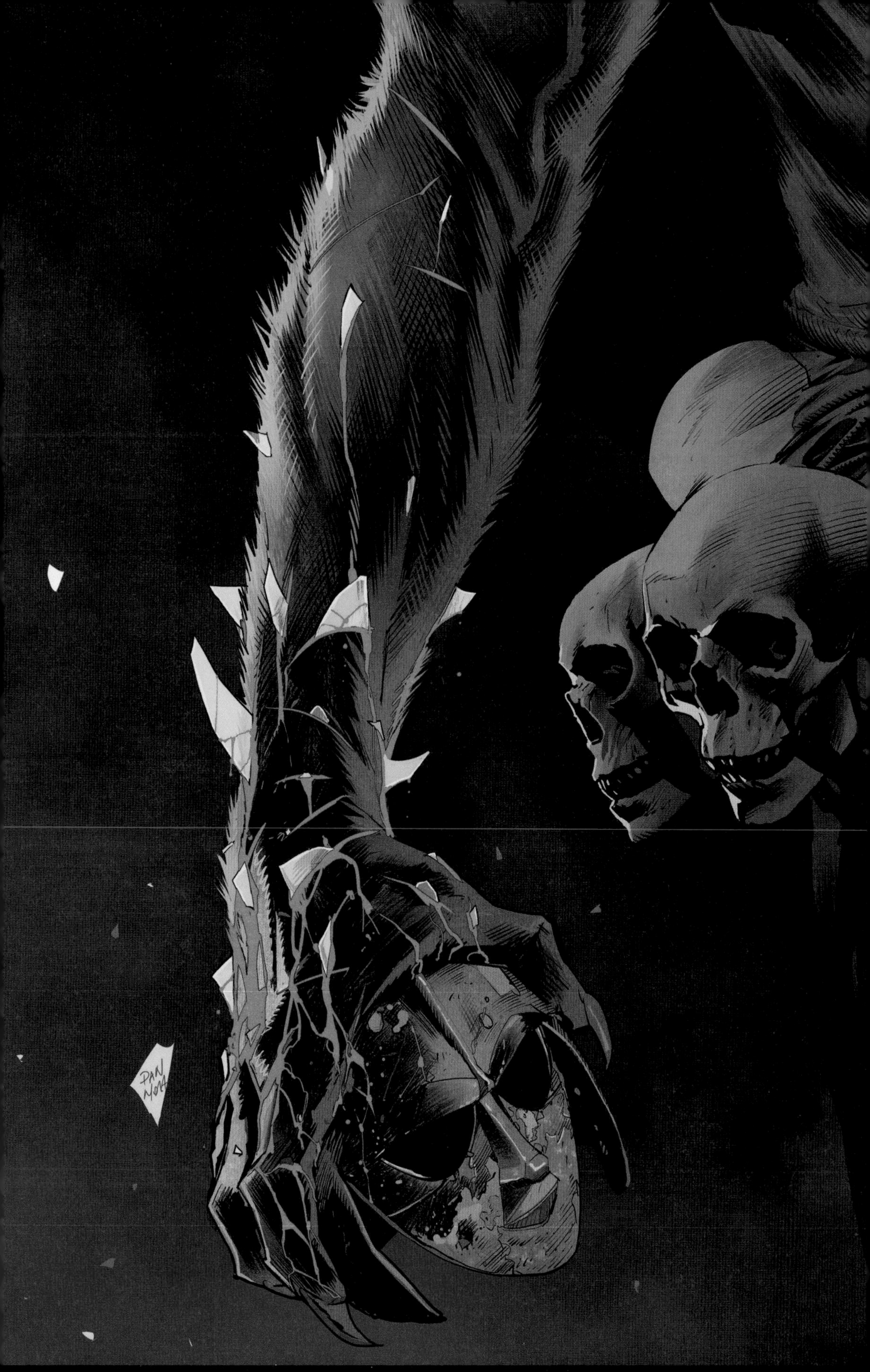

ISSUE NINE COVER BY **DAN MORA**

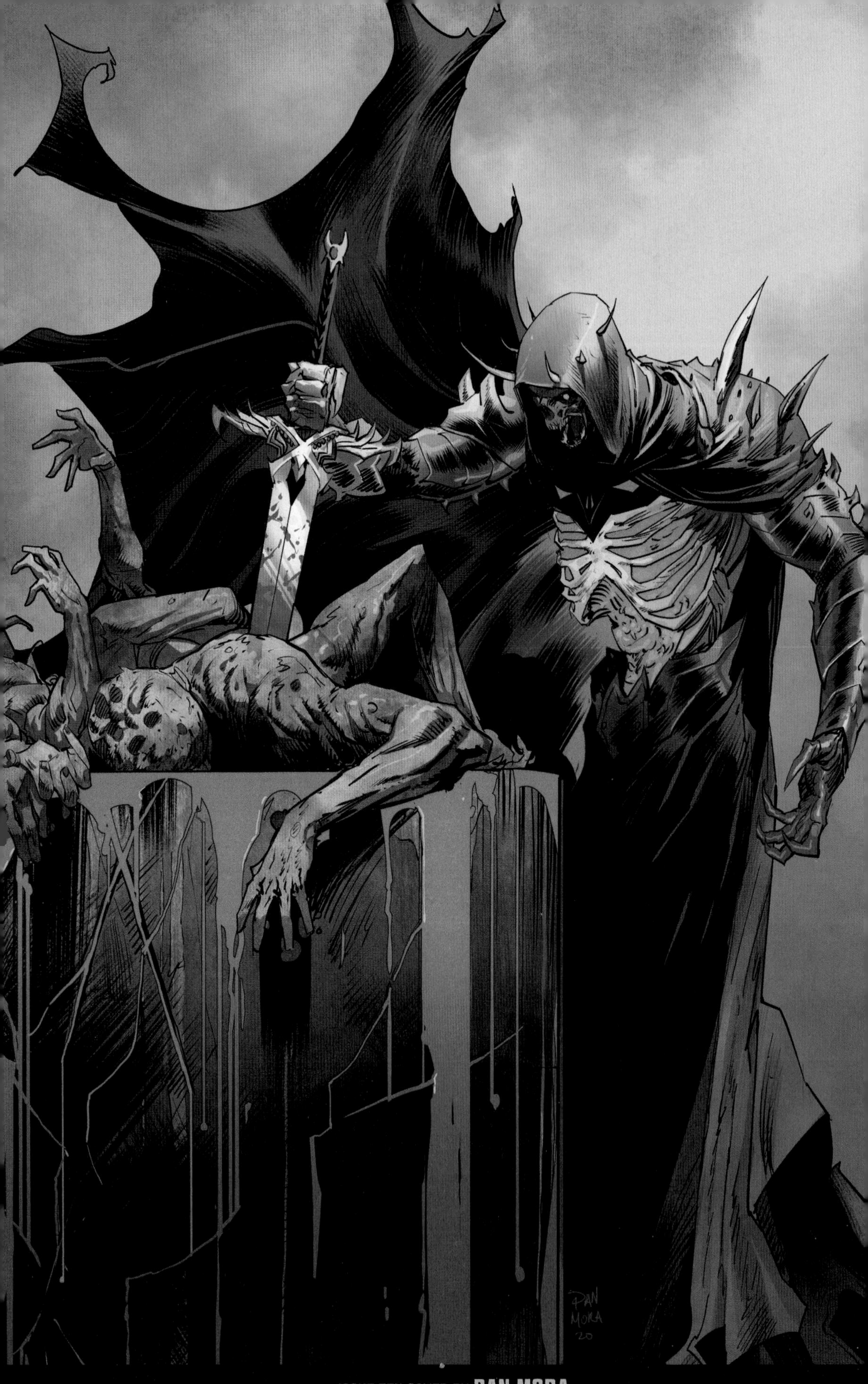
DAN MORA '20

ISSUE TEN COVER BY **DAN MORA**

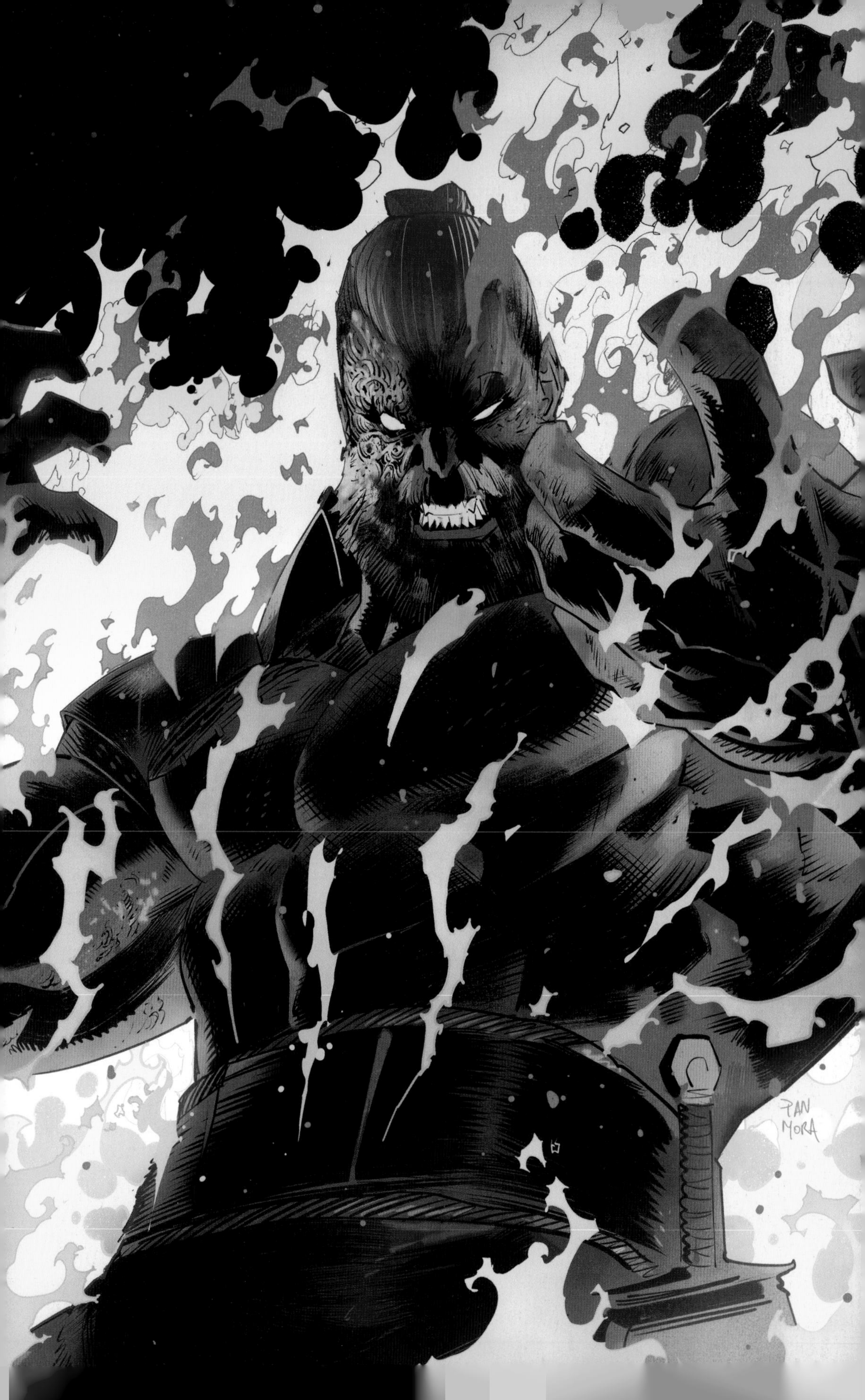
DAN MORA

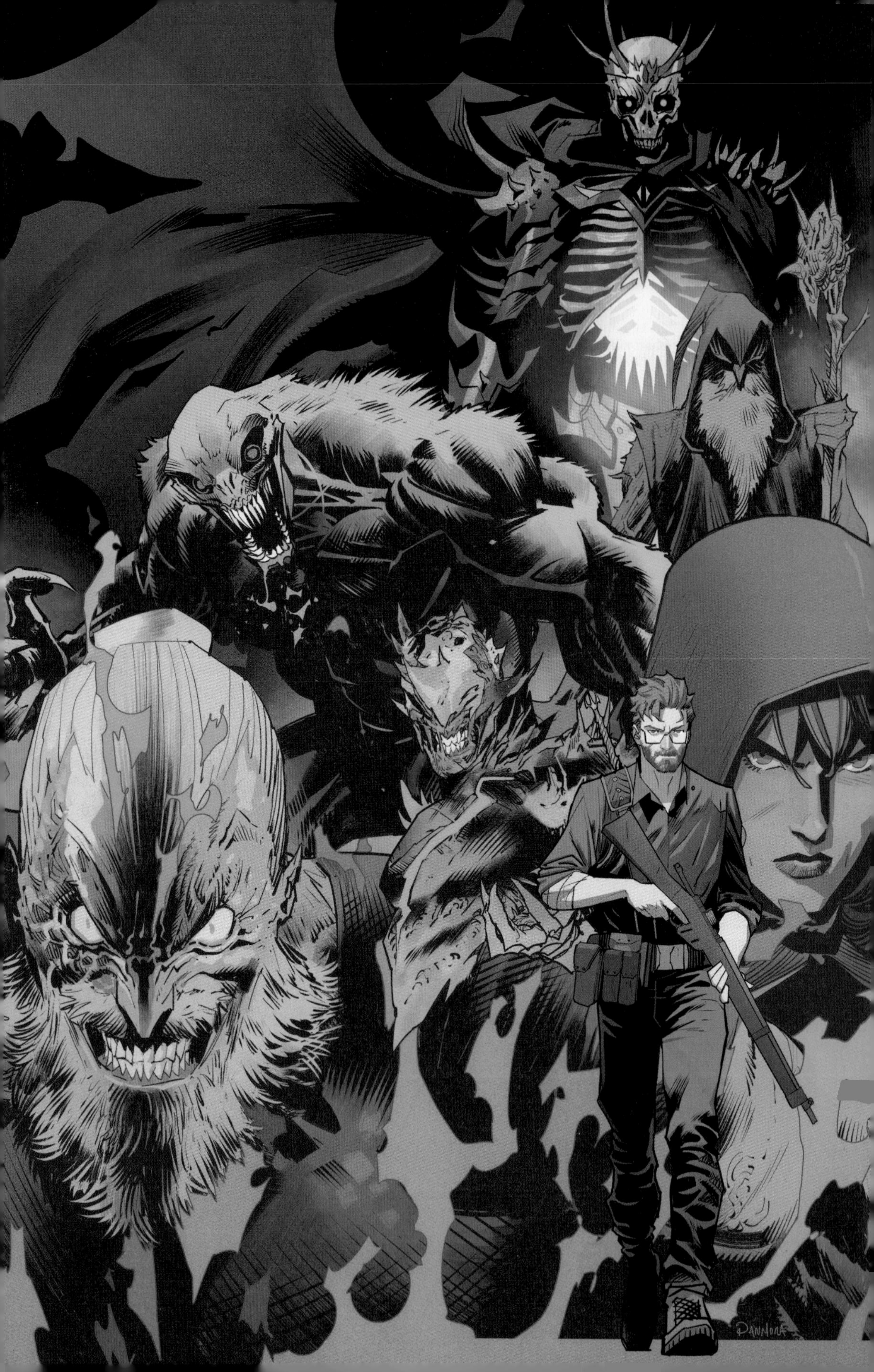
DANNORA